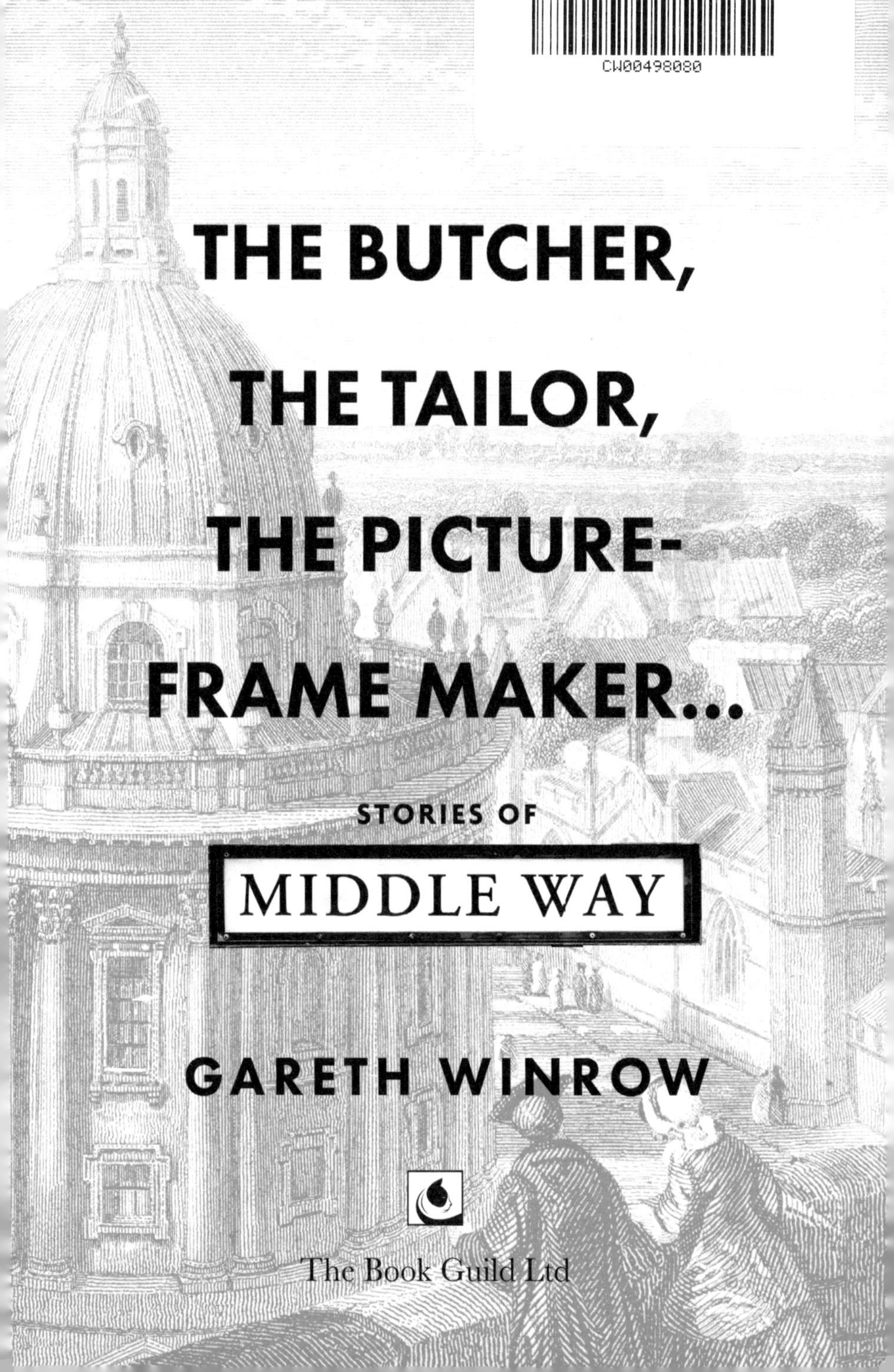

THE BUTCHER, THE TAILOR, THE PICTURE-FRAME MAKER...

STORIES OF

MIDDLE WAY

GARETH WINROW

The Book Guild Ltd

First published in Great Britain in 2023 by
The Book Guild Ltd
Unit E2 Airfield Business Park,
Harrison Road, Market Harborough,
Leicestershire. LE16 7UL
Tel: 0116 2792299
www.bookguild.co.uk
Email: info@bookguild.co.uk
Twitter: @bookguild

Typeset in 12pt Adobe Caslon Pro

Printed and bound in the UK by TJ Books LTD, Padstow, Cornwall

ISBN 978 1915352 729

British Library Cataloguing in Publication Data.
A catalogue record for this book is available from the British Library.

MIX
Paper from
responsible sources
FSC® C013056

THE BUTCHER, THE TAILOR, THE PICTURE-FRAME MAKER...

STORIES OF

MIDDLE WAY

CONTENTS

Centre of Summertown

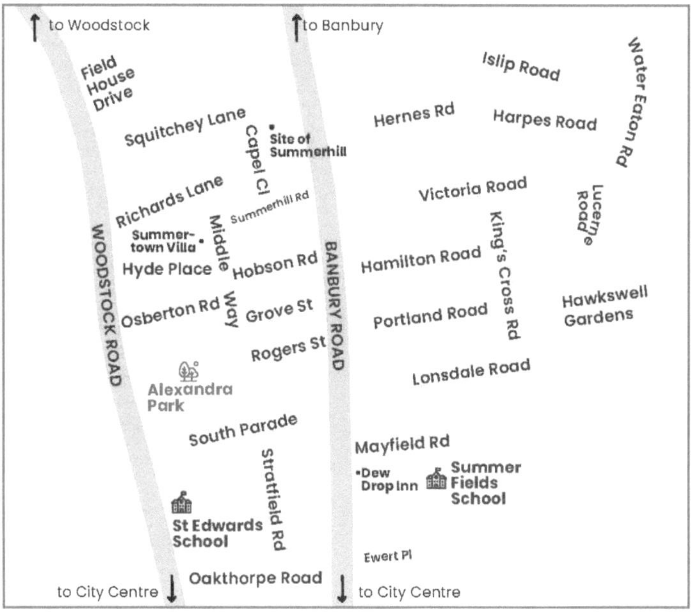

LIST OF ILLUSTRATIONS

TIMELINE – OWNERS OF LAND AND PROPERTY

St Frideswide Monastery/Priory and Godstow Abbey

Early 1000s–c.1122	St Frideswide Monastery
c.1086	Roger D'Ivri or Siward/St Frideswide Monastery
1139	St Frideswide Priory
1358	Godstow Abbey
1541–1558	George Owen

Whorestone Farm

Early 1600s–1659	Ryves family
1659–1692	Christopher Blower Senior
1692–c.1725 (?)	Christopher Blower Junior
c.1725 (?) –1760	Robert Buswell Senior
1760–1780	Robert Buswell Junior
1780–1786	Joseph Tyrrell
1786–c.1806	George Knapp
c.1806–1820/1	Henry John North
1821–1822 (?)	Crews Dudley and George Kimber

Summerhill

c.1822–1824	John Mobley
c.1824–?	John Brain(e)
c. 1840 (?) –1881	James Ryman
1881–1925	Frank Ryman Hall
1925–c.1925	Noah, Aubrey and Harry Capel
c.1925–1952	Horace William Adamson

73 George Street (Middle Way)

1925–1927	Aubrey and Harry Capel
1927–1928	Hinkins and Frewin
1928–1951	Eva Catley – renting to:
1932–1933	Mrs Jenkins
1933–1939	Harry Garnett
1939–1951	Edward George Leslie Hone
1951–1991	William and Florence Lecky-Thompson
1991–1996	Stratford Caldecott
1996–2018	Paul and Catherine Matthews
2018–	Gareth and Nazan Winrow

ONE

INTRODUCTION

'A home is not a mere transient shelter: its essence lies in the personalities of the people who live in it'

(H.L. Mencken)

This story of 73 Middle Way begins with a suspected murder in the mid-eighteenth century. Apparently motivated by jealousy, a newlywed young woman from what appeared to be a respectable and God-fearing family was accused of poisoning her maidservant. The case attracted great publicity. As she was arrested, placed on trial, found guilty and about to be hanged in Oxford Castle, King George II personally intervened at the last minute to pardon the young lady. The repercussions of this trial would have an impact on claims to the ownership of land on what is now Middle Way.

There are other stories about the individuals who owned or occupied the land and property where 73 Middle Way now stands in Summertown, a suburb of Oxford. For example, in the 1820s and 1830s there are the tales of two unfortunate butchers. One fell into serious debt after purchasing the land and as a result soon found himself a guest in one of His Majesty's prisons. The second butcher, after the death of his wife, suddenly disappeared. Only after he had died was it discovered that he had for some reason changed his identity, remarried and found other employment in another part of the country.

The 'richest man in Oxford' at one time owned the substantial estate on which the house on Middle Way is now located. Originally a picture-frame maker with a shop on the High Street in the centre of the city, this dealer mixed with the connoisseurs and cognoscenti of the Victorian art world and became an associate of luminaries such as Turner and Ruskin. Bankers, tailors, post office workers and retired police officers who had worked in Burma when it was part of British-ruled India are among others who would be connected with the land and later house on Middle Way.

This book is not simply the history of a house and the land on which it is situated. In tracing the lives of people with ties to the property it is possible to gain particular insights to understand how the community in Summertown itself evolved. Following the stories of these individuals and their families – some of whom are not at all well-known – also provides an alternative means to look at how Oxford itself, and, indeed, the villages around it, developed. Not surprisingly, many histories of Oxford tend to focus on the university or on the well-documented tensions between town and gown. In this book, the university is present but remains firmly in the background and the relations between town and gown are seen to be complementary rather than adversarial.

Several people who owned the land and property on Middle Way sought to make a tidy profit. There were the bold land speculators of the late eighteenth and early nineteenth centuries who purchased and then quickly resold the freehold land. Later, with the break-up of what was then the Summerhill estate, so-called speculative builders benefitted from acquiring and then reselling plots of land on which new housing would be built. Landlords could then collect rents from young newlywed couples who had just moved to Oxford. Relocating to Summertown to advance careers, these couples eventually moved on again in response to the demands of the job market.

The land and property at what would become 73 Middle Way also served other functions. In the first half of the nineteenth century, the large, open space that could be exploited provided ideal conditions for butchers. At that time butchers required considerable acreage to rear and then slaughter their livestock. In the second half of the nineteenth century Summerhill was radically transformed. No longer primarily a place of utility, its pleasure grounds and reconfigured villa made the estate a location which was admired for its aesthetic value. The estate became the centre of the local community where parades, exhibitions and tea parties were held. After the break-up of the Summerhill estate in the mid-1920s, the house which was constructed on Middle Way became a home for families.

73 Middle Way is situated near the top, northern end of the road. Semi-detached and three-storeyed, with a tiled roof and walls of solid, partly rendered brickwork, the house is to be found on the east side. Next to a gravelled entrance is a tiny front garden with a small crab apple

tree. When in full blossom in spring, the tree's splendid, overhanging pinkish canopy catches the attention of the passing pedestrian. Apart from the tree when in full flower, with its unassuming frontage you would probably pass by the house without noticing it.

As the name suggests, Middle Way runs parallel between two major roads. These busy highways connect Oxford with Banbury and Woodstock. The northern and southern ends of Middle Way link up with Squitchey Lane and South Parade respectively. The road does not quite run in a straight line but curves gently across largely flat terrain. Middle Way can be negotiated in a comfortable five- to ten-minute walk. According to a recent report prepared by a local neighbourhood forum for Oxford City Council, Middle Way is 'an eclectic mix of houses from different periods with no architectural theme'.[1]

Walking down from the memorably named Squitchey Lane, one immediately comes across detached and semi-detached housing on both sides of Middle Way. The above-mentioned report casually observes that these houses are 'less interesting in architectural terms' when compared to buildings further down the road.[2] Most of these 'less interesting' houses – which include 73 Middle Way – were constructed immediately after the sale of the Summerhill estate. They stand on land which would either have been previously part of the estate's pleasure grounds or would have been open space. A little further down the east side of the road stands a block of flats known as Martin Court. An impressive house known as 'The Firs' had occupied this land prior to its demolition in the early 1960s. This was once the property of the nurseryman Joseph Bates, who had a particular interest in conifers. The large, majestic trees which tower gracefully above the road towards the top end of Middle Way are the products of the work of Bates.

Across the road from Martin Court and behind its high walls, stands Summertown Villa. One of the most expensive houses in Oxford, it is the last of the grand Regency and Victorian villas to remain on Middle Way. Its late Regency neighbour, The Avenue, also known as Beaumont House, was demolished some time ago to be replaced by a school and then by new housing and roads. The Avenue was originally the residence of the land speculator George Kimber, one of the key characters in this book. A stone's throw away from Summertown Villa on the same side of the road stands a house which was once the home of Agent Sonya – a German-born spy who had provided crucial military intelligence to the Soviets at the time of the Second World War.

Moving southwards, stretches of terracing fill both sides of Middle Way until one approaches Dudley Court to the east and Summertown Pavilion to the west. Although now difficult to imagine, this was once the hub of Summertown. Dudley Court is a block of flats named after Crews Dudley, another land speculator and working partner of George Kimber. The flats occupy the land where St John the Baptist Church and its school had previously stood. The grass verge skirting the flats is now the playground for families of squirrels. Summertown Pavilion, currently accommodating several offices, formerly housed a famous bakery established by two cooks working at Keble College. The sweet aroma from cakes being baked once wafted up and down Middle Way and along its side streets.[3]

Many of the oldest houses on Middle Way are to be found on the final stretch of road running south to South Parade. At one time Protestant dissenters assembled in a meeting house among the clutch of cottages and later a Congregationalist chapel was founded on the other side of the road. The history of Middle Way is steeped in religion. According to one commentator writing in the 1930s, the parish of Summertown 'must hold the record in England for a persistent ringing of church bells'.[4] In the midst of these cottages and next to the North Oxford Spiritual Church, and looking perhaps out of place, are two very modern-looking houses built at the turn of the century. A patch of greenery and the tennis courts of Alexandra Park may be accessed from across the road. A local butcher once kept his pigs in the field here. Summertown was at one time a village where butchers were clearly prominent members of the local community.

The development of Middle Way to some extent reflects the evolution and growth of Summertown itself. Summertown did not exist before 1820. There had been open fields dotted with the occasional farm. The village of Summertown gradually took shape and in 1832 the Church of St John the Baptist was constructed and consecrated by the road which would later become known as Middle Way. Shops, schools and other facilities were established along the side roads and to the east of the highway running to Banbury. By the late 1880s the village had in effect become a suburb of Oxford with the expansion of housing along the Banbury Road from the city centre. This change in identity was formalised with Summertown being included within the city boundaries in 1889. The original village of Summertown had centred on clusters of housing along the Banbury and Woodstock Roads and in the intersecting streets running between. Much later, housing was constructed around the so-called 'Seven Roads' and in the adjoining districts of Sunnymead and Cutteslowe. These areas to the north and east of the Banbury Road are today, with the possible exception of Cutteslowe, generally regarded as being a part of Summertown.

Although it is situated to the north of the centre of Oxford, one may contend that Summertown is not north Oxford. Both 'Summertown' and 'north Oxford' have positive or negative connotations for different people and the two terms are often used interchangeably. But, arguably, Summertown has been able to maintain its own separate character. It is exceedingly difficult for people in Oxford to remain neutral or to have no opinion about Summertown and/or 'north Oxford'. They are not simply geographical markers which are open to interpretation. They are also contested and loaded terms.

In 2016 a local newspaper article referred to a piece in *The Times* which noted that Summertown was one of the top ten suburbs in the country in which to live. Attention was drawn in particular to the quality of its schools and to the recent addition of the Oxford Parkway Station just to the north which provided the commuter quicker rail access to the centre of London.[5] The area covered by the OX2 postcode, which includes Summertown, has one of the highest life expectations in the UK.[6] The items on offer in its several charity shops scattered along the Banbury Road have been much praised – 'It's the Sotheby's of charity shopping'.[7] The ladies in charge of some of these establishments are distinctly picky about what items to accept from the public at large. The neighbourhood has been depicted – with some justification –

as 'prime academic and retired academic territory'.[8] It is also, undeniably, on the whole an expensive place in which to live. This has led some people to associate the area with snobbery and with 'yummy mummies' supposedly frequenting if not commandeering its several coffee shops.

However, Summertown is a place which is continually evolving. It has a history separate from that of north Oxford. Summertown was once primarily an artisans' village which had in its midst a sprinkling of larger and grander houses and villas surrounded by much humbler dwellings and also ramshackle hovels. There was even a workhouse in the village in the 1820s and 1830s. Although past and present academics have become charmed with what Summertown has to offer, students of the university had tended to give a wide berth to this particular suburb. But now town and gown are literally cheek by jowl in Summertown with the development of student housing. In recent years university examinations have been held in Ewart House in the very centre of Summertown. At the time of writing the local community is attempting to adapt to the presence of a fresh intruder after the opening of a large EasyHotel on the Banbury Road.

As a geographic term, for many people who live in the city or for those who are familiar with Oxford, 'north Oxford' refers to the area north of St Giles' Church, near the centre of the city, up to the roads around Summertown.[9] Territory to the north of Summertown should be clearly distinguished from this traditional use of the expression, 'north Oxford'. The classic 'north Oxford' is looked upon as 'legendary don-land'.[10] Indeed, its cultural roots are partly academic, but prosperous industrialists and other successful tradespeople also lived in the large houses which sprang up in the 1860s and 1870s in

Park Town and Norham Manor off the Banbury Road. The predominant Gothic architecture of these imposing edifices has had its critics. According to Penelope Lively, for example, they were not houses 'but flights of fancy' which reeked of 'hymns and the Empire'.[11] John Ruskin, on the other hand, was enamoured with north Oxford. He encouraged his fellow writer Frederick Harrison, 'in the name of all that's human and progressive' to promenade 'up and down the elongating suburb of the married Fellows, on the cock-horse road to Banbury'.[12] St John's College, the major landowner in north Oxford, insisted that trees, gardens and shrubs should be meticulously maintained, and this has given the area a pleasing verdant look which persists today.[13]

This 'north Oxford', especially in its early manifestation, was definitely more snobby than the neighbourhood of Summertown to its immediate north. There was much more wealth in this 'north Oxford', and in the late nineteenth century the wives of the dons and senior administrators in the university were most reluctant to mingle socially with their counterparts and possible neighbours whose husbands were successful businessmen.[14] The traditions and customs of this 'north Oxford' should certainly not be confused with the supposed nouveau riche and 'lumpenbourgeoisie' living to the north of Summertown who were so scurrilously depicted in a novel by Michael Dibdin.[15]

The aim of this book is not to seek to further classify or rebrand Summertown, and, indeed, other parts of Oxford including 'north Oxford'. But, through examining the lives of individuals and families who owned or occupied the land and property on Middle Way, it is hoped that the reader may gain an understanding of how this particular corner of

Oxford emerged, developed and was transformed. The stories of some of the individuals recounted here are fascinating in themselves.

In my previous book I focused on studying the lives of members of a particular family who over the course of time and across different generations had become scattered across the globe.[16] The scope of this book is somewhat different, concentrating rather on the history of a fixed location. I have unashamedly made liberal use of the work of a past local historian, Ruth Fasnacht, the doyen of writers about Summertown. Rewarding hours spent in archives and in the Bodleian Library have been reinforced by useful information provided by popular family history search engines.

More importantly, however, this book has been enriched by details and observations that have been kindly offered by the living relatives of people once associated with the land and house at 73 Middle Way. Such voices from the present helps one to reinterpret and reexamine the events of the past. I have been directed along paths which I may not have noticed or might have chosen to ignore. This process has also turned out to be a reciprocal one. Occasionally, I have been able to provide these relatives with previously unknown information or recounted to them stories which had presumably long since been forgotten. Most satisfying of all, I have in some instances been able to reunite family members who for various reasons had lost contact with one another.

This book is dedicated to all the relatives of those connected with the land and property at 73 Middle Way who have each made important contributions to this book.

TWO

EARLY LANDOWNERS

'Make money and the whole nation will conspire to call you a gentleman'

(G.B. Shaw)

Introduction:

A fourteenth-century map of Oxford referred to a piece of land which was known as 'The Furlong called Twene the Weys'.[17] This was an early reference to an area later known as Whorestone Farm through which would run a road between the two highways leading to Banbury and Woodstock. For many years this road, the later Middle Way, was little more than a dirt track extending across open fields. The village of Summertown did not exist until the 1820s. By the early eighteenth century Whorestone Farm covered roughly eighty acres of freehold land at the northern end of the Oxford parish of St Giles. The farm lay immediately beyond the 455 acres of land which St John's College had purchased in north Oxford in 1573. Whorestone Farm took its name from the six hoar-stones or boundary stones which marked the division between the parishes of St Giles and Wolvercote. Four of the stones were located on the northern boundary of the farm, and two stones were to be found on the farm's western periphery.[18]

As late as the early nineteenth century the area to the north of the St Giles' Church would have quickly opened up to nursery gardens and pastureland. There was little incentive at the time for St John's College to build housing in what was known as St Giles' Field in north Oxford. The college would have received little profit. This was because of so-called short-term beneficial leases which the college had been encouraged to adopt by legislation passed in the late sixteenth century. For such leases, only a nominal rent was paid each year rather than a rent based on the value of the market. The lifespan of these leases was a mere twenty years for land and forty years for housing.[19]

On the other hand, if new housing was to be built in Oxford, the ideal location would be land in north Oxford. The crowded old city was constructed on gravel soil in a compact area where the rivers Thames and Cherwell converged. The meadow land to the immediate east, west and south of the city was low-lying and especially prone to flooding. However, there was a gradually sloping gravel terrace stretching to the north of the city with natural drainage which provided much more suitable land for building. The Banbury and Woodstock turnpike roads ran along this narrow strip of gravel, and the buildings which were eventually constructed to the east and west of these roads came to an abrupt halt when the gravel gave way to clay.[20] The shape of the city of Oxford was hence determined by the features of the gravel bank. Jan Morris noted in her trademark florid style that because of the topography of the land, the city was six miles in length and rarely more than one mile across, making Oxford look 'like a spiral nebula, with a hub at the centre where the roads cross, and gaseous extensions thrown off'.[21]

With sparse housing and open fields, the area immediately to the north of the city was one in which highwaymen were encouraged to roam. Close to Whorestone Farm and a little nearer to the city was the site of Diamond House (also known as Diamond Hall), a notorious inn. Before 1820 Diamond House had been one of the few properties located in the neighbourhood on the eastern side of the Banbury turnpike road. In the eighteenth century, the stone-built Diamond House had acquired a reputation as a hostelry frequented by thieves and other unsavoury characters. According to one commentator writing in the early 1830s, the 'lone Public House' had apparently 'been the source of many a dark deed'.[22] The Woodstock turnpike road was not much safer. It was much closer to the city centre and as late as in 1777 a lone highwayman was emboldened enough to hold up and rob the Birmingham coach on the road opposite the recently built Radcliffe Infirmary.[23]

By the early eighteenth century, the land at Whorestone Farm had been acquired by the Buswell family of Westcott Barton in Oxfordshire. Various branches of this well-to-do family lived in Westcott Barton and earlier generations had resided in the manor house in the village of Hailey near Witney in the same county. Some of the Buswells were yeomans – a status just below that of the landed gentry – who resided in the manor house at Westcott Barton. William

Boseville, the High Sheriff of Oxfordshire in 1650 and 'a learned civilian', was reputedly a member of the family.[24] It is not clear when exactly the family gained possession of Whorestone Farm. However, a settlement dated 1726 which concerned the family referred to the use of the land and buildings at Whorestone and an adjoining close of ground called Great Whorestone.[25]

The settlement was drawn up by Robert Buswell, clerk, and later rector of the Oxfordshire village of Kiddington. The Buswells were related to the Knapps and Tyrrells, who later owned Whorestone Farm. Upon the 'presentation' (i.e. nomination) of a Robert Buswell of 'Westcote Barton' (Westcott Barton), 'gentleman' – Robert's father, it seems – and John Knapp of 'Ensham' (Eynsham), 'gentleman', Robert Buswell was appointed the rector of Kiddington in 1729.[26] John Knapp was the son of George Knapp and Mary Buswell. Mary was a relative of Robert Buswell, the above-mentioned gentleman. John came from the Cumnor branch of the Knapp family which originated from Chilton in Berkshire.[27] The Knapps later intermarried with the Tyrrell family.

The 1726 settlement concerning Whorestone Farm listed other family members, and they, together with Robert Buswell, the future vicar, effectively acted as trustees for Robert's young children. But the settlement did not make fully clear what would happen to the land after the death of Robert Buswell, the then clerk.

The Reverend Robert Buswell died in 1760. His will, prepared in 1734 and not updated, did not refer in detail to the future disposition of Whorestone Farm. Nevertheless, according to the will, property owned by Robert Buswell was again to be held in trust by his relatives for Robert's three children, Elizabeth, Anne and Robert junior. Apart from Robert Buswell junior obtaining his father's books, the will stated that all goods, chattels and the personal estate of Robert Buswell senior should in future be apportioned equally between the children.[28] This seemed to imply that the land at Whorestone Farm should be distributed equally among the children of the Reverend Robert Buswell. However, after his father's death, and having got hold of the title deeds, Robert Buswell junior, then a farmer, took possession of the whole estate at Whorestone. Continuing to ignore the terms of his father's will, before his death Robert Buswell junior had sold the land he claimed to own at Whorestone Farm.

In 1809 the Reverend Thomas Wisdom (or Wisdome), Rector of Farnham in Essex and formerly Fellow of Trinity College at Oxford University, petitioned the Treasury to claim part of the land at Whorestone Farm for himself and his mother, then known as Elizabeth Slatter.[29] Thomas was Elizabeth's elder son from her first marriage. Wisdom's mother was one of the daughters of Robert Buswell senior, who had not been able to secure her share of the Whorestone Farm according to the terms of the will of 1734 and seemingly counter to the provisions of the settlement made in 1726. However, the case was complicated by the fact that in 1749 Elizabeth had been convicted of murder. Although she was pardoned by King George II, it was argued that because of her initial conviction Elizabeth had lost her right to claim her share of the land. There was also a dispute over whether the land claimed by Elizabeth should have been escheated (i.e. transferred) to the Crown after her conviction. The 'murder' – overlooked in local history books – sparked great interest at the time and attracted the attention of local gentry and government officials as well as the Hanoverian court.

Elizabeth Buswell (1725–1815): The Chipping Norton Murderess?

I met Tommy Bull together with one of his daughters in Oxford in May 2022. A computer consultant based in Florida, Tommy was the first relative of a person connected with the land at Middle Way that I was able to meet in person. Largely because of Covid restrictions, my previous contacts with Tommy and other ancestors had been either by telephone, mail or via the internet. Elizabeth Buswell was the six-times great-grandmother of Tommy. An avid researcher into his own family history, Tommy had regularly visited Westcott Barton and other sleepy Oxfordshire villages which were connected to the Buswells. He had earlier sent me a photograph of the Wisdome family trunk. A solid piece of work carved in 1691, a cousin of Tommy's living in England was tasked with maintaining and handing on this valued piece of family heritage.

Tommy and I had exchanged numerous email messages about the Buswells and their relations with other families such as the Terrys and the Norgroves. I was able to introduce to Tommy via email a distant relative in Australia who had also long pursued an interest in the Buswells of Westcott Barton. However, in spite of his close interest in family history, Tommy had been completely unaware of the life story of Elizabeth Buswell and her conviction for murder. This was perhaps not surprising given how the story behind Elizabeth's suspected poisoning of her maidservant had failed to catch the attention of historians.

On 25 March 1749 Elizabeth Wisdom (née Buswell) received the rites of the last supper in the county gaol housed in the castle of Oxford. She was about to be hanged in the gallows in the castle courtyard. In attendance with her was the Reverend Edmund Trott of St Alban Hall, a university residence then connected to Merton College. Also present was the wife of the keeper of the gaol. With Trott and the keeper of the gaol's wife as her witnesses, Elizabeth repeated once again that she was not guilty of poisoning and murdering her maidservant, Grace Hall. This was in spite of Trott's concerted attempts to pressure Elizabeth to confess to the deed and thereby supposedly save her soul before her impending execution.[30]

Elizabeth had been detained in the prison at the castle for several weeks. Conditions in the gaol at that time were dire for most of those who were incarcerated. Formerly a functioning military establishment as well as a prison, much of the castle had fallen into disrepair with the end of the Civil War. Two decades after Elizabeth's imprisonment, a report by John Howard, the prison reformer and former Sheriff of Bedfordshire, condemned the state of neglect of the buildings which were deemed not suitable for human habitation. The women's night room was very small and had no window. Deprived of sunlight, straw for bedding and basic medical facilities, and with only a small courtyard in which to exercise, it was not surprising that eleven inmates had died of smallpox in 1773.[31] Prisoners were forced to hand over money to their gaolers to obtain basic food.

In the period between 1650 and 1766 only eleven women were executed in Oxford – either at the castle itself or at the so-called Green Ditch (today's St Margaret's Road), located one mile north by the Banbury road turnpike. Most of these women were found guilty of infanticide. Convicted for killing their new-born illegitimate children, the majority of these women came from poor backgrounds.[32]

Because Elizabeth came from a family of a certain social status, she probably received more favourable treatment than other female prisoners and she may well have been allocated a room of her own in the gaol. Two years later Mary Blandy, the daughter of an attorney and town clerk of Henley, who was convicted of poisoning her father, had been granted her own room in the prison. She was apparently housed in the lodging of the keeper of the gaol. Allowed to have a maid in attendance, Mary had received visitors for tea and to play cards and had been allowed to stroll in the garden of the keeper of the gaol together with a guard. Because of a delay in her trial, Mary had remained in the prison for six months.[33] Perhaps Elizabeth did not receive the full privileges accorded to Mary Blandy, given that her time in prison was much shorter. In spite of her social standing and a general sympathy for her case, Mary Blandy would eventually be hanged. The situation for Elizabeth Wisdom, therefore, must have been particularly grim, even though she did not appear to have the background and credentials of a would-be murderer.

Baptised in May 1725 in the small Hampshire village of Cliddesden, Elizabeth was the daughter of Robert and Elizabeth Buswell. Religion was deeply entrenched in the family. Elizabeth Wisdom's mother was the daughter of the Reverend Thomas Terry of Dummer in Hampshire. In his will prepared in 1715, the reverend had given his brother, Stephen Terry, guardianship over his young children, including Elizabeth Terry, the future mother of Elizabeth Wisdom. Specific instructions were given for the children to be properly educated and raised in the Church of England.[34]

Almost a century later, the Terry family of Dummer would feature prominently in the letters of Jane Austen. This later generation of Terrys was altogether more worldly. The diarist and Squire of Dummer, another Stephen Terry, offered himself as a regular dance partner for Jane Austen at the numerous balls held in the district. Austen noted somewhat flippantly that the Terrys of Dummer were a 'noisy family'.[35]

In October 1748 Elizabeth Buswell married Thomas Rose Wisdom, a grocer who had a shop in the thriving Oxfordshire market town of Chipping Norton. The Wisdoms were a well-established family in the town. The upholsterer, Philip Wisdom, was a grandfather of Thomas Rose. Philip, who died in 1709, had been a man of some wealth living in a comfortable house in the centre of Chipping Norton. His kitchen was fully equipped with the latest conveniences and his bedroom, a chamber above the parlour warmed by a fireplace, had been pleasantly furnished with a feather mattress bed, a looking glass, cane chairs and a chest of drawers. Philip's son, Thomas, the father of Thomas Rose, had married well. His wife, Elizabeth Norgrove, came from a family which had acquired ownership of the town's two largest tan yards. One-time followers of Puritanism, the Norgroves were known to be religiously devout.[36]

Elizabeth's husband was well known to the Buswell family. In the will of Thomas Rose's father, who died in 1746, it was noted how his son '...is unhappily afflicted by being disordered in his senses...' and so he was not able to manage his own affairs. The father had therefore named two guardians to maintain a watchful eye on his son. One of these was '…my good friend the Reverend Mr Robert Buswell of Kiddington'.[37] The marriage of Elizabeth Buswell and Thomas Rose Wisdom would thus have been a highly convenient one, enabling the Buswells to continue to monitor closely the life of the troubled Thomas Rose.

Given these circumstances, it would have come as a major surprise to learn that on 22 February 1749 Elizabeth Wisdom was indicted for murdering Grace Hall. A later report which summarised the proceedings stated that exactly one week earlier, '…moved and seduced by the instigation of the Devil…' Elizabeth had mixed and mingled '…a great quantity of mortal poison into a certain pudding…' which was then given to Grace Hall. The twenty-two-year-old maidservant fell sick and died several days later. Following her arrest, Elizabeth again and again pleaded her innocence. But after examining various testimonies and affidavits, a jury found her guilty, and Elizabeth was sentenced '…to be hanged by the neck until she be dead'.[38]

The case attracted considerable attention. Presumably, the interest of the general public was aroused by the horror of such a heinous crime supposedly committed by a woman who came from such an undoubtedly respectable, Christian family. The trial was also closely followed by leading officials of the day. Details of the trial were presented by Charles Clarke, the wealthy judge, barrister and Whig politician, who held the senior judicial post of Baron of the Exchequer – the title for a court which monitored cases of equity and common pleas. Clarke, a formidable lawyer who had been appointed to his post back in 1742, regularly attended and presided over cases which sparked public interest. It was no surprise, therefore, that Clarke should be present at the trial of Elizabeth Wisdom which was held at the Oxford assizes in the presence of senior judges. Sir Michael Foster, a judge of the King's Bench, was another distinguished justice in attendance at the trial.[39] According to the much-quoted jurist Sir William Blackstone, who was a contemporary of Foster, Sir Michael was 'a very great master of the Crown-law'.[40] The presence of such an eminent judge must have lent further gravitas to the occasion. Clarke reported details of the case to the Duke of Newcastle, the Whig grandee and then Secretary of State who later served two terms of office as Prime Minister.

In his report discussing what had happened at court Charles Clarke declared that he was convinced that Elizabeth was guilty of murdering Grace Hall, a healthy young woman who had recently moved into the Wisdom household. He noted that just before two in the afternoon on the 15 February Grace had run to the nearby house of Mrs Tinson. Violently vomiting and with pains in her stomach, a distressed Grace claimed that she had been poisoned by her mistress. Mrs Tinson immediately sought help from the local apothecary, Mr Mackarness. Grace remained ill for several days and the local doctor was called. While not confirming that Grace had indeed been poisoned, Dr Smith did acknowledge that it was quite likely.

Grace had told Mackarness that she had consumed one end of the pudding prepared by Elizabeth Wisdom which had a reddish colour that contrasted with the rest of the dessert. Her master and mistress had both eaten the other end of the pudding. The apothecary tested what remained of the food but could not find anything amiss. Questioned why her mistress may have poisoned her, Grace had told Mackarness that it was because of jealousy. Grace's previous mistress, a Mrs Elkington, confirmed that Grace had said to her that Elizabeth was jealous of her relationship with Mr Wisdom. Charles Clarke referred in passing to the testimonies of other witnesses and then agreed with the jury that in the light of the evidence available Elizabeth was guilty of murder.[41]

Charles Clarke may have been convinced of Elizabeth's guilt, but there were statements from others in court which cast doubt on the verdict of the jury. There were several references to Elizabeth's good behaviour and how, therefore, it was inconceivable that she could have committed such a terrible crime. In an affidavit, John Buswell, a cousin of Elizabeth and a yeoman living in Westcott Barton, declared that he had known Elizabeth since childhood and that she was a person 'of good extraction' and 'always esteemed'.[42] According to Mary Smith, a former servant of Elizabeth's father, Elizabeth was a person with 'great humanity' who regularly attended church, was charitable to the poor and was a dutiful daughter.[43] Other statements signed by a group of villagers from Kiddington, which was near Chipping Norton, emphasised how she was a religious and charitable person who had never harmed anybody.[44] Another affidavit of support for Elizabeth included the name Thomas Mackarness – the apothecary who had given evidence at the trial.[45] Further doubts were raised by the statements of two local women who claimed that Grace actually had a record of previous poor health.[46]

Elizabeth Wisdom also had the backing of much more influential people. Edward Ryves was the town clerk of Woodstock and was a wealthy landowner. He was also an agent of Charles Spencer, the third Duke of Marlborough who had his seat at Blenheim Palace. Ryves informed the duke about the trial and noted how the public believed that the verdict was too harsh. He added that the judges involved had come to regret the ruling and that the general feeling was that there was no evidence of poisoning.[47] It is not clear why the Duke of Marlborough would have taken such a close interest in Elizabeth's case. More significantly, the case attracted the interest and concern of Lady Susan Keck. Lady Susan's husband, Anthony Tracy Keck, was a protégé of the Dukes of Marlborough, and he would become an MP for Woodstock in 1753.[48] But Lady Susan, herself, was also a formidable force to be reckoned with.

Lady Susan Keck was the daughter of the fourth Duke of Hamilton. Her father's first wife had been the aunt of the Duke of Marlborough, and so the Kecks were not surprisingly frequent dinner guests at Blenheim. Prior to her marriage, Lady Susan had been a lady of the bedchamber to King George II's three eldest daughters for four years from 1732. A hunter of stags in her youth, the tomboyish, brash and supremely confident Lady Susan, a staunch advocate of the Whigs, was derided by the Tories, who called her 'Lord Sue'. She is perhaps best known for her personal involvement in campaigning and canvassing in the parliamentary election in Oxfordshire in 1754 when she successfully promoted the more reform-minded New Interest Whigs against the Old Interest Tories.[49]

In March 1749 Lady Susan penned a long letter about the case of Elizabeth Wisdom to the Countess of Yarmouth, a woman of even greater influence. She pleaded for support from the Countess, declaring that she was convinced that Elizabeth was not guilty. Lady Susan referred to separate reports from her own physician and from the Reverend Trott. Her doctor believed that Grace had not been poisoned. And the Reverend Trott, who was present with Elizabeth throughout much of her confinement, noted again how Elizabeth had repeatedly announced that she was innocent. Interestingly, perhaps to balance somewhat these accounts, Lady Susan also included a less favourable affidavit from Grace's 'sweetheart and lover', Isaiah Smith.[50]

Why had Lady Susan rallied to support Elizabeth? Perhaps she had known the Buswells and the Wisdoms for some time, given that the Kecks resided at the estate at Great Tew, which was not far from Westcott Barton and Chipping Norton. Or Lady Susan's interest in the case may have been prompted through her close connection with the Duke of Marlborough and the duke's apparent interest in the trial. She may also have taken up the case simply because of her conviction that an innocent woman was being wronged and was about to lose her life.

The letter to the Countess of Yarmouth most probably ultimately resulted in the last-minute pardoning of Elizabeth Wisdom. Amalie Sophie Marianne von Wallmoden – the Countess of Yarmouth – was King George II's favourite mistress at the time. She would also become his most longstanding mistress. Her affair with the monarch had started in 1735 when the King had made one of his regular visits to Hanover. The affair was made public after the death of Queen Caroline two years later, and in 1740 Amalie was made Countess after divorcing her husband. She was the last of the British royal mistresses to be granted a peerage title. The Countess was provided with luxurious apartments at St James's Palace and at Kensington Palace.

The Countess of Yarmouth was heavily involved in politics and highly influential in the royal court. She became a main channel of communication between ministers and the King. Knowing well the King's temper, according to the clergyman and historian Archdeacon Coxe, 'she knew how to introduce memorials, petitions, letters and recommendations at the proper season'. Ministers depended on the Countess to make applications on their behalf which they knew the King would not like.[51] The Countess also had an alliance with the Duke of Newcastle, with the duke exploiting his ties with Amalie to learn about the views of the King on certain matters. King George II, himself, would occasionally use the Countess as his personal secretary.[52]

The Countess of Yarmouth, therefore, was an important conduit through whom petitions were sent to King George II for him to intercede and grant clemency in certain cases. With the backing and clout of Lady Keck, it would appear that the Countess favoured clemency for Elizabeth Wisdom. King George II certainly intervened and pardoned Elizabeth very shortly before she was about to be hanged. In this particular instance, the Countess's leverage over the Duke of Newcastle may have had more clout than Charles Clarke's connection with the Whig grandee.

However, the royal pardon did not ensure that Elizabeth and her heirs would inherit their share of Whorestone Farm. Elizabeth was still alive – although 'very old' and 'infirm' – when in 1809 her son, the Reverend Thomas Wisdom, made a petition to claim a part of the Whorestone estate on behalf of his mother and himself. After the death of her first husband in 1759, seven years later Elizabeth had married John Slatter, a yeoman living at Stratford on Avon.[53] The conviction and all the negative publicity associated with it may have made Elizabeth loathe to challenge her brother's seizure of all the property at Whorestone in 1760. Elizabeth eventually died in 1815 and was buried in Shipton-under-Wychwood, the Oxfordshire village from where the Wisdom family had originated.

The petition made by the Reverend Wisdom also had to contend with another serious problem. This concerned the charge that the share of the property claimed by Elizabeth should have been escheated to the Crown as a result of Elizabeth's conviction – in spite of the ensuing royal pardon. The details of this are presented in the next chapter. A later owner of Whorestone Farm, Henry John North, a lawyer from Woodstock, would become directly involved in the legal dispute with the Reverend Wisdom and other lawyers over whether the land should be escheated to the Crown.

Joseph Tyrrell (c.1728–1786): 'Gentleman of Kidlington'

The property at Whorestone Farm was put up for sale by Robert Buswell, Elizabeth's brother, in 1780. The newspaper advertisement gave details about the eighty acres of freehold estate. The rich, arable land was enclosed in a ring-fence and was divided into five grounds by quickset hedges. Situated on the property was a barn, a stable and other conveniences, and some timber was also growing on the land. The property was tithe-free.[54]

The farm was bought by Joseph Tyrrell, a gentleman of means living in nearby Kidlington.[55] Frustratingly, in spite of his great wealth, not much is known about Joseph, and the few available references to him and his sister, Katherine, are open to question. There were suggestions that Joseph and Katherine were immediately related to the Tyrrells, who had owned the Hanslope estate in Buckinghamshire, but the evidence at hand does not appear to substantiate this.[56]

Joseph Tyrrell's father, also called Joseph, and likewise referred to as a 'gentleman', had lived in the village of Drayton in Berkshire before moving to Kidlington. Joseph Tyrrell junior appeared to be one of four children but seems to have been the only son. The family were quite wealthy. By 1766 Joseph Tyrrell junior had acquired part of the old manor house and estate in the Oxfordshire village of Hampton Poyle, which was situated by Kidlington, but across the other side of the River Cherwell.[57] When Tyrrell died in 1786, a local newspaper referred to Joseph as 'a gentleman of very considerable fortune'.[58]

In 1753 Katherine Tyrrell, one of Joseph's sisters, married George Knapp, a grocer from the then Berkshire town of Abingdon. This George Knapp was a relative of John Knapp of 'Ensham'. Katherine and George were soon the parents of George Knapp junior, who would follow in his father's footsteps and become mayor of Abingdon. He would also serve as member of parliament for his hometown. George Knapp junior was destined to inherit Whorestone Farm and other properties previously owned by his uncle.

George Knapp (1754–1809): The Abingdon Radical

Doubts have been raised as to the exact circumstances of the cause of death of George Knapp, banker, mayor and member of parliament. According to press reports at the time, he had died in his house in London on the morning of 12 November 1809, two weeks after being thrown from his gig when travelling through Oxfordshire. The serious head injuries he had sustained had not been properly treated. There followed an infection of the brain which resulted in a fever that proved to be fatal.[59]

However, it has also been suggested that George Knapp may actually have perished as a result of a duel, and that this may have been linked to his addiction to gambling which could have resulted in a dispute with a fellow gambler. Suspiciously, there were no reports of an inquest into his death, and only days before he died George had added a codicil to his will to increase financial provision for his two 'natural' daughters, Anne and Harriet. A cover-up would have also avoided a likely public scandal. This would have suited the interests of the Knapp, Tomkins and Goodall banking enterprise, of which George was a key member. The good reputation of the Abingdon High Street bank would have been kept intact.[60]

It was common knowledge that George Knapp was a heavy gambler. What made matters worse was that he was also not very good at the gambling table. In 1792 he had lost the exorbitant sum of £1,300 in two wild gambling sessions.[61] His addiction was well known to his longstanding good friend, William Bagshaw Stevens, the diarist, poet and chaplain, and headmaster of Repton School in Derbyshire. Like Knapp, Stevens was a graduate of Roysse's School in Abingdon. On 21 September 1792, acknowledging a letter he had just received from Knapp, Stevens commented on his friend's weakness and lack of skill at gambling:

'Pity that he should be such a Dupe to Gamesters. Without temper, skill or knavery, he is fool enough to believe himself a Match for Them. Ruinous Infatuation!'[62]

Stevens was also fully aware of his friend's other major shortcoming – his obsession with a certain 'Miss Keymore' of Manchester. According to the diarist, Knapp had little prospect of winning over the heart of the young lady in question. Writing in his diary on 19 November 1793, Stevens noted that Knapp had 'unexpectedly' come to visit him in Derbyshire direct from one of his excursions to Manchester. The chaplain wrote: '…his amorous hopes seem to me to have little to lean upon – Miss Keymore will continue to refuse him'.[63] A year later, Stevens was much more scathing as Knapp continued to vacillate over how to approach the 'Attraction of Manchester'. It seemed that Knapp was then being challenged by a younger suitor who lived locally. Stevens questioned if Knapp had 'given over the chase'. He bluntly wrote to Knapp that if he really did think that he was too old, then he should leave '…the Manchester fortress to be attacked by some more vigorous Swordsman'.[64]

The identity of this 'Miss Keymore' remains unclear. Perhaps Stevens was actually referring to a Miss Susannah Keymer, an inhabitant of Manchester who was the sister of Robert Keymer. Robert was a successful small-ware manufacturer who eventually took up residence at Culcheth Hall in Cheshire. This particular lady died in 1833 without having married. Knapp could have met Susannah through his brother Joseph, who had relocated to Manchester from Abingdon in 1789 to expand his drapery business. Ultimately, it seems that Knapp failed to woo the elusive Miss Keymore or Keymer. Although he had two daughters, George Knapp did not marry, and the mother of his offspring is not known. His weaknesses notwithstanding, Knapp was an enterprising businessman and an astute and determined politician at both the local and national levels. He also became a substantial property owner.

Several earlier generations of the Knapp family had lived in Berkshire. For example, George's great-great-great-grandfather, also named George, was a yeoman from Chilton in the county. Some later descendants were yeomen residing in the Berkshire village of Blewbury.[65] George Knapp's father, the brother-in-law of Joseph Tyrrell, as well being a grocer also served in local politics. He was the mayor of Abingdon in 1759 and 1767. After George Knapp junior died, his remains were buried in the family vault under an altar-tomb in the Church of All Saints at Chilton.[66]

George Knapp junior followed in the footsteps of his father. Together with a younger brother, Henry, George became a grocer and was then made a freeman of Abingdon in 1780. He quickly advanced in local government, serving as a burgess, then as a bailiff, before becoming a chamberlain and then eventually being chosen as mayor. In fact, George Knapp held the position of Mayor of Abingdon on five occasions in the 1790s and 1800s. In 1794 he had supported the setting up of a local militia in Abingdon against possible French invasion in the time of the Napoleonic Wars. As mayor he had to deal with the local riots of 1799 and 1800. The Riot Act was read and troops were stationed in the town to crush escalating unrest at the steep rise in bread prices.[67] George Knapp may have been a lovestruck middle-aged man with a penchant for squandering his time and money at the gambling table, but he could also be a ruthless politician when needs required.

By the 1780s George Knapp had shifted his commercial interests from groceries to banking. The Knapp, Tomkins and

Goodall banking enterprise set up its offices on the High Street in Abingdon. The Tomkins brothers, Joseph and William, were wealthy local maltsters involved in the town's brewing industry. They were also leading Baptists. Their standing among nonconformist voters would help George eventually fulfil his ambition to become an elected member of parliament for Abingdon in 1807.[68]

In 1802, and again in 1806, George Knapp, representing the Whig party, had mounted unsuccessful campaigns to be elected to the House of Commons. Standing in his way was the 'nabob', Sir Thomas Theophilus Metcalfe. The term 'nabob' referred to young, ambitious men who travelled to India with little money and returned to England in their middle age with considerable wealth at their disposal. Initially serving in the army of the East India Company, Metcalfe made his fortune in India and later became a director of the Company.[69] In the early nineteenth century standing in parliamentary elections was an expensive undertaking, and George Knapp would have had to expend considerable sums of money to attempt to unseat Metcalfe.

Knapp and Metcalfe had to canvass the support of an electorate in Abingdon which totalled only about 260. Although the Tomkins brothers helped Knapp to secure the vote of the nonconformists, Knapp was also greatly dependent on the support of Edward Loveden Loveden. A former member of parliament representing Abingdon, Loveden, the owner of nearby Buscot Park with its mansion and extensive grounds, was a very rich and successful businessman. He was also an occasional supporter of the Whigs, and it seems that it was Loveden who urged Knapp to stand again for election in 1807.[70] Ultimately, though, Knapp was only able to prevail with a particular sleight of hand from the sitting mayor of Abingdon.

In 1807, the 'purples', backing Knapp, would eventually prevail over the 'blues' who supported Metcalfe, but only through controversial means. Knapp had stood on a platform which advocated economy, retrenchment and religious toleration.[71] The vote was very close and was disputed by Knapp. Fortunately, at the time Knapp's old schoolfriend, Thomas Knight, as the mayor, was responsible for adjudicating the vote. Knight proceeded to disqualify nine of the votes cast for Metcalfe, thereby enabling Knapp to secure election on a vote which had swung to 120 to 113 in his favour.

Shortly after, Knapp was once more elected mayor, which meant that for over two years he was simultaneously mayor and member of parliament for Abingdon. Celebrating his triumph in the mayoral election, Knapp distributed among the locals bread and cheese together with 'several barrels of strong beer'.[72] He was evidently a much-loved politician in Abingdon. 'Mayor-dressing' was a popular custom in the town in the eighteenth and nineteenth centuries. When a mayor was newly elected, the streets of Abingdon were decked with flowers and pumpkins and the arches of branches. At the time Knapp was elected again as mayor in September 1807, the mayor-dressing for the occasion was an especially lavish and spectacular one. A 'most expensive bower' was made which extended along and across the main streets in the centre of the town.[73]

Although George Knapp did not sit for long in parliament, he was quite active in this short period. He had moved from the mainstream of the Whig party in the 1790s to become one of the party's more radical members by the time he served as member of parliament. He voted for inquiries into alleged parliamentary abuses by prominent members, including a call for an investigation into the activities of Spencer Perceval, the future prime minister. More significantly, he threw his support behind the radical Whig member Francis Burdett, who was also a close friend of William Bagshaw Stevens. On 15 June 1809 Burdett presented his plan for parliamentary reform. The aim was to eventually dismantle the 'rotten-borough system', which was referred to by Burdett as 'this ill-shaped monster'. In rotten or so-called pocket boroughs, only a very small electorate voted. Typically, one family continued to be re-elected in these constituencies. Burdett was careful to note that the plan was not intended to be immediately adopted, but he had tabled it for future consideration. The plan promoted the extension of the franchise so that all men who were freeholders and who were householders subject to tax should be awarded the vote.[74] Here, Burdett was a forerunner to the Chartists who a few decades later were demanding universal male suffrage as well as annual parliaments and vote by secret ballot. The rotten boroughs would be abolished with the Reform Act of 1832. Knapp was one of only fifteen members of parliament who dared to openly back Burdett's plan. Perhaps Knapp would have become much better known as a follower of the Burdettite radical camp if it had not been for his untimely and suspicious death later in 1809.

George Knapp was a major landowner. From his father, he inherited property at East Hanney, a village then located in Berkshire. He also greatly benefitted from his father's marriage to Katherine Tyrrell. Katherine brought to her husband a lease at the rectory at Kidlington, which George Knapp senior then renewed.[75] An agreement was also made in 1753 between Katherine, her husband, her brother Joseph Tyrrell and Dr Charles Nourse, an eminent medical man, with regard to the lease of the corner house on Ock Street in the centre of Abingdon.[76] This would become one of the main residences of George Knapp junior, together with what had been his mother's home in Kidlington. An observer at the time noted how the best modern houses in Abingdon were made of brick. The exception, though, was the house of George Knapp 'which is handsomely built of stone'.[77] With Joseph Tyrrell dying childless, Knapp also inherited his uncle's property at Hampton Poyle.[78] And George Knapp also became the new owner of Whorestone Farm in 1786 with the death of his uncle. Knapp held the farm for the next twenty years.

In the summer of 1805 George Knapp attempted to sell Whorestone Farm. A newspaper advertisement about the sale provided much more details of the farm. Rather than eighty acres as in the case of the 1780 sale, fifty-eight acres of 'very valuable freehold estate' was put up for sale and partitioned into five lots. The first lot covered over twenty-seven acres and was called 'Great Ground'. This enclosed area included a barn and other buildings. The first lot may have involved the close of the ground referred to as Great Whorestone in the 1726 settlement. The remaining lots involved smaller plots of land which were labelled 'Trough Ground', 'Harelow', 'Barn Piece' and 'Clay Piece'.[79] This sale would not be realised because of objections raised over the issue of tithes, even though the land had been advertised as tithe-free.[80] However, by 1806 Whorestone Farm would eventually be sold to the Woodstock solicitor Henry John North.

As with the cases of Robert Buswell and Joseph Tyrrell, George Knapp had become a substantial property owner.

But none of these individuals had actually lived and worked on Whorestone Farm. Instead, they rented out the farm. Records show that Buswell, Tyrrell and Knapp had each in turn rented out Whorestone Farm to John Rowland, a yeoman from the nearby village of Water Eaton.

John Rowland paid rent for the land at Whorestone Farm between the years 1777 and 1806. Throughout this period, the annual rent amounted to £85.[81] It seems, though, that Rowland himself probably did not spend much time at the farm. Rowland must have had a team of labourers to manage the property given that he continued to also rent and work on a large tract of land at nearby Water Eaton. The Rowlands were themselves a wealthy family. John's father, Richard, had been a gamekeeper to the Lord of the Manor at Water Eaton. In 1774, the local press referred to Richard as 'a very opulent farmer of WaterEaton'.[82] John Rowland also worked as a gamekeeper for the local Lord of the Manor, and rented land at Water Eaton from him.

At Water Eaton John Rowland owned 'many and great beasts'. His preference was for short-horned Yorkshire cows, and Mrs Rowland herself was reported to milk a large number of them. John Rowland was known to prefer Hereford draught oxen to horses to plough the land. He believed that two oxen were equal to one horse and were much cheaper to maintain.[83] There may have been a connection between the Rowlands and the Buswells of Westcott Barton. A John Buswell was one of the executors of John Rowland's will.[84] According to newspaper reports, John Rowland died in June 1817 after falling from his horse.[85]

Conclusion

In practice, it is exceedingly difficult to trace the actual occupants of the land at Whorestone Farm in the eighteenth century. The farm was in the hands of rich absentee landowners who owned other property in the neighbourhood. These landowners – the Buswells, Tyrrells and Knapps – came from families which had intermarried. They rented the land at Whorestone Farm to other well-off individuals such as John Rowland, who could afford to pay the substantial annual rent. These individuals, in turn, would have employed others of lower social status and lesser economic means to manage and live on the farm.

Henry John North became the next owner of the land at Whorestone Farm following George Knapp. Ruthless property speculators rather than gentlemen of leisure or individuals more concerned with national politics were about to take an interest in the estate. This new generation of landowners were often eager to acquire land and then swiftly resell it for a profit. They were the products of what was in effect a new age of land speculation in Oxford beginning in the early nineteenth century.

THREE

LAWYERS AND LAND SPECULATORS

'Don't buy the house: buy the neighbourhood'

(Russian proverb)

Introduction

Two key periods in English history allow one to trace the early owners of the property which would become Whorestone Farm. Between 1085 and 1086 a national survey of land was carried out by William the Conqueror. Eager to raise taxes, the Norman ruler wanted to know who owned the land in his kingdom and what was the value of this land. The result was the publication of the Domesday Book. Four and a half centuries later, following his break with Rome, King Henry VIII proceeded to expropriate the assets and income of the monasteries, priories, nunneries and convents throughout his realm. In the Dissolution, substantial amounts of territory and properties were confiscated and then sold to families who had supported the monarch.

In preparing his defence to maintain the ownership of Whorestone Farm, the Woodstock-based solicitor Henry John North argued that the Crown had relinquished its title to the farm when King Henry VIII had allowed his physician to purchase land which had previously belonged to the abbey/nunnery at Godstow.[86] According to the Domesday Book, the owner of this land in 1086 was either Roger d'Ivri or Siward. Prior to the Norman Conquest, the land had been owned since the start of the eleventh century by St Frideswide Monastery as part of its Cutteslowe estate. By 1086, a piece of the monastery's land had come into the possession of Roger d'Ivri, an aristocrat and chief butler to King William I, who owned the manors of Walton and Wolvercote.[87] However, the nobleman Siward, who had held territory in the area at the time of Edward the Confessor, still also nominally held control of a part of the land allotted to the monastery in 'Codeslam' (Cutteslowe).[88]

By 1122 St Frideswide Monastery had been dissolved, and in its place stood St Frideswide Priory run by Augustinian monks. Within seventeen years the priory was in full control of all the territory in Cutteslowe once owned by the monastery. This was after Roger, the Bishop of Salisbury, had restored to the priory land previously allocated to the manor of Walton, and land once under Siward's ownership had been handed over.[89] In 1358 the priory struck an agreement with the abbey at Godstow to exchange lands. The abbey acquired land at 'Horston'.[90] It continued to own Horston until King Henry

VIII dissolved the monasteries and religious foundations in 1541.

In 1537, together with two other physicians, George Owen was present at the birth of the future King Edward VI, the long-hoped-for heir to the throne. Owen had only recently been appointed one of the physicians to King Henry VIII. It was Owen who signed the letter which announced the serious condition of Edward's mother, Jane Seymour, who died shortly after. In the next two years Owen was regularly summoned 'to prescribe' for the infant prince.[91] Contrary to received opinion, in general the young Edward remained in reasonable health apart from the final six months before his death in 1553. A witness to the will of King Henry VIII in which he was bequeathed £100, Owen was one of the last persons to speak to the King while he was alive and he was present at the monarch's death.[92]

King Henry VIII generously rewarded George Owen for his services in the birth and then monitoring of the well-being of the heir to the Crown.[93] Owen was granted the right to purchase land in north Oxford from the King. As a result, the physician became the greatest landowner in the neighbourhood. In 1541, the King permitted Owen to buy the abbey/nunnery at Godstow and convert the building into a house, which became his main residence. At the same time, Owen also gained ownership of all the land which had been under the control of Godstow Abbey. The King also permitted Owen to obtain the manors of Walton and Wolvercote, and the house and site of Rewley Abbey for £1,174. Earlier, in 1538, Owen had purchased the manor at nearby Yarnton.[94]

The doctor later entered politics and before his death was briefly a member of parliament for Oxfordshire in 1558.

The author of a treatise on the treatment of ague, ironically Owen himself died of fever. Godstow House was later sold by Owen's grandson, George, in 1616.[95] In 1573 George Owen's son, Richard, had earlier disposed of Walton Manor and its estate to St John's College. The advowson of St Giles' was also included in the sale (i.e., in theory, the right to present to the bishop a nominee for a vacant post in the Church), enabling the college to acquire substantial areas of land and various buildings and to become the major landowner in north Oxford.[96]

It has been suggested that the land which later became known as Whorestone Farm may have been sold by the Owen family some time in the period between 1549 and 1573.[97] By the early 1600s, the land called 'Great Horestowne' and other lands in the parishes of St Giles and in neighbouring Marston and Wolvercote had come into the possession of William Ryves (1570–1647). A distinguished lawyer, knighted in 1629, Ryves later settled in Ireland, where he became the King's Attorney General and Speaker of the Irish House of Lords. In 1606, as a taxpayer in Oxford, he was registered as 'William Ryves, Esquier in the Suburbs'.[98] Twenty years later it was noted that the land owned by St John's College 'abutteth northward on a hedge or mound of Sir William Ryves'.[99] Ryves was related to the previously mentioned Edward Ryves, the Woodstock-based town clerk.[100]

After Sir William's death his property was inherited by a relation – another William Ryves who resided in Rathsallagh in County Wicklow in Ireland. In 1659, this William Ryves sold Great Hoarstone Close and Little Hoarstone Close to the gentleman and lawyer Christopher Blower (c.1632–1692), who lived in the Berkshire village of Sunningwell near Abingdon. The sale took place when a start was made to enclose some of the fields in the area. At the time, a house was located in Great Hoarstone Close.[101]

The Blower family owned the land at Great Hoarstone Close and Little Hoarstone Close for at least the next fifty years, but it seems that Christopher Blower himself continued to reside in Sunningwell as a tenant of Hannibal Baskerville, the Lord of the Manor there.[102] Baskerville was an eccentric who was well known at the time for his generosity in providing succour to local beggars.[103] Blower got on well with Baskerville. In his letters penned from Staple Inn in Holborn in London – an Inn of Chancery where lawyers were trained and had their offices – Blower referred to Baskerville as 'my honorary friend and landlord'.[104]

A little more about the character of Blower may be gleaned from the fact that he was a close associate of Peter Heylyn, the distinguished Abingdon-based clergyman and intellectual.[105] Towards the end of the Civil War and in its immediate aftermath, Abingdon had become a stronghold for Puritans, who were bitter enemies of the Royalists and who were also vehemently opposed to the rites of the established Church. Heylyn had been ousted from his parish in the town when Anglican worship was banned by Oliver Cromwell. With the restoration of the Stuart Dynasty in 1660 and the suppression of the nonconformists, Heylyn was able again to promote his religious and political views in Abingdon.[106] This would seem to suggest that Blower's sympathies, like those of Heylyn, lay with the traditional Church and Crown. As previously noted, though, the nonconformists would maintain a strong presence in the town with influential families such as the Tomkins.

Great Hoarstone Close was converted from arable land to pasture in the mid-seventeenth century before becoming mainly arable again by 1707. In that year a one-year lease was concluded between the then owner, Christopher Blower junior (1657–1727), and two other parties.[107] Like his father before him, Christopher Blower junior continued to live at Sunningwell and was a practising lawyer and scholar who also had some knowledge in antiquity.[108] It would seem then that the Buswells had not been owners of Whorestone Farm for long before the preparation of the settlement in 1726. Indeed, perhaps the settlement was drawn up immediately upon the Buswells taking possession of the land.

In a petition of June 1813, Henry John North argued – justifiably, it seems – that the land which King Henry VIII had permitted George Owen to purchase in north Oxford would have included the property which would come to be known as Whorestone Farm. North contended that the Crown had thereby permanently surrendered its title to this land. However, other lawyers believed that with the conviction of Elizabeth Wisdom, an 'undivided fourth part' of the farm should have been automatically escheated or transferred to the Crown. As the new owner, North was determined to ensure that he would keep control over the whole of Whorestone Farm.

Henry John North (1756–1831): Lawyer and Land Speculator of Woodstock

By the late eighteenth century, the small Oxfordshire town of Woodstock was in serious economic, political and social decline. A falling population and a drop in property values had led to the virtual collapse of its steel jewellery manufacture and there were also serious problems in the local glove industry which was another key source of employment.[109] This was in marked contrast to the start of the century when the town had flourished and work had commenced on the building of Blenheim Palace. The new seat of the Dukes of Marlborough with its much-admired landscaped gardens had provided a welcome source of income for local innkeepers, shopkeepers and other tradespeople as tourists flocked to Woodstock. The town became the focus of markets and fairs, and the new wealth was displayed in the construction of grand houses in the centre of Woodstock. However, in a reflection of the times, by 1817 the new fifth Duke of Marlborough, George Spencer Churchill, was in grave financial trouble. The duke had debts amounting to over £600,000. His estates were seized and he was obliged to sell much of his library and art collection. Separated from his wife, the duke was forced to retire to Blenheim in semi-disgrace with his mistress and live on an annuity which had been originally granted by Queen Anne to the first Duke of Marlborough. The fifth duke died in the palace in 1840, surrounded by bailiffs who were disguised as footmen.[110]

Local government in the town had become rife with corruption and sleaze. Increasingly out of touch with the needs of its population, the town council squandered funds instead of investing in infrastructure and properly representing the inhabitants of Woodstock. The council, for example, frittered away money by buying lottery tickets. In 1793, the council spent £3 and 12 shillings on the distribution of a hogshead of ale to celebrate the burning of an effigy of the radical reformer, Thomas Paine. Opposed to reforms such as Catholic Emancipation and hostile to nonconformists, officials in Woodstock were determined to cling to power through populist measures.[111]

The situation further deteriorated in the first decades of the nineteenth century. Local politics had become hotly contested, with the supporters of the duke generally hostile to parliamentary reform.[112] In the parliamentary election of 1826, 'the most shameful scenes ever remembered in the town' occurred when the three sons of the Duke of Marlborough were embroiled in street riots against their opponents. One of the sons, Lord Charles Spencer, fought stripped to the waist. The three behaved so badly 'that their supporters cried shame, and many declared that they were the greatest blackguards at the election'.[113] Through much of the 1830s, local government in Woodstock came to a standstill when the anti-Blenheim members of the town council opposed the Duke of Marlborough's nominee for the position of recorder.[114] The recorder worked as a key legal adviser for the town corporation. Without a recorder in place, little business could be conducted by the town council.

It is not clear what role was played by Henry John North in these proceedings. The local solicitor held the influential post of town clerk in the period between 1804 and 1829, and, being one of the wealthiest inhabitants of Woodstock, North would have undoubtedly been involved in key decision-making in local government.[115] However, his reputation seems to have emerged unscathed in spite of the gross incompetence and negligence of the town council. His son, Henry North, took over as town clerk when ailing health had compelled Henry John North to resign. In contrast to his father, Henry North was not a supporter of the Duke of

Marlborough. Henry North would become a key ringleader of the anti-Blenheim faction in the 1830s.[116]

What is certain is that the career of Henry John North prospered while the conditions in Woodstock declined. North got on well with the Dukes of Marlborough. Here, he followed in the footsteps of one of his predecessors, Edward Ryves, the town clerk and agent of the third Duke of Marlborough. In 1808 North sold the town's water supply to the fourth Duke of Marlborough. Nine years earlier North had secured joint ownership of the water undertaking of Woodstock when he had acted as an executor and trustee for the will of John Chapman, carpenter and joiner, and previous owner of the town's water supply. North had become the sole owner of the piped water system in 1805.[117] Presumably, he made a handsome profit in disposing of the water undertaking. And North had also held the post and title of Steward of the Court of the Duke of Marlborough's Manor for ten years until 1829.[118]

Together with a local steelmaker around 1775 Henry John North purchased the site which would become known as 5–9 Park Street.[119] North took up residence at 9 Park Street in what became the most fashionable quarter of Woodstock in the centre of the town. He remodelled much of the interior of the building and upgraded its façade. In the mid-twentieth century the property was known as the Old Town House.[120] 9 Park Street was certainly an appropriate home for one of Woodstock's richest townspeople.

Today, the local museum, which is situated almost immediately across from 9 Park Street, has in its collection a portrait of Henry John North. Commissioned in 1808, the portrait was painted by Sir William Beechey, a close friend of North's. Before becoming a well-known artist, Beechey had briefly trained to become a solicitor, apparently with the encouragement and support of North. According to one story, Beechey's uncle, his guardian after the death of his father, was so determined to ensure that the young William should continue with his studies to become a law clerk that each night he would lock up his nephew in his bedroom in a house on Stow-on-the-Wold. One night, though, William evaded the clutches of his uncle by climbing out through the window and escaping down a pear tree before swimming across the nearby river and then fleeing to London.[121] The friendship between Beechey and North continued after Beechey became an important portrait painter for members of the royal family. There is also another memorial to Henry John North. Two years after his death, a stained-glass window was installed in his memory in the south aisle of the Woodstock Parish Church. The church is located opposite the local museum and is very close to 9 Park Street.[122]

Henry John North came from a wealthy and respectable family. His father, John, a 'gentleman', was also a solicitor at Woodstock, having previously practised in London. Henry John's mother, Gladys Baily, was quite possibly related to Dr Walter Bayley, the personal physician of Queen Elizabeth I.[123] One of Bayley's acclaimed published works was a treatise on the preservation of eyesight. Henry John's grandfather, William, had worked on land in the Headington area of Oxford.

Mary Ann Lenthall married Henry John North in the Oxfordshire town of Burford in 1791. The Lenthalls were a family who for several generations had lived at Burford Priory. They could be traced back to Sir Rowland Lenthall, the yeoman of the robes to King Henry IV, and 'one of the most distinguished warriors of Agincourt'. The Lenthall family was 'of considerable antiquity and historical renown'.[124] Mary Ann's great-great-great-grandfather was William Lenthall, who held the post of the Speaker of the House of Commons immediately before and after the execution of King Charles I. It was William Lenthall who on 4 January 1642 had defied the King who had entered parliament with four hundred armed men to demand the arrest of five members whom he accused of treason. Lenthall refused to tell the King the whereabouts of the five men. This was the first occasion when a Speaker had declared allegiance to the liberty of parliament rather than bowing to the will of the monarch.

William Lenthall acquired ownership of Burford Priory in 1634, and the Lenthalls then remained occupants of the Priory for the next two centuries. The Priory had been built in the 1580s and is said to be haunted by a gamekeeper and a small monk dressed in brown. One of the dominant families in the area, several of the Lenthalls became Sheriffs of Oxfordshire. Although still wealthy, by the time Mary Ann was born in 1770 the Lenthalls were starting to gradually lose their power and influence. Mary Ann's brother, John, was struggling to maintain the expense of managing large areas of estate while also maintaining his son, William John, who was serving as an officer in the Third Dragoons. Under increasing financial pressure, John was forced to mortgage certain properties.[125] William John Lenthall eventually sold Burford Priory in 1828. Twenty years earlier, parts of the house had been demolished and the famous Lenthall pictures had to be auctioned. It seems that William Lenthall had obtained ownership of these paintings from King Charles I. Among the collection of around 145 works was a well-known painting of Sir Thomas More and his family which would later come into possession of the National Portrait Gallery.[126] The Lenthall pictures had attracted a number of visitors to Burford Priory.

In spite of the financial problems of the Lenthall family, Henry John North's will revealed that Mary had brought a thousand-pound settlement to their marriage.[127] Given his comfortable background, North certainly had the financial means to become a significant landowner. His will recorded that he owned property in New Woodstock as well as having a house in Kidlington and land in the parish of nearby Thrupp. He had also owned a freehold farm in the Oxfordshire village of North Leigh, as well as an estate in Bladon near to Blenheim Palace.

His knowledge of the neighbourhood would have also given North certain advantages with regard to the acquisition and sale of property. As a solicitor he was closely involved in the Kidlington Enclosure of 1810 when various local proprietors staked their claims to secure land which had been previously held in common.[128] He had also served for many years as one of the clerks for the Trust of the Stokenchurch, Wheatley, Begbroke and New Woodstock Turnpike.[129] By 1806 Henry John North had also acquired ownership of Whorestone Farm, although he had for some time been interested in the estate.

It is significant to note that North's dealings with Elizabeth Slatter – the former Elizabeth Wisdom – stretched back as far as 1776. In that year the young Henry John North was in attendance and wrote his signature when Elizabeth and her second husband, John, in a written statement renounced all rights to the goods and property of Thomas

Rose Wisdom, Elizabeth's first husband. This followed the death of Elizabeth's daughter, also called Elizabeth. The estate of Elizabeth Slatter's first husband was to be inherited by Thomas Wisdom, Elizabeth's elder son.[130] The precocious Henry John North had already received his articles of clerkship back in 1770 when attached to his father John and he would take over his father's practice in 1786 when John died.[131]

More significantly, Henry John North was later heavily involved in the case over whether an undivided fourth part of Whorestone Farm should be escheated to the Crown instead of being inherited by Elizabeth Slatter, as a result of Elizabeth's earlier conviction for murder. In the documents made available, some details of this fourth part of the estate were not provided. For example, it was not clear what amount of acreage was involved over which part of the estate. The case would become a protracted one.

On 24 February 1804 North addressed a letter to the then Reverend Thomas Wisdom. Noting that all the family members of his late uncle – i.e. Robert Buswell – were advanced in years, North believed that it was 'desirable for all parties to dispose of the estate at Wolvercote' and declared that he was ready to be of assistance.[132] This indicated that Thomas Wisdom had been interested in obtaining for his mother and himself what he considered to be their rightful share of Whorestone Farm – i.e. the undivided fourth part – several years before he had petitioned the Treasury.

On 16 June 1807 North wrote a letter to the lawyer, William Gee of Bishop's Stortford, who was then representing the interests of the Wisdom family. The Woodstock solicitor expressed his concern for the Wisdoms and informed Gee that he was no doubt that they were entitled to their share of the land according to the settlement of 1726, but in his opinion they were barred because of the statute of limitations. The two lawyers then exchanged correspondence. According to Gee, North had offered him £400 to include Elizabeth and her son 'in the conveyance', but this was opposed by Gee. It is not clear, here, what exactly North was suggesting given that by this time he himself had taken over ownership of the whole of the Whorestone Farm from George Knapp.[133] North's attention would then turn to ensuring that he would not be forced to escheat to the Crown the undivided fourth part of the estate which had been claimed by the Wisdoms.

Quite extraordinarily, it was Elizabeth Slatter herself who had informed the Crown that the land should be escheated to it because 'of the tainted descent of the property'.[134] In the words of one of North's lawyers, the legal reformer Sir Samuel Romilly, Elizabeth Slatter had 'turned informer'.[135] Clearly, the Wisdom family was furious that they were not able to inherit what they believed to be rightfully theirs and their anger was channelled directly at North. If the Wisdoms could not gain possession of the land, they were then determined to ensure that North should be compelled by the Crown to relinquish it. Responding to Elizabeth's request, a group of five commissioners were granted a warrant by the Attorney General to launch an inquiry into the property. The commissioners held a number of meetings in the King's Arms in Oxford in April 1813.[136] They eventually resolved that the fourth part of the estate should indeed be transferred back to the Crown.

On 22 June 1813 North moved against this ruling. North and his lawyers appealed to the Court of Chancery to traverse the inquisition – i.e. overcome the ruling of the commissioners. Romilly, a member of the Court of Chancery as well as being a member of parliament, was one of the key lawyers who represented North. Romilly had been campaigning for a reform of the legislation with regard to the so-called law of the corruption of blood which had prevented the relatives of those convicted of certain crimes from inheriting land, goods and property. Ironically, Romilly was working against the interests of a family which had been direct victims of the law of the corruption of blood.

North and his team of lawyers argued that the Crown had surrendered its rights to the property when Henry VIII had allowed George Owen to become owner of large areas of land in north Oxford. Some details of the fourth part of the estate at Whorestone Farm were disclosed. Its annual value, including tithes, amounted to £36. Between 1777 and 1780 Robert Buswell had taken profits from this portion of the estate which totalled £54. In the years 1780 to 1786, Joseph Tyrrell had made a profit of £118, and between 1786 and 1806 George Knapp had earned £346 from the land. North himself, between 1806 and 1812, had made a profit of £192. Following North's petition, on 11 August 1813 the Court of Chancery made an initial ruling. The court argued that North's appeal was justified and that he was entitled to own the fourth part of the estate. Calling for a traverse of the inquisition, the court declared that all of the Whorestone Farm had been properly conveyed to the Woodstock lawyer.[137] In spite of the ruling of the Court of Chancery, the case dragged on.

Addressing the House of Commons on 25 April 1814, Romilly noted how his client had not been properly treated.

He argued that North had faced the 'most expensive proceedings'. Romilly added that North had previously given a 'fair and valuable price' for the land at Whorestone Farm.[138] The Assize Courts were to decide in a trial if there should be a possible traverse of the inquisition, but then the trial was for some reason postponed.[139] Was the previous decision in favour of the Crown eventually reversed? This seems to have been so because in 1820 North was evidently able to sell the whole of Whorestone Farm.

The case of Elizabeth Slatter with regard to the fate of Whorestone Farm turned out to be a landmark one. Through the efforts of Romilly, Parliament passed the Corruption of Blood Act in 1814. According to the Act, the impact of the so-called corruption of blood on family members seeking to claim their inheritance rights was abolished except for crimes of high and petty treason and murder. Previously, felonies came within the remit of the application of the so-called corruption of blood.

As with the examples of Buswell, Tyrrell and Knapp, Henry John North did not reside at Whorestone Farm. In 1813 William Rowland, a 'mealman' from the parish of St Thomas in Oxford, was paying North a yearly rent of £159 and ten shillings, subject to a land tax of £12, to manage the farm.[140] Interestingly, Rowland was present at one and perhaps more of the meetings of the Commissioners of Inquiry in Oxford in April 1813.[141] Rowland – evidently not an immediate relative to John Rowland of Water Eaton, the previous tenant – may have started to rent the farm in 1807. In November of that year a local newspaper advertised to be let 'several truly eligible fields' between the Woodstock and Kidlington roads known as 'Whoreston's Grounds'. Applications were to be made to Mr North.[142]

William Rowland was a successful businessman who lived and worked near the centre of Oxford. This meant that as in the case of his predecessor as tenant, Whorestone Farm would have been managed by others employed by Rowland. The Rowlands of the parish of St Thomas were a family of bakers and maltsters. As a mealman, William Rowland handled grain, meal and flour, and he ran a malthouse which processed malt for the local brewers. The malthouse was located in the ruins of Rewley Abbey. The former Cistercian Abbey was founded in 1280 by Edmund, the Earl of Cornwall. The monks had previously used the water power and transport provided by the nearby Castle Mill Stream and the Trill Mill Stream to operate the malthouse. The parish of St Thomas was noted for its poverty, and so the Rowlands would have been one of the dominant families in the neighbourhood.[143]

In December 1805 William Rowland had married Ann Bush, the eldest daughter of the ironmonger, Thomas Bush. Bush was the owner of a shop at 5 High Street in the centre of Oxford. The shop later became the site of Gill's Ironmongers, which eventually relocated to the nearby Wheatsheaf Yard. When the shop was finally closed in 2010 the local media reported that this marked the end of England's oldest ironmongering business, which had been operating for 480 years.[144]

William Rowland died a wealthy man in 1836. His 'excellent Dwelling house' at St Thomas's with its extensive corn granaries, stabling and a yard was advertised to be let.[145] He had acquired from the fourth Duke of Marlborough a large estate at Shabbington in Buckinghamshire.[146] William Rowland also had property near the Kidlington turnpike as well as at Water Eaton[147] – suggesting that he may have had distant family ties with the Rowlands of that area.

It is not known for how long William Rowland rented the property at Whorestone Farm. What is known, though, is that in 1820 Henry John North decided to sell the estate and in October of that year two land speculators, Crews Dudley and George Kimber, purchased the sixty-two acres that were advertised for sale at a cost of approximately £70 per acre. The conveyance was executed, and Dudley and Kimber gained possession of the farm on 27 August 1821.[148]

Crews Dudley (1781–1846): Lawyer and 'Pure Speculator'

The Oxford-based solicitor Crews Dudley was a so-called 'pure speculator'. He perfected a method of buying and then selling land to make a quick profit. Much of the land he acquired was sold within a few weeks or months.[149] Working as a solicitor, Crews Dudley would have been privy to inside information on local property markets. Some of his clients were involved in the mortgage, sale and renting of land. Conveyancing was a potentially highly lucrative business, dealing with agreements, assignments, leases, loans and mortgages. Skilled lawyers could act as accountants and brokers, advising their clients how they should invest their money. Such lawyers were in a position to secure credit, which they could then use to purchase and sell land for their personal gain. Because of its price volatility, the acquisition of land was particularly attractive to any lawyer who was prepared to speculate.[150]

By the start of the nineteenth century, with the growth of population in the Oxford area, new housing was urgently required, and this made the purchase of land especially attractive to speculators. People like Crews Dudley had the means and know-how to benefit from these changing circumstances. In 1811 a total of 2,092 houses were occupied in the city and in the bordering parish of St Clement's. But in the 'boom decade' of the 1820s at least 1,190 houses around the city were constructed.[151] The British economy was expanding after the final defeat of Napoleon in 1815. In Oxford, together with an increase in the population there was an 'internal migration' within the city as colleges took over housing they owned in the congested centre to extend their buildings and upgrade their facilities. The poor were forced out of the city centre and driven to the nearby suburbs.[152] A depression in the countryside in the 1820s and 1830s had also encouraged a wave of labourers to relocate to the Oxford area, and cheap housing was quickly built in the parishes of St Ebbe's and St Thomas's immediately beyond the old city walls to accommodate them.[153]

Crews Dudley played an instrumental role in the development of the parish of St Ebbe's which lay to the south of the city centre. Known for its garden nurseries and orchards, the area had traditionally been populated by labourers. Land here was available to build on. Dudley's name appeared on the deeds of a number of the land sales in 1822, usually as a trustee for the lease and release process of the conveyance of property, but he was also involved in the purchasing of land. Dudley participated in the sale of forty-four freehold lots in St Ebbe's on 31 August 1822 and made quick profits. For example, he purchased lot 37 for £28 but then swiftly sold the lot to a local hairdresser for over £36 before the conveyance was complete. Dudley also procured lot 11 for £70 and then resold the land to a carpenter for £105 in May 1823. The housing was of poor quality and the area quickly became overcrowded. Cesspools appeared and sewage from overloaded ditches and streams contaminated local wells. Ideal conditions were created for the spread of cholera and other diseases and infections. The St Ebbe's district suffered in particular in the three cholera outbreaks in Oxford in 1832, 1849 and 1859. Ironically, as a member of the Paving Commissioners of Oxford, Dudley was supposedly responsible for improving drainage in the city and its surrounds.[154] But the Paving Commissioners had little power in practice. Conditions in the district further deteriorated with air pollution caused by the smoke and fumes belching from the local gas works which was erected in 1818.[155]

In stark contrast to St Ebbe's, the development of the land around Beaumont Street near Worcester College entailed the construction of superior housing in what would become a much more salubrious area immediately beyond the city walls to the north of the city centre. This was part of a scheme to improve access to Worcester College from the city centre. Today's Beaumont Street is a thoroughfare populated by the offices of upmarket lawyers and business professionals and the surgeries of successful dentists and general practitioners. Houses were erected and then leased between 1823 and 1831 on land near Worcester College which was owned by St John's College. Dudley worked in partnership with George Kimber to take possession of several building plots. The first plots of land were advertised for sale in April 1823, so this enabled Dudley to swiftly make use of profits he had accrued from the resale of land at St Ebbe's.[156]

In October 1824 Dudley and Kimber purchased all five plots of land on the north side of Beaumont Street east of St John Street, one plot of land on St John Street and five plots of land 'intended for the building of stables' in what is now Pusey Lane. Three years later they acquired the remaining plots on the north side of Beaumont Street west of St John Street. In February 1828 Dudley and Kimber then promptly sold their leases on the land where houses had been built in order to make quick profits. Within a short four-year period Dudley and Kimber had become the largest land speculators in the development of the area around Beaumont Street.[157]

Not always the pure speculator, instead of quickly reselling Crews Dudley also maintained possession of other parcels of land which he leased from St John's College. On one occasion working together with Richard Carr, yeoman, in 1833 Dudley participated in the auction for the sale of forty-two lots of land in St Giles' parish near today's North Parade Avenue – about midway along the Banbury Road between Oxford city centre and Summertown.[158] Ten years later, St John's College decided not to renew the leases on property Dudley had acquired on land to the immediate north and south of North Parade Avenue. Dudley may have been relieved to have been freed from the leases. The costs for renewing leases on land owned by St John's College had been steeply rising.[159]

Sufficient available capital was essential in order to speculate on land. Crews Dudley came from a family which was rising up the social ladder. His father was a draper and tailor based in the Oxfordshire market town of Banbury. Earlier generations of the Dudley family had also lived in Banbury. His mother was the daughter of a master butcher from Long Crendon in Buckinghamshire. Several of the siblings of Crews Dudley seemed to prosper. Two brothers were successful tradesmen. One was a silversmith and jeweller living in Portsmouth, and another established a business on the High Street in Oxford working as a plumber and glazier. A third brother, Samuel, had served in the Dragoons in the Peninsular War against Napoleon and had been aide de camp to Lord Combermere. The Duke of Wellington had entrusted Samuel Dudley to take command of a castle in the course of the war.[160]

Crews Dudley married into the wealthy Castell family of North Leigh in Oxfordshire. After he had married in 1805 his wife, Jane, the Castell family took possession of Wilcote House, which was also known as 'Castle House' or 'the great house near Wilcote'. The house was situated among over two hundred acres of meadow, pasture and land for sheep. Queen Elizabeth I had originally granted the title of the land to Robert Devereux, the Earl of Essex. The previously mentioned Lenthall family then briefly owned the estate at the turn of the sixteenth century.[161] The Castell family owned other substantial property in the neighbourhood.

Dudley's legal practice was located at 6 Broad Street, which was a prime location in the very centre of Oxford. As well as being a solicitor and land speculator, Crews Dudley was also involved in public service. He was a vestry clerk for the parish of St Michael's in Oxford and he held the post of warden of the Incorporated Company of Cordwainers of Oxford. At the time of his death, Dudley was a councillor for the Liberals in the West Ward of Oxford.[162] An obituary in a local newspaper noted that he had worked as a solicitor for nearly forty years and 'was universally respected by the members of his profession'. He had held the then important offices of Chamberlain and

Bailiff in local government and was a representative of the town council.[163] John Crews Dudley, the son of Crews, was also trained as a lawyer and became mayor of Oxford in the early 1850s.

According to an account of the first years of Summertown produced by John Badcock, the local churchwarden, Crews Dudley and George Kimber made a threefold profit from the sale of Whorestone Farm which they had quickly put up for resale after completing the purchase of the property in August 1821.[164] The sixty-two acres were divided into seventy-two lots and two major public auctions were held in December 1821 and June 1822.

There were two maps which showed the layout of the seventy-two lots. A sketch of the auctioneer's advertisement for the sale with the various plots was drawn in 1859 by Edward Palin, the then vicar of St John the Baptist Church in Summertown. This was actually an updated version of a map produced by Badcock himself in 1832. In Badcock's map, the lot numbers 71 and 72 are not inserted in the plan.[165] In Palin's depiction, both ends of the track running along the north of the estate – today's Squitchey Lane – and the south end of the path running across the farm – today's Middle Way – were gated. At the time these were private 'roads' and those who purchased adjoining lots to them were provided with keys. By 1832, these roads had become public rights of way.[166] Plot 62 covered the piece of land on which 73 Middle Way would later be constructed. It was not clear when this particular plot was actually sold. The plot may have been purchased in the June 1822 sale given that it and other plots neighbouring it would form part of the property of the Summerhill estate. The construction of the main building on the Summerhill estate was not completed until 1823.

The first sale of Whorestone Farm had been originally scheduled for 6 November 1821 but was delayed for two weeks because the construction of roads and other works were not completed. Bad weather led to another postponement of the sale until 4 December.[167] The advertisement for the sale noted that the land was situated on a 'gentle rise' from the south and commanded 'most interesting views' of Oxford. The land was 'admirably calculated for villas or other buildings' with the soil being 'extremely fertile' resting mostly on 'fine gravel' 'under a rich loam'. The spring water was excellent and 'commodious roads' were about to be opened on the estate.[168] This probably referred to the upgrading of the future Squitchey Lane (previously known as North Road or Victoria Road) and the development of 'Green Lane' – i.e. Middle Way.[169]

A second sale was held in June 1822 to dispose of around thirty lots of land which had not attracted offers in the first auction. Apparently, the smaller lots had been easier to sell.[170] Dudley and Kimber decided to keep eight acres each for themselves and this land was not offered in the second auction. Crews Dudley kept possession of lots 47, 48, 49, 51 and 52 before he then 'disposed' of his eight acres to Joseph Bates, the gardener.[171] Acquiring another four acres from Kimber, Bates then managed a twelve-acre nursery garden which would extend southwards along 'Green Lane'. Bates himself took up residence in the property called 'The Firs' (plot 51), named after the trees which grew in the garden of the house.

Dudley also rented out land he had acquired just beyond Whorestone Farm on the corner of today's Banbury Road and

South Parade in Summertown. The property named 'South Lawn' was built on this land in 1822.[172] According to Badcock, this was an impressive building which was one of the most desirable in the village of Summertown. It commanded good views, with a garden surrounded by 'a neatly trimmed white-thorn hedge' and it was 'ever cheerful in the morning sun'.[173] Its attractions notwithstanding, Dudley preferred to continue to live in the centre of Oxford. The first tenant of South Lawn was a Miss Varney, who started a school in the property. By the early 1830s, South Lawn was occupied by Mrs Hobson, who as governess ran a school for the education of young ladies in the house.[174] South Lawn was later demolished and in its place now stands the less imposing Prama House.

Lot 71 proved to be the most difficult to sell. It was also the largest plot of land. Dudley and Kimber had shared ownership rights to the lot, but in 1835 Dudley allowed Kimber to take full control of the plot. The peddler Robert Richards, who may have been a squatter, occupied a dwelling within the plot, but his presence did not appear to be the major factor in the delay to sell the land. His house is today known as Richards Cottage and is situated on a picturesque narrow road fringed with tall trees called Richards Lane.[175]

In line with his previous land transactions, presumably Dudley made considerable profits from the resale and disposal of plots of land on Whorestone Farm. A tree was planted around 1830 near the north end of Green Lane (Middle Way) to delineate the boundary of the land initially acquired by Dudley. This impressive tree came to be known as Dudley's Oak.[176] It dominated the top end of Green Lane and the location of properties nearby were referred to by their distance from the tree. The top part of what would become

Middle Way was often known as Oak Lane. Much to the outrage of locals, the tree was felled in 1919.[177] Dudley's name, though, is still remembered on Middle Way. Following the demolition of a school previously linked to the church of St John the Baptist, in the early 1970s a block of flats called Dudley Court was built on the road.

George Kimber (1780–1835): Tallow Chandler, Speculator and Nonconformist

George Kimber was the proud owner and occupant of the grand residence which was known initially as 'Beaumont House' and then commonly referred to as 'The Avenue'. The house was built in 1823 in the area covered by lot 72 in the sale of Whorestone Farm. It was set in an eight-acre garden which lay between the Woodstock turnpike and Green Lane (Middle Way). The 1832 map placed Kimber's property much closer to Green Lane. Badcock was certainly impressed by Kimber's new home and called it 'a handsome white house of the first magnitude in Summertown'. The Avenue could be accessed from both Green Lane and the Woodstock turnpike. On Green Lane large gates opened to the back of the premises. The entrance from the Woodstock turnpike followed a pleasant carriage drive with flower beds and dwarf shrubs 'adorning the side all the way along'.[178] A later newspaper advertisement for the sale of the property in 1836 noted that it was 'a delightful genteel freehold villa residence'. There was a farmyard, stabling, cowsheds, a servant's cottage and other outbuildings 'placed at an agreeable distance from the dwelling'. The villa was situated at a 'pleasing distance' from the Woodstock turnpike 'where coaches are frequently passing'.[179] Kimber's then young son, Alfred, had laid the foundation stone for the building of The Avenue.

In contrast to his business partner Crews Dudley, George Kimber was not a pure speculator. He lived on land which he had purchased. Kimber was one of those successful, upwardly mobile entrepreneurs who was eager to make use of and enjoy the land he had acquired to enhance and secure his social standing.[180] As in the case of his partner, Kimber had his workplace in the centre of Oxford, but, unlike Dudley, as a result of his property dealings Kimber relocated to Summertown to begin a new life in his imposing new mansion.

The Avenue had been originally called Beaumont House on account of the ancient doorway which Kimber had taken from the ruins of Beaumont Palace at the time when he had become interested in obtaining leases to the land near Worcester College. Beaumont Palace had been built immediately beyond the north gate of Oxford in 1132 in the reign of King Henry I. The king had been eager for a palace to be constructed close to the royal hunting lodge which was located at Woodstock. Both King John and King Richard I (Richard the Lionheart) would be born at Beaumont Palace, but by the end of the thirteenth century the building no longer served as a royal residence. In 1318 King Edward II allowed a group of Carmelite monks (White Friars) to make use of the palace. After the Reformation, the building became increasingly dilapidated and it was finally demolished in the 1820s to allow the development of the Beaumont Street area.[181] Kimber seized the opportunity to acquire part of the east wall of the palace which had a doorway with a rose window over it. This doorway was then reconstructed in the grounds of The Avenue.[182]

Kimber did buy and then swiftly resell other land that he had acquired, but, in contrast to Crews Dudley, he was more prepared to hold on to the lease of properties and rent out these properties. Kimber also built on land he obtained. In the Beaumont Street area, he had built 'four tenements and a brewhouse' on land leased from St John's College near to the passageway known as Friar's Entry. The brewhouse probably later became the Gloucester Arms (at the time of writing renamed The White Rabbit). Kimber also became the leaseholder of two plots of land on the south side of Beaumont Street, and he had a house built on land he leased on St John Street which he then offered for sale in 1828.[183]

Prior to relocating to The Avenue, Kimber had lived and worked at Friar's Entry. He ran his tallow chandler business from a shop on the alleyway. Friar's Entry was originally an old medieval route which provided access for the Carmelite monks in their friary at Beaumont Palace. By the early nineteenth century, the alleyway was a shabby crowded side street which connected to the city centre. Kimber's move to The Avenue would have certainly been perceived as a major step up the social ladder.

In the sale of Whorestone Farm George Kimber purchased several other lots. He acquired lots 69 and 70 which covered an area of three acres. This part of the estate was arguably the least attractive. Known as Squitchey (i.e. Couchy) Piece, as late as 1832 the land here was of poor quality – of squitch and couch grass – and was not properly cultivated. Nevertheless, Kimber was able to sell this land to a Mr Green, the builder of The Avenue, for the sum of three hundred guineas. Green himself then made a quick profit by reselling the land for £470.[184] One of Kimber's sons was eventually able to dispose of the problematic lot 71, for which Dudley had abandoned any responsibility. This was the land upon which the Regency villa Summertown Lodge (now known as Summertown Villa) would be built.

George Kimber came from a family which had property and some wealth. His father had been a yeoman living in Kidlington. An uncle was a yeoman and farmer with land at Northmoor in Oxfordshire. In addition to living and working in his shop at Friar's Entry, George Kimber himself also spent a portion of his time managing his farm at Water Eaton. After his death, there was a sale of the stock at Kimber's farm in 1836. One hundred and seventeen southdown and longer wool ewes, together with cows, heifers and calves, a horse and colts, and an assortment of farm implements were advertised.[185] Clearly, Kimber had been a successful grazier as well as a tallow chandler and a land speculator.

A nonconformist, George Kimber had married Catherine Hayes in June 1801 in the village of Stanford-on-the-Vale in Berkshire. Catherine's father, William, was well known as an outspoken and practising nonconformist. William Hayes was also a tallow chandler and grocer, and in 1803 he had generously handed over his shop, stock and trade to his son-in-law.[186] Kimber kept his grocery business running until his death, and the shop was then taken over by his son, Alfred.[187] Unlike Henry John North and Crews Dudley, George Kimber was not an active participant in civic affairs. His nonconformist background would have made it more difficult for him to be successful in local government.

Nonconformists were not always welcomed in Oxford. As in the case of nearby Abingdon, they had established a firm presence in the city when Parliamentarian soldiers were quartered there in the Civil War. At the time the university had remained staunchly loyal to the Crown. The Meeting House Riots in the city in May 1715 against local Presbyterians, Baptists and Quakers had led to the imposition of martial law. The disturbances had been stirred up by students of the university, although townspeople had also participated. The Anglican-dominated university was especially hostile to the nonconformist community. Undergraduates attended gatherings in the meeting houses to act as troublemakers and ridicule those who were worshipping. The university could even prevent nonconformists from earning a living. Shopkeepers and businesses who were dependent on the colleges for their income were loath to provide employment to nonconformists through fear of causing offence to the university and thereby losing revenue.[188]

A key representative of the local nonconformist community at the turn of the nineteenth century was James Hinton, the pastor of the New Road Baptist Church in Oxford. His ministry at New Road – at the site of a church earlier erected by the Presbyterians – commenced in 1787 and spanned a thirty-six-year period. In that time Hinton succeeded in bringing together local Baptists and Presbyterians, who were traditionally fiercely at odds with one another, and the membership of the church increased dramatically from around twenty-five members in 1787 to about 250 in 1821. The meeting house had to be expanded twice to accommodate the larger number of worshippers.[189] A skilled preacher, moderate in his views and beliefs, and willing to reach out and embrace nonconformists of all persuasions, Hinton was a powerful force in the local community. However, the unity among the nonconformists in Oxford was short-lived.

The Congregationalists broke away from New Road Baptist Church after the conclusion of Hinton's ministry.

George Kimber's father-in-law was a member of Hinton's congregation. William Hayes served as a chamberlain in local government in Oxford and in 1806 he was elected to the position of bailiff. But Hayes refused to take up the post, apparently because he objected to making the customary oath. He then resigned as a member of the council chamber.[190] This prompted James Hinton to send a letter to a local newspaper explaining in detail why Hayes had decided not to become a bailiff. According to Hinton, the problem was not the swearing of an oath but instead involved passing a religious test.[191] The requirement to take the sacrament of the Lord's Supper in line with the rites of the Church of England prevented Protestant dissenters from accepting certain offices. The Corporation Act of 1661 and the Test Act of 1663, with their provisions for the receiving of the sacrament in order to hold certain posts, were not repealed until 1828. And it was only in 1871 that nonconformists were allowed to attend the universities of Oxford and Cambridge.

James Hinton personally knew George Kimber. The birth of Kimber's son, George Kimber junior, was registered by Hinton himself at the New Road Baptist Church in August 1808. However, there is no evidence to suggest that George Kimber senior was an active member of the local nonconformist community. It was mainly through the efforts of families such as the Lindsays, the Pharoahs and the Kingerlees that the Congregationalists established a presence in Summertown.[192] A group of Congregationalists had established a meeting house in Summertown as early as 1824. This was 'a small brick Dissenting Meeting House' at the south end of Green Lane.[193] It is not known if Kimber regularly attended their assemblies. According to Badcock writing in 1832, the Meeting House on the west side of Green Lane had been closed for some time.[194] Apparently, though, the Meeting House in 1835 had continued to serve as a preaching station with services held there on Sunday evenings.[195] A Congregational Chapel was later established in Summertown by 1843.[196] Kimber, though, had died eight years earlier. His final resting place was at the Protestant Dissenters' burial ground in the parish of St Peter's in Oxford near to the New Road Baptist Church.

Intriguingly, it seems that George Kimber had had a serious disagreement with his father-in-law sometime after taking over control of the tallow chandler business. In 1820 William Hayes had died a wealthy man. The total value of his estate was almost £4,000. In his will, he left his leasehold properties in Holywell, Oxford, to his daughter, Catherine – Kimber's wife – 'for her sole and separate use and benefit independent of her husband'. In the event of Catherine's death, her children were to take advantage from the outgoings of the properties. If Catherine did not have children, the estate would have gone to the tea dealer, John Bland of Newington Causeway, Surrey, who was the husband of Catherine's sister, Elizabeth.[197] The cause of the friction between George Kimber and William Hayes is not known.

Perhaps because of his nonconformist background, Kimber does not appear to have been remembered in Summertown, unlike his partner, Crews Dudley. The Avenue was eventually demolished in 1964 and was replaced by a school named after a former Bishop of Oxford, Kenneth Kirk. This school, in turn, was later torn down and its place was taken by a new residential development called Bishop Kirk Place. Another road named Hyde Place, which connects to Middle Way, was built adjoining Bishop Kirk Place. Thomas Hyde, who in 1839 established the Oxford Clothing Establishment on Queen Street in central Oxford, which would soon become a thriving business, was the next resident of The Avenue after Kimber's death.[198] Between 1850 and 1871 Hyde had served as a churchwarden in Summertown, and this may have contributed to the decision to name the road after the clothing merchant.[199]

The doorway which Kimber had rescued from the ruins of Beaumont Palace is no longer in Summertown. The arch is back in the possession of the Carmelite monks who established a priory at Boars Hill on the outskirts of Oxford.[200]

Conclusion

The longstanding dispute over the ownership of Whorestone Farm only seems to have been resolved sometime after 1814. This friction over control of the land was perhaps not surprising given that the farm occupied a prized location between the two main highways leading out of Oxford. Immediately after its sale in 1820 it was inevitable that the land would be quickly parcelled into a significant number of lots for the construction of properties given the demand for new housing. Because of their know-how and access to influential people, lawyers played a prominent role in the fate of Whorestone Farm. Lawyers could flourish in an age of speculation when a demand for housing at a time of economic growth meant that the ownership, sale and leasing of land had become commercially attractive. However, lawyers did not have a monopoly over the purchase and sale of land in Oxford at this time. As the example of George Kimber attested, skilful entrepreneurs from other professions could also successfully partake in the acquisition and redistribution of property.

The break-up of Whorestone Farm went in parallel with the emergence and development of the village of Summertown. A new era was dawning. The age of grand landowners and ruthless property speculators would eventually come to a close. Lot 62, the later site of 73 Middle Way, formed part of what would become the Summerhill estate. The first inhabitants of this new estate were two butchers and their families. These butchers were certainly not as well-known as North, Dudley and Kimber, but their lives would be equally interesting. In contrast to the previous anonymous occupants of Whorestone Farm – as opposed to the farm's landlords and tenants – it now became possible to trace the lives of the actual residents of the Summerhill estate.

FOUR
THE BUTCHERS

'One does not love a place the less for having suffered in it, unless it has been all suffering, nothing but suffering'

(Jane Austen)

Introduction

The story goes that Summertown owes its name to one James Lambourne, also known as 'Gipsy Jim', a horse dealer whose family came from the nearby village of Cumnor. A later resident of Summertown who got to know Lambourne personally, referred to him as a 'light, firm built active man', who was 'round as a baker's rolling pin'. Lambourne had been keen to settle down with his gypsy wife, Sinetta, whom he had met at the Warwick races. Sinetta, a seller of 'various articles of merchandise', was apparently a woman of striking beauty – '…of fine slim form, tall figure, good nut brown countenance and hazel eyes piercingly moving beneath her stylish black Beaver'.[201] Her mother had gone by the name 'Prettybody Smith'. It seems that Sinetta may have been born in Curraple in Italy.[202]

James and Sinetta were married in the village of Shipston-on-Stour in 1816. The couple quickly had three children before then deciding to settle down. In autumn 1820 a start was made on constructing a house on open land north of Oxford facing the Banbury turnpike on the east side of the road. Continuing to live in their caravan as the house was being built, the couple were hence reputedly the first settlers in what would become the village of Summertown. Sinetta was largely responsible for the house's construction, ensuring that building materials were carried from a distant stone pit. James, meanwhile, continued to ply his trade at local fairs.[203]

After the house was finally erected, James needed an address to promote his business. With the help of a certain Costar, and at the cost of 4s 6d, a sign board was put up in a conspicuous location in front of the new home. On the sign board were the words: 'James Lambourne, Horse Dealer Somer's Town'.[204] Apparently, James, who could neither read nor write, had wanted the words 'Summer Town' to be written on the sign board. He believed that his house was situated in 'the pleasant place in all England' if not 'in all the world', and, according to James, summer was the most delightful season of the year.[205]

For several years, maps referred to 'Somer's Town' or 'Summer's Town', and it was only in the 1840s that the village came to be commonly known as 'Summertown'.[206] The Lambournes have another indirect claim to fame. Their daughter, Sineta Lambourne, who was evidently another woman of eye-catching beauty by all accounts, married

Charley Cavendish Bentinck, the eldest son of Lord and Lady Charles Bentinck. Unfortunately, the two children from this marriage died in their infancy and Sineta also passed away in her youth. Charley would remarry and one of the daughters of his second marriage was destined to become the grandmother of Queen Elizabeth II.

The Lambournes may have been the first people to start to build a house on the freehold land immediately north of the corn fields and pastures belonging to St John's College. However, the historian Fasnacht believed that it was the raised footpath on the east side of the Banbury turnpike, completed in 1820, that 'was probably the main factor in making Summertown possible as the site of a village'.[207] This footpath ran as far north as the Horslow Field Road and then curved round to return to Oxford along the west side of the Woodstock turnpike. The purpose of the footpath was to provide university students with a bracing five-mile walk commencing from St Giles. This led to the saying – 'a walk round the five mile' – and, more recently, gave the name to the road known today as 'Five Mile Drive'.[208] The footpath also provided ready access from the city centre to the future Summertown.

The development of the village really first started with the sale in November 1820 of over seven acres of tithe-free, freehold land on the east side of the Banbury turnpike near to Diamond House. The owner of the land was Thomas Baylis, a well-to-do baker from Holywell in the centre of Oxford. The pasture and fields which were put to auction were parcelled out into forty-five lots. In the advertisement for the sale, it was noted that the land was located in one of the most 'eligible' situations in Oxford 'being elevated and dry, commanding pleasant and extensive views'.[209] The sale of Whorestone Farm, one year later, marked, as it were, the start of the second phase of expansion of the village.

Much of our knowledge of the first years of Summertown come from the writings of John Badcock, a widower and originally a tanner from Abingdon. He arrived in Summertown in 1830 to be near to one of his sons who was studying at Pembroke College at the University of Oxford. Two years later, Badcock was the author of the text: 'Origin, History and Description of Summer-town'. He had been commissioned by the first vicar of the village to provide details of the parishioners, and in particular to learn if they read the bible and if they belonged to any religious denomination. The first churchwarden of the village prepared what turned out to be a colourful commentary from his 'humble cott' – this was part of a double house which today is known as The Dewdrop Inn on Banbury Road. From the window of his then simple residence, Badcock would have been ideally placed to witness the villagers going about their daily business.[210]

Following the sale of the land owned by Baylis, twenty-five houses were swiftly erected on the east side of the Banbury turnpike. The first house to be completed in Summertown, on 24 March 1821 – before the Lambournes would settle in their new cottage – was called 'Mayfield'. This house was later purchased by the Summer Fields School.[211] Many of the properties on the east side of the Banbury turnpike had small slips of land at the front and larger gardens in the rear. There was a string of tenements known as Pharoah's Row. These were named after the Pharoah family, the nonconformists who plied their trade as tailors, coal merchants and draymen. The original centre of the emerging village was the large, open gravel space in front of the King's Arms Inn by the Banbury turnpike. Here the men of the village assembled and exchanged gossip.[212] At this time there was only a scattering of houses immediately to the west of the Banbury turnpike.

By 1830 Summertown consisted of around ninety houses and had a population of 517.[213] With no town planning, building was haphazard, and dwellings had sprung up with little sense of order around the Banbury and Woodstock turnpikes. There was a mixture of housing. As well as a few impressive properties for wealthy local businessmen, there was a number of much smaller cottages for tradesmen. There was also a slum area centred around a brewhouse on the east side of the Woodstock turnpike. People of various occupations resided in what had quickly become a functioning village. For example, there were labourers, glaziers, gardeners, shoemakers, coachmen, tailors, bakers, plasterers, masons, wheelwrights, laundry workers, teachers and butchers. These were the sort of jobs that helped to support an established community. More surprising, perhaps, was the resident Angelo Campino, 'an Italian maker of weather glasses' who lived on the Banbury turnpike.[214]

In these first years there was no public transportation to connect Summertown with the centre of Oxford. A few of the village's wealthier inhabitants were able to make the commute from the comfort of their own coaches. But the majority of the residents had to make do with horse-drawn buses which only ran as far as the street lighting from the city centre to St Margaret's Road. The villagers would then wait to cluster together in the safety of a group before braving themselves to then proceed northwards on a twenty-minute walk through the darkness to the village. With Summertown initially not being served by a post office, one of the villagers made the trek to the city centre each day to collect the mail.[215]

West of the Banbury turnpike, 'Middle Way' developed in parallel with the emergence and growth of Summertown. A variety of buildings popped up along what was then known as Green Lane. Moving downwards or southwards from Dudley's Oak, one would have passed The Avenue occupied by Kimber, the land speculator, and the twelve-acre nursery garden belonging to Joseph Bates. A pedestrian would eventually come across the Church of St John the Baptist on the east side of the road. The church was opened in 1832 and originally served as a chapel-at-ease before becoming a parish church in 1864 when Summertown became a parish. The church was built on a plot of land which was purchased by St John's College and which was situated on the corner of today's Middle Way and Rogers Street. The church quickly became the focal point of Summertown. The centre of the village had shifted away from the gravel frontage by The King's Arms. A school was built next to the church together with shops, a much-needed post office and the popular public house known as The Rose and Crown. The stretch of Green Lane which ran from just north of the church down to Double Ditch (today's South Parade) was called Church Street or Chapel Street.[216]

In Badcock's time the village schoolmaster, William Green, owned a cottage on the west side of Green Lane. James Hainge, a coachman, was another resident on this side of the road. His wife ran a grocery store next to their cottage, and the couple later set up a beer shop on the street. Arguably the first cottages built on Green Lane belonged to William Bolton, a successful local farmer who also owned 'a comfortable stone fronted house' immediately opposite the church. At the end of Green Lane on the east side of the road by Double Ditch was an open space known as Thurland's piece. This belonged to William Thurland, a cook employed by Jesus College. William Rogers, a labourer employed by George Kimber, occupied one of the few small dwellings located by Thurland's piece.[217]

According to Badcock's account, 'Summerhill' was one of the few houses built on the west side of the Banbury turnpike. He noted that 'far beyond, on rising ground, stands a cheerful (*thin*, like many more in Sumr. T.) brick house with pasture land before it'.[218] Summerhill was built in 1823 on a gently elevated slope running north from Summertown. According to Palin's plan of 1859, the Summerhill estate covered lots 52, 57, 58, 59, 61 and 62 which had been offered for sale by Kimber and Dudley – lot 62 being the site of today's 73 Middle Way. It seems, though, that the original building known as Summerhill was located in lot 56. Badcock's plan of 1832 positioned the house of the Brain family – the second household to reside in the property – in land allocated to lot 56.[219] James Ryman, the owner of the estate in 1859, had by that time apparently extended the grounds adjoining Summerhill.[220] It is not clear, then, if lot 62 was originally attached to Summerhill.

The first occupants of Summerhill were butchers. Butchers have played an infamous role in the history of Oxford. As early as the thirteenth century there were complaints from the public against the killing of cattle by butchers in the centre of the city at Carfax. These butchers then sold the meat in open stalls on the main street. An ordnance of King Edward III forbade the slaying of any beast within the city walls, and so slaughtering took place instead for a period below the castle.[221]

The public slaughter of livestock continued up to the mid-seventeenth century. Blood poured into street gutters and the town ditch and also polluted nearby streams. The slaughtering of livestock also continued just beyond the city walls in today's Brewer Street, which was once known as Slaying Lane.[222]

Regulations eventually prohibited the slaughter of cattle on streets, but unhygienic outdoor stalls continued to sell meat. Permanent stalls, known as The Shambles, were erected on Butcher Row (today's Queen Street) in the city centre until they were forced to close with the Oxford Mileways Act of 1771. With the passage of this act, which also addressed other pressing issues such as the widening of roads in the crowded city centre and the repairing of dilapidated bridges, butchers could only sell their produce in the newly constructed Covered Market which opened for business in central Oxford in 1772. Butchers were obliged to slaughter livestock on their own premises. At this time, butchers also carried out tasks that are associated with the modern farmer. They bred and raised cattle and pigs prior to their killing. This meant that butchers required a substantial area of land to perform their work. It was not surprising, therefore, that a number of butchers soon settled in the expanding village of Summertown. In 1832, there were at least five butchers resident in the village. And Summerhill, in particular, seemed to provide an ideal location for a butcher.

John Mobley (1785–1853): A Butcher in Debt

One year after occupying Summerhill, the butcher John Mobley was a prisoner of debt in the infamous King's Bench prison in London.[223] The prison was situated in Southwark in reclaimed marsh land south of the Thames. Conditions in the prison for those who had sufficient means at their disposal were quite reasonable. They may have stayed in comfortable rooms or could have lived within three miles of the prison after paying a fee to the marshal of the prison. This system of liberties, known as the Rules, was often abused. Many 'prisoners' ran a shop or business close to the prison, rented their rooms, got drunk and generally behaved in whatever way they wanted. In one particularly glowing account published by an anonymous writer in 1823, one learns how the King's Bench prison had reading rooms, a bakehouse and excellent apartments in which older prisoners who had not caused any trouble could stay for one shilling per week.[224]

Those prisoners who were not so wealthy were much less fortunate. Given his background and circumstances John Mobley was most probably one such prisoner. Unable to pay the necessary fees, these inhabitants of the King's Bench prison lived in crowded small cells which were rife with disease. They had to provide their own bedding and food and drink.[225] As of 1 December 1824, six hundred of the 837 'inmates' of the King's Bench prison were incarcerated within the walls of the jail. They were imprisoned in cells which were only supposed to accommodate around two hundred prisoners at most. There was no medical attendant, and prisoners were obliged to pay 'extremely high' fees to secure their release.[226]

How had John Mobley found himself in the King's Bench prison? It seems that he had bankrupted himself by purchasing the land and building of Summerhill. He did not appear to come from a family which had wealth and property. Acquiring Summerhill was a risk which had quickly backfired against Mobley. It was reported that Thomas Hunt, a 'bookseller' from Oxford, had petitioned the courts to attempt to recover money apparently owed to him by Mobley.[227] The exact amount involved was not declared. Bankrupts were usually imprisoned if petitioning creditors failed to secure their money after repeatedly appealing to the courts.

The name Thomas Hunt does not appear in the lists of booksellers working in Oxford at that time. It is quite possible that this particular Thomas Hunt was actually the one-time baker and later gentleman of St Giles, Oxford, who seemed to have an interest in books. By the early 1840s, Hunt had leased one of his properties in Summertown to the Reverend Philip Bliss.[228] The Reverend was a well-known antiquary and book collector. For over thirty years Bliss worked as Registrar of the University of Oxford and Keeper of the Archives. Given Hunt's wealth, his connections to the world of books and his ties to Summertown, it is quite conceivable that the former baker was the individual to whom Mobley was in debt.

One of the first mentions of John Mobley in the local press was in 1818. Some men were driving a bull belonging to Mr Mobley, the butcher, into the city. It seems that the bull had been grazing in what was then unenclosed and undeveloped land known as Cowley Field. While crossing Magdalen Bridge, the bull went out of control and in a rampage attacked Lady Sewell and her companion, Mrs Page. The bull took hold on its horns the shawl from the neck of Lady Sewell and then '…ran most furiously into Merton-fields, [and] attacked and gored a horse belonging to

Mr Taylor of Long Wall'. Eventually, the bull was restrained after a rope was thrown around its horns, and the two ladies, 'though much alarmed, were not seriously hurt'.[229]

One of at least ten children, John Mobley was born in 1785 in the small Oxfordshire village of Elsfield. He was the son of Samuel Mobley (also known as Moberly, Mobberly and Meublin) and Catherine Cleydon (or Claydon). The census of 1851 noted that John Mobley was born at Sescot. It was quite possible, then, that John Mobley's father had been a labourer working at Sescot (Suscot/Suscut) farm at Elsfield. The farm lay on lush low-lying land by the banks of the River Cherwell. In the late eighteenth century, apart from the occupants of the local manor house and a few farmers, most of the occupants of Elsfield would have struggled to make a living. The author John Buchan was a later resident at the manor house in Elsfield after the end of the First World War. Little is also known about the Cleydons, though it seems that the family had been resident at Twyford in Buckinghamshire for several generations. In 1808 John Mobley, butcher, married Ann Barrett at Great Marlow in Buckinghamshire. By this time Mobley was living in the parish of St Peter-le-Bailey in the centre of Oxford. Ann seems to have been the daughter of a carpenter who lived and worked in the same parish.

John Mobley may have attempted to move up the social ladder by becoming the first occupant of Summerhill in 1823. Details of the property were given in the advertised sale of the property only one year later. It was announced that an auction would take place on 5 August 1824 for the sale of twelve lots of land which were freehold and tithe-free, and which were 'delightfully situated on an elevated slope'. Blessed with springs of 'good water', the lots were suitable for building on. For further particulars, those interested could apply to Mr Mobley on the premises.[230]

There was a delay in selling the property and so in November 1824 Summerhill was advertised again together with a close of land adjoining it. The property was described as 'a valuable freehold dwelling house' with a stable, a slaughterhouse and 'convenient out-buildings' which were 'recently erected at a great expence'. A 'very desirable situation' for a butcher, the dwelling house had four 'very capital bedrooms', 'two excellent sitting rooms', a paved kitchen, a servant's bedroom, a cellar and other facilities. The house came with a 'good garden' and a large piece of ground, together with the unexpired lease of twelve and a half years of the close of land next to it. Clearly, John Mobley had spared no expense in constructing Summerhill. Mobley himself was now referred to as 'bankrupt'.[231] The two and a half acres of close of land was put up for auction again in February 1825.[232]

By January 1826, John Mobley had been released from the King's Bench prison and was working as a butcher in the St Clement's district of Oxford. His son, Thomas, was baptised that month in the parish. All of John Mobley's five sons would become local butchers. At the time, the parish of St Clement's attracted artisans and labourers. The population of the district had greatly expanded in the 1820s as a result of slum clearance in the city centre as streets were widened and the colleges erected new buildings. Conditions in St Clement's were far from salubrious. Sewers discharged their filth into the waters of the River Cherwell which flowed through the parish. Not surprisingly, the area was particularly devastated by the cholera epidemic of 1832. St Clement's accounted for around one third of all deaths in the Oxford area.[233]

In 1847 John Mobley was once more in trouble. Summons were taken out against John Mobley, senior, of St Giles, and two other butchers, who were accused of selling meat outside the covered market in Oxford. Contrary to the Oxford Mileways Act of 1771, a growing number of butchers were selling their produce from their houses and shops and the law was proving difficult to enforce. In 1848, twenty-seven butchers had petitioned for the right to sell their meat outside the covered market. The petition was rejected.[234]

In the case of John Mobley and his two associates, to the 'utmost astonishment' of those inside and outside the court, the butchers were reprieved. They had been convicted and fined nine shillings' costs, but the prosecutor had agreed not to press charges provided that the parties involved promised not to offend again. The butchers had confessed to selling meat outside the covered market, even though they had rented stalls there. Apparently, the prosecutor was not present to demand a conviction, and some of the magistrates in attendance were evidently not sufficiently acquainted with the nature of the case.[235]

Two of John Mobley's sons were much less fortunate. In March 1848 Richard and Thomas Mobley were charged with stealing sheep and were sentenced to be transported to Australia for ten years. The brothers had been living in Burford, where they had made a living selling black puddings and sausages. They were charged with obtaining a horse and cart and then stealing seven sheep from a farmer at Shipton-under-Wychwood on 18 December 1847. John Mobley himself testified in court. He admitted that he had seen his sons with several long-woolled sheep at six in the morning on 18 December, but this was not unusual since Richard and Thomas had a habit of using his slaughterhouse before selling their produce on the market in Oxford or London. John Mobley gave the court assurances that he had not been a partner to the crime.[236] After their sentencing, the sons arrived in Tasmania in November 1850. They were granted conditional pardons in 1853, but Richard and Thomas decided to remain in Australia and raised families there.

As for John Mobley, he did not seem to fully recover from his bankruptcy. In spite of continuing to work as a butcher for many years, according to the census of 1851 John Mobley was receiving parish relief while living with his wife, one daughter and a granddaughter on Nelson Street in the parish of St Clement's. Another son of John Mobley was living immediately next door with his family. John Mobley died on 17 August 1853 after a long and painful illness.[237]

With the benefit of hindsight, clearly the purchase of land and the building of Summerhill had proven to be an extremely costly and risky undertaking for John Mobley. Here was a failed attempt at social mobility. Bankruptcy had resulted from Mobley over-extending himself and getting into serious debt. The Mobley family was then plagued with further ill fortune. The next occupant of Summerhill, the butcher John Brain, would also suffer his share of trauma and personal hardship.

John Brain(e) (1798–1855): The Butcher Who Disappeared

The life of John Brain is shrouded in mystery. According to Fasnacht, the Summertown historian, Brain lived at Summerhill until 1846. In that year the well-known picture-frame maker and art dealer James Ryman had taken over the property.[238] This was actually not the case. After the death of his first wife, at the end of 1832 John Brain sold his household items and livestock and disappeared. He took on a new identity and relocated out of the county. This was only discovered after his death in January 1855. One may only speculate as to why John Brain had decided to take such a drastic course of action. In contrast to his predecessor living at Summerhill, John Brain had come from quite a comfortable background. He had also married into a distinguished family.

Confusion over the life of John Brain, who was originally a butcher, is compounded by the fact that there was another John Brain who resided in the Oxford area at the same time. This other John Brain, an agricultural labourer, lived, worked and died in the Oxfordshire village of Nuneham Courtenay. A number of family historians interested in the Brain family have mistakenly conflated the lives of these two individuals. This seems to be because John Brain the butcher was actually married in Nuneham Courtenay.

Thomas Brain, the father of John, was also a butcher who had lived and worked in Eynsham in Oxfordshire, where he had run a farm. Thomas Brain had owned substantial portions of land in the Oxford area. In 1817 he advertised to let about twenty-four acres of 'excellent meadow' or pasture land in three enclosed grounds land on the east side of the Banbury turnpike near Diamond House.[239] He had probably purchased this land seven years earlier from another butcher, the late William Forty, whose executors offered for sale almost twenty-four acres of grass land close to Diamond House.[240] It is not clear if this was the same land later acquired by Thomas Baylis. If not, the property of Thomas Brain would have most probably adjoined land owned by Baylis. Unlike the Mobleys, therefore, the Brain family had connections with the area which became known as Summertown prior to the acquisition of Summerhill. Indeed, this familiarity with the neighbourhood may have encouraged John Brain to purchase Summerhill in late 1824/early 1825.

In his will prepared in 1829, Thomas Brain, gentleman of St Giles, referred to meadow and pastureland he owned in the small village of Binsey, just to the west of Oxford, and to various properties he was renting out in the parish of St Peter-le-Bailey. His son, John, was at the time a butcher based in the same parish. The will made detailed provisions with regard to whom should inherit property and benefit from other proceeds of the family estate after the deaths of various members of the family including John.[241] The Brains were undoubtedly a family which enjoyed significant wealth. Thomas Brain eventually died eight years after preparing his will.

One grandson of Thomas was the well-known anaesthetist Francis Woodhouse Braine. Francis, an able boxer, whip and rider of hounds, spoke of how he had inherited his grandfather's love of sport. According to Francis, Thomas Brain was a wealthy gentleman farmer who lived in Oxfordshire.[242] Francis was the son of James Williams Braine, who was himself a reputable surgeon and member of the Royal College of Surgeons. James had married the daughter of a prominent barrister who became Advocate-General of Bombay. The couple resided in the most fashionable quarters of London, including in Mayfair.

The Brains were a large family. Thomas Brain was the father of at least six girls and four boys. Two of the boys became butchers – one of which was John – one was a surgeon (James Williams) and the other a saddler.

In September 1819 John Brain married Ann(e) Maria Lucy (1792–1831) at Nuneham Courtenay. In a number of communications with John de Lucy, I came to learn much more about the Lucy family. Ann's grandfather was the first cousin of the master carpenter and wheelwright William Lucy. John de Lucy was a direct descendant of this William. John informed me that the Lucy family could trace its roots back to before the Norman Conquest. Originally from Luce in Normandy, the family name was later Anglicised to Lucy. Very much interested in learning more about his family background, John discovered that his family was connected to Sir Richard de Lucy, the Chief Justiciar in England at the time of King Henry II.

Sir Richard de Lucy was implicated in the murder in 1170 of Thomas Beckett, the Archbishop of Canterbury. Beckett had clashed with the king on the issue of whether clerics who were convicted of felony in the ecclesiastical courts should be punished by the secular authorities. King Henry II supposedly declared: 'Who will rid me of this turbulent priest?' Sir Richard de Lucy had previously been twice excommunicated by Beckett for supporting the king. Sir Richard was one of the authors of the Constitutions of Clarendon (1164) which had stipulated that the clergy should be tried in lay courts. Apparently, it was Sir Richard who assembled together the knights who were despatched to murder the Archbishop. Later, feeling remorse over the death of Beckett, in 1179 Richard de Lucy resigned from high office and spent his final months doing penance at Lesnes Abbey in Kent. One year earlier Sir Richard had given instructions for the construction of the abbey.[243] The Lucy family later acquired the Elizabethan mansion at Charlecote in Warwickshire, and Queen Elizabeth I herself was a visitor to the estate.[244]

According to John de Lucy, a branch of the family who had lived at Charlecote went out to make its own way in the world, and William Lucy (1538–1593) became involved in the building trade in Ledbury in Herefordshire. Ann Maria Lucy was descended from this family branch. Although well informed about his ancestors, John de Lucy would still be very surprised to hear from me details of what happened to Ann Maria's husband, John Brain.

Ann Maria's father, Charles, was a highly successful flax farmer from Colwall in Herefordshire. It was reported in 1815 that he had managed for twenty-eight years the 210-acre Brockbury farm in the county, which had a mixture of meadow and arable land and almost thirty acres of orchard.[245] By the time of the marriage of his second daughter to John Brain in 1819, Charles Lucy had left Herefordshire and was running Lower Farm at Nuneham Courtenay.[246]

In 1831 John Brain was struck by a double tragedy. His baby son John perished. Two other sons had previously died in their infancy in 1820 and 1827. And one month before the passing away of John Brain junior, Ann Maria died at the age of thirty-eight. Badcock noted, with reference to John Brain, that 'in losing his wife he truly lost his better part'. With the death of Ann, John was left living at Summerhill in 1832 with his three remaining children, James, Jane and Harry, together with two young apprentices and a female servant.[247]

By December 1832 John Brain was advertising the sale of his livestock and household effects. His sows and pigs and a 'useful Hackney mare' were to be auctioned. The sale of his furniture included a 'handsome full-sized four-post, tent and other bedsteads', mattresses and blankets, chests of drawers, a dressing table, a bookcase, carpets and rugs, a pianoforte, table linen, cutlery, china, glass, prints, tableware, candlesticks, chimney ornaments, brewery tubs and beer casks amongst other items.[248] This was a sale on a grand scale in which John Brain appeared to be divesting himself of almost all his trappings and belongings. Intriguingly, there was no mention in the newspaper advertisement of the actual sale of Summerhill, and there seemed to be no obvious financial reason for John Brain to dispose of most of his effects. Perhaps devastated by his recent losses, John Brain may have decided to abandon Summerhill. What is certain, is that he would at some time relocate, change his name, abandon his profession as a butcher and begin a new life.

A notice appeared in *The London Gazette* in June 1856. In line with an Order of the High Court of Chancery with regard to the trust of the will of Thomas Brain, an appeal was made to all the children of John Brain to come forward to prove their claim to be beneficiaries of their grandfather's will. It was noted that John Brain had died on or around 2 January 1855. The notice went on to add that John Brain had moved from Oxford to Lambeth in Surrey and then had resided at Sydenham in Kent, where he had assumed the name of John William Smith. No longer a butcher, in his later years John had become an assistant to one of the messengers of the London Court of Bankruptcy. There was also a reference to Jane Lucy Brain, his daughter, who had not been heard of since 1844.[249] No other children were mentioned in the notice. The eighteen-month gap between John Brain's death and the publication of the notice suggested that it had not been easy to retrace the footsteps of the former butcher after he had left Oxford.

In practice, it seems that John Brain had also used the names James Smith and William Smith. For example, the census of 1851 referred to a John Smith, widower, living at Sydenham Place in Lewisham, Kent. Born in 1798 in Witney in Oxfordshire – Eynsham and Witney were neighbouring villages – this John Smith was employed as a clerk in the Court of Bankruptcy. Together with him was an eleven-year-old daughter called 'Fload' – presumably, 'Flora' – who had been born in Lambeth. The third member of the household was a young female house-servant from Tetsworth in Oxfordshire. The death of a John William Smith from Lewisham was later recorded in the first quarter of 1855.

It appeared that John Brain had remarried and had at least one child from this marriage. His second wife was apparently called Martha. There were various local newspaper reports which referred to Martha and William Smith residing at Sydenham Place in Lewisham. In September 1849 the couple accused a labourer, with whom they were acquainted, of stealing money from them. This was after the three had spent a night out together drinking heavily.[250] There were several advertisements – the earliest dating October 1844 – of a Mr or Mrs Smith from 1, 3 or 4 Sydenham Place seeking to let a four-bedroomed cottage with a garden close to the local railway station.[251] This implied that the couple were reasonably well off and had been married for several years.

There are records of a Flora E. Smith or a Flora E.A. Smith who remained single who was born around 1840. This woman, who claimed to have been born in Sydenham in Kent, was quite probably the daughter of John Brain. In 1881 Flora appeared to be prospering. She was the manageress of a bakery on the High Street in Croydon. Ten years later, listed as a domestic housekeeper, Flora was a lodger in Fulham. There then appeared to be a downturn in her fortune and in her final years Flora was an inmate in the Guildford Union Workhouse. A Flora Smith from Guildford died in 1915.

It is not clear if any of John Brain's children were able to benefit from the will of Thomas Brain. Neither Jane Lucy nor Harry (Henry Francis) are able to be traced. There is much more information about John's oldest son, James Brain (1821–1866), but it was quite likely that James was not able to claim his inheritance rights given his particular circumstances.

In 1841 James Brain was working for the Abingdon-based butcher John Vindon Collingwood, who was a former mayor of the town. Collingwood was also the owner of a substantial farm of some five hundred acres. Soon after, though, James Brain decided to migrate to South America. He spent the remainder of his life in Peru and Chile and came to be known as 'Santiago Brain Lucy'. In 1845 James Brain married Juana Capriol, the daughter of a mariner from Europe who had arrived in Valparaiso with his pregnant wife. Juana's mother soon died from the plague and the infant was adopted by the Capriol family. After his marriage, James Brain became a successful businessman running a shipping company which operated from Panama to Peru and Chile.[252]

James Brain would have benefitted from Britain's increasing commercial interest in Latin America and in Chile in particular. The export of fertilisers such as guano was an especially profitable business. There was also extensive British involvement in railways, construction and public utilities. A niche role was also provided by the British in chartering, insuring and repairing ships.[253] James and Juana had a large family and several generations of Brains have lived and worked in South America. There is no evidence to suggest that James Brain returned to England after his decision to emigrate and so he may never have been aware of the details of his grandfather's will. James Brain died in Iquique, then in Peru, in 1866.

Why, then, did John Brain decide to adopt a new identity? Was it connected with the death of his young wife? The name he chose would seem to suggest that John was determined to disappear, reinvent himself and not be traced. At that time, people who decided to change their names often made an announcement in the press – usually in *The Times* – or the change in name was published in *The London Gazette*. This did not appear to be the case with regard to John Brain.

Perhaps John decided to disappear after the death of his father, Thomas. The will of Thomas Brain was proved on 5 April 1838 by one of John's sisters.[254] Interestingly, no revisions or additions had been made to the will even though it had been prepared in 1829. Quite possibly John – and his children? – may have been removed as beneficiaries from the will if he had left Oxford before his father's death.

And what then of John's young children, James, Jane Lucy and Harry? Harry would have only been about seven years old at the time his father decided to sell his livestock and goods. Were the children looked after by their grandfather or by their uncles or aunts? And what of Summerhill? Was the property rented out or sold? One would assume that the property would have been eventually sold in order for John Brain to effectively carry out his change of identity. In contrast to John Mobley, there does not seem to have been pressing financial problems which may have forced John Brain to sell up and then disappear. And how did John Brain's well-to-do relatives – his illustrious brother, James Williams, and nephew, Francis Woodhouse – react to this chain of events? Here is a mystery which still remains to be solved.

Conclusion

Two butchers and their families were the first occupants of Summerhill. Both John Mobley and John Brain suffered considerable grief and misfortune The art dealer James Ryman was definitely in residence at Summerhill by 1846, and he had probably acquired the property some time before then. The house may have remained vacant for a period before its acquisition by Ryman, or someone else may have resided there for a period after John Brain. The 1841 census is not very helpful given the minimal details that were recorded in what was the first countrywide register of inhabitants. Perhaps another butcher may have lived and worked at Summerhill given the facilities that the property offered. There were several butchers residing in the village in 1841.

Previously farmland, for several years the property and grounds around the newly built Summerhill had become a place of utility as well as a family home. This was about to change. Under the next owners, the Summerhill estate became one which was treasured much more for its aesthetic value. Summerhill would also become a focal point for grand parties and other large social gatherings for the expanding Summertown community.

FIVE

PICTURE-FRAME MAKERS AND ART DEALERS

'Just in the four-mile radius where hackney carriages run
Solid Italianate houses for the solid commercial mind'

(Sir John Betjemin)

Introduction

In 1872 the Reverend Algernon Barrington Simeon, the headmaster of St Edward's School, described Summertown as 'a miserable dirty little village'. The remark was prompted by the school being forced to relocate its premises from the centre of Oxford at New Inn Hall Street after serious damage caused by a storm. Having failed to find a ready-made building to accommodate the school, the only appropriate site which was immediately available for the headmaster was five acres of turnip field by the side of Woodstock Road in Summertown. After paying £7,000 to acquire the land, in the spring of 1872 Simeon and the 'well-wishing' Miss Felicia Skene – the writer and philanthropist and 'a dear friend of St Edward's' – cut the first sod for a new building for the school in the middle of the turnip field. By August 1873 the school was ready to reopen in its new location.[255] Summertown was rapidly becoming a centre for educational excellence. Summer Fields school on the eastern side of the Banbury Road was gradually expanding and incorporated Mayfield, the first house built in the village.

Why, in stark contrast to the enthusiasm and praise of James Lambourne, was Simeon so scathing of Summertown? Certainly, the village had expanded in size since Lambourne's time. Fasnacht argued that in 1851, with its 228 inhabited houses, Summertown could still be referred to as 'a tradesmen's village'.[256] But a few decades later, with the construction of new roads and further housing development, Summertown had, in effect, become a suburb of Oxford.

The land owned by St John's College, which stretched between St Giles and Summertown, had been largely arable and pasture, with vegetable plots and gardens. The area had also catered for leisure activities such as fishing and archery practice.[257] But from the mid-nineteenth century, the college supported the construction of new housing on this land. A start had already been made to build housing north of St Giles' Church with the separate development of Park Town just off Banbury Road. Imposing detached Italianate villas for the wealthy and handsome terraced town houses designed by the architect S.L. Seckham were erected on a patch of land owned by New College in the 1850s. But Park Town was almost not built. The original plan had been to construct a workhouse on the site to be run by the Guardians of the Poor.[258]

The decision to build Park Town had an immediate impact on the development of north Oxford. St John's College was encouraged to lobby for an Act of Parliament, passed in 1855, which granted longer-term building leases of ninety-nine years.[259] Previously, the college could only lease land for twenty years and housing for forty years. This had not encouraged urban development as the short term of the lease was not enough for the builder to get his return from the house purchaser. With the longer leases, the builder could benefit from selling the lease with enough years to make it also worth the buyer's while. This change in the leasing system encouraged the building of first-class housing in north Oxford which attracted those with money.[260] Industrialists, businessmen and other successful professionals purchased properties in the area. A further spur to development was the passing of the Universities Act of 1877 which made it possible for fellows of the university to marry. College staff started to look for suitable housing to accommodate their families, and the large neo-Gothic houses which were springing up in north Oxford were becoming affordable to many academics by 1914.[261] These houses lay within one and a half miles of Carfax Tower in the centre of Oxford – a limit beyond which university faculty were not supposed to reside. The city was increasingly encroaching on the fields and land which bordered Summertown.

A key year was 1889, when it could be argued that Summertown had officially become a suburb. With the redrawing of the municipal boundary, Summertown was for the first time included within the Oxford City area. This would enable the inhabitants of Summertown to benefit from public services which had been hitherto largely lacking. Previously, all houses had earth closets and there was no proper sanitation. With the absence of mains water, water came from wells. One resident of Summertown remembered how: 'Summer nights were made loathsome by the emptying of cess-pools'.[262] The provision of drains, the handling of sewerage and the supply of mains water would come at a cost with higher rents and rates to be paid by the locals.

The transport network between Summertown and the city centre also greatly improved, and the population of Summertown no longer felt isolated and cut off. In 1877 conditions on the Banbury Road as it approached Summertown were referred to as 'a bog, a morass, a great dismal swamp'. This led to the Oxford Local Board – which had in 1865 replaced the Mileways Improvement Commissioners – being granted special powers in 1878 to improve the highways. Even before the redrawing of the municipal boundary, property owners in Summertown were forced to pay for work on Banbury Road through the levy of a rate.[263] This was a harbinger of things to come. And, in 1898 the horse tramway service was extended from the city centre to South Parade in the heart of Summertown. Before, the service, which had opened in 1882, and which should be distinguished from earlier horse-drawn buses, had only run from Carfax to Rackham's Lane (i.e. St Margaret's Road). Finally, a proper public transport system had been established to connect Oxford with Summertown.[264] In 1900 an observer noted how the motor car was becoming a familiar sight in the city, and Banbury Road was 'its peculiar exercising ground'.[265]

At the end of the nineteenth century, the Reverend William Tuckwell depicted north Oxford as 'a tremendous irruption' with 'intermediate streets of villadom, converging insatiably protuberant upon distant Wolvercote [sic] and Summertown'.[266] The village of Summertown was no more. As a result of extensive house-building, the population in Summertown increased from 1,421 in 1881 to 4,307 in 1911.[267] Between 1890 and 1894, eight new roads were constructed. These were to the immediate south of 'Middle Way' and in the far northeastern part of Summertown across Banbury Road and just inside the new city boundary, where a start was made at the same time to develop the Sunnymead estate.

Sunnymead was developed on land purchased by Owen Grimbly, the upmarket grocer, who lived for almost forty years at the majestic Summertown Villa (also known as the Lodge) on Green Lane (i.e. Middle Way). Grimbly would travel each day from his grand residence '...in his low carriage drawn by a plodding horse which seemed more accustomed to farmwork'.[268] Grimbly was forced to mortgage his villa to pay for the acquisition of the land. Sunnymead would become famous for providing laundry services for its north Oxford clientele. As late as the 1950s it was a common sight to observe women loaded with heavy laundry struggling up the Banbury Road to carry the dirty linen of the Oxford dons to their laundries. Sunnymead became known as 'Soapsud Island' because soap suds were often seen bubbling out of the street drains.[269]

It was no longer possible to easily detect where north Oxford ended and Summertown began. There was further urban development on the eastern side of Banbury Road after 1905. This provoked Fasnacht to note that in the years 1890–1910 the middle classes had taken possession of Summertown.[270] The redrawing of the municipal boundary in 1889 had enabled Summertown to extend northwards. In this period, Summertown also became a shopping hub. Along the west side of Banbury Road in particular, the ground floor of a number of houses were converted into shops as the suburb of Summertown further developed.[271]

The term 'suburb' is a loaded and contested one. Writing in 1891, the historian and journalist Sidney Low attempted to spin a positive account by explaining how the supposed order and rationality of the suburb, in contrast to life in the urban jungle, produced superior citizens in both mind and body who would be more fit for national service.[272] This was, in effect, open praise for the suburb by looking through what was clearly an imperialist lens. At the same time, though, the purported humdrum life of suburbia was mocked by George and Weedon Grossmith in their bestseller *The Diary of a Nobody*. This novel focused on the life of the Pooter family and the petty concerns of the lower middle classes with their feelings of self-importance, snobbishness and misplaced grandeur. More recently, suburbs have been criticised for their homogeneity and for being bastions of conservativism, and have been labelled as 'empires of consumerism' and sites where 'gigantic boredom' prevailed.[273] But in a world plagued by Covid, suburbs have been arguably reinvented and are viewed more as welcome areas of refuge offering comfort and a sense of belonging to people living there.

In practice, there are many types of suburbs. They may be differentiated, for example, according to their history and location, the nature of their inhabitants and the facilities and services they might provide.[274] The suburb of Summertown developed its own particular traits. The village may have disappeared, but aspects of village life lingered for several decades in Summertown. The Summerhill estate would continue to provide a much-appreciated venue for summer fetes and garden parties open to the local community. Summertown was able to keep its sense of identity as the city encroached on its borders and then enveloped it. This was not a community running according to some sort of clockwork order and harmony or exclusively centred on families filled with Pooterish ambitions. The society remained a mixed one, where the poorer elements and those struggling to make a living continued to share the same space with those who had the means to live in splendid villas. There were also subtle changes as more families with direct ties to the university were embraced, thereby further enhancing the community's previously established links to schooling and education.

'Middle Way' itself was gradually transformed in the latter half of the nineteenth century and in the years before the outbreak of the First World War. With the appearance of shops on the Banbury Road the centre of Summertown shifted away from the Church of St John the Baptist to focus again on the main highway. Apparently becoming too small to accommodate parishioners, the church was eventually demolished in 1924 after the building of a new parish church of St Michael on the Banbury Road. Previously known as Green Lane, by 1859 'Middle Way' was referred to as Centre Road by Edward Palin, the local vicar. It later became known as George Street, named presumably after King George IV, although the king had long passed away in 1830. The nursery gardens of Joseph Bates, which had at one time extended from the Woodstock Turnpike to the Banbury Turnpike, were divided and new housing erected there and along other sections of the road.[275] 'Middle Way', in effect, was becoming less green. One exception to this was the development of the Summerhill estate under its new owner, the art dealer James Ryman. Within the grounds of the estate exotic plants and trees were cultivated and a large garden was fashioned which would become effectively a hub for the local community.

James Ryman (c.1795–1880): From Rags to Riches?

On 15 August 1848 the much-anticipated auction of the art collection and other effects of the Second Duke of Buckingham and Chandos took place at Stowe House in Buckinghamshire. The month-long auction became a significant event with what were in effect national treasures being put on sale. There was immense interest from the art world, the press and the public at large. Railway timetables had to be readjusted to ensure that crowds could come and tour the grand estate at Stowe before its dismantling. The auction itself, conducted by Christie's, took place in the State Dining Room at the impressive neo-classical mansion. The sale was looked upon as a 'national catastrophe'. Somewhat exaggeratedly, according to an editorial in *The Times*, the bankruptcy of the duke was comparable to 'the overthrow of a nation or a throne'.[276]

Bailiffs had arrived at Stowe House as early as August 1847. By the summer of 1848, the debts of Richard Grenville, the duke, who, through his mother, was a direct descendant of the Plantagenets, exceeded £1,500,000. Much of this was at an exorbitant interest rate of five per cent. The lavish expense splashed to cover a visit and stayover of Queen Victoria and Prince Albert to Stowe in June 1845 would certainly not have helped matters. The duke was referred to as 'the Greatest Debtor in the World'. Much money had been frittered away speculating on land and on the railways. At the auction at Stowe House even the deer in the park were placed on sale. The auction turned out to be a major disappointment. Prices were low and only £75,000 was collected.[277] There were expectations that the sale of the famous Chandos Portrait of Shakespeare would raise substantial funds, but these hopes were also dashed.

The Chandos Portrait was an oil work on canvas which was painted in the period between 1600–1610 when Shakespeare was still alive. Its origins remain obscure, but it was perhaps the work of John Taylor, an artist and key member of the Painter-Stainer's Company – one of the oldest Livery Companies of the City of London. The painting was allegedly first in the possession of Shakespeare's godson, the poet laureate Sir William Davanant. It then fell into the hands of several owners, including Robert Keck, a lawyer and relative of Anthony Keck of Great Tew. The painting was inherited by John Nicholl, who married into the Keck family. Nicholl's daughter married the third Duke of Chandos, and the painting then passed down the Chandos and Chandos/Buckingham line. Over the years the painting suffered from general wear and tear – it had been displayed in the Duke's Theatre in London in the 1660s – and had been damaged by clumsy varnishing and less than careful cleaning.[278]

Bidding for lot 382 – the Chandos Portrait – took place on the twenty-third day of the auction. The competition was fierce between five art dealers, one of whom was James Ryman. The other bidders were Henry Blore, a picture dealer from Regent Street in London who had been insolvent and imprisoned because of his debts only five years previously. Mr Farrer from Wardour Street in London was one of the major purchasers at Stowe and was bidding for the First Earl of Dudley. Joseph Nicholl, who was also a member of the Company of Monayers at the Royal Mint, was a descendant of the Nicholls who had at one time owned the Chandos Portrait. Also participating in the bid for the painting was Horatio Rodd, picture dealer and bookseller, who was bidding for the First Earl of Ellesmere, a self-styled poet and politician. Rodd was reported to have in his possession a small portrait of Shakespeare produced around 1700 which resembled the Chandos work.[279] Ryman himself purchased many items at Stowe for the Countess of Jersey – Sarah Sophia Child-Villiers – who was one of the richest women in England at the time.

Edward Manson, in charge of the bidding, first addressed his audience. He announced that bids should be 'in character with the high worth of the interesting relic'.[280] A large and expectant crowd had congregated for the occasion. Ryman opened the bidding with a paltry £50. This provoked a gentle and good-humoured reprimand from Manson – 'That is not as it ought to be, Mr Ryman, but I will take your bidding nevertheless [laughter]'. Both Blore and Farrer had given way when the bidding reached £200. Nicholl pulled out when the bidding came to £300, leaving a head-to-head contest between Rodd and Ryman. Manson was obliged to use 'his most persuasive powers' to coax Ryman, 'who is generally a very bold purchaser' to continue in the bidding. But Ryman eventually retired when Rodd offered 355 guineas for the Chandos Portrait.[281]

The Earl of Ellesmere, a founding member of the National Portrait Gallery, would donate the painting to the gallery when it opened in 1856. The Chandos Portrait was listed as the first painting in the collection of the National Portrait Gallery.

In spite of failing to secure the Chandos Portrait, Ryman was one of the largest purchasers at the auction at Stowe House. He bought at least fifty-one lots, many on behalf of the Countess of Jersey. These included paintings by Rembrandt, Rubens and da Vinci, and items such as a silver table and mirror and various vases, a cabinet and a toilet table. Ryman also acquired items for his personal collection. This included lot 311 – Mireveldt's paintings of King Frederick of Bohemia and his wife, Queen Elizabeth – 'two of the best portraits in the whole collection' – for less than £72.[282]

In one obituary of James Ryman it was claimed that in his lifetime he became one of the richest men in Oxford.[283] Here was a definite example of social mobility. Ryman was baptised in Oxford in March 1795. Little is known about his parents, William and Sarah. His aunt, Elizabeth, married John English, a blacksmith from the parish of St Giles in Oxford. James Ryman attended the Blue Coat Boys' School in the city. This was a well-known charity maintained by the local authority in Oxford. Pupils were provided with clothes and given lodgings. After becoming a successful art dealer, Ryman provided almost £200 in donations to the school.[284] He also held regular parties at Summerhill for children from both the Blue Coat Boys' School and Girls' School. Ryman did not appear to marry into a wealthy family. James and Ann Helme, the parents of his wife, Jane, were Presbyterians from Cripplegate in London. Jane Helme's sister, Charlotte, would marry a butcher.

There were brief mentions of James Ryman with regard to his work as early as 1816. He was at that time apparently a client of George Jackson who was a composition ornament maker and a supplier of glue.[285] And, in an auction for an oil painting by George Morland which was titled 'Horses & Figures Outside a Tavern', there was a label on the back of the painting which referred to James Ryman, 'picture frame maker, carver and gilder'.[286] However, Ryman was only made a freeman of Oxford – thereby being able to do business within the city – on 6 September 1819. One could become a freeman in Oxford by various means. Many became freemen by serving a seven-year apprenticeship, usually from the age of fourteen. Others became freemen by gift (honorary), through purchasing the title or by being the son of a freeman. In exceptional cases, one could become a freeman by an act of council approved by the Lord Mayor. This was the means by which Ryman became a freeman.[287]

Originally, Ryman had a small shop on Pembroke Street in St Aldate's.[288] But, in 1823, one year after marrying Jane, he took over the larger premises of the picture-frame maker, John Williams, at the much more prestigious address of 24/25 High Street. At this time, Ryman referred to himself as a carver, gilder, picture frame and looking-glass manufacturer.[289] In the previous year he had been initiated as a freemason at the Lodge of Concord. The print seller and dealer James Wyatt appeared to play a crucial role in Ryman's rise to fame in the art world.

James Wyatt had been an apprentice to Robert Archer, carver and gilder, and had then worked with him as a partner for four years before establishing his own business on 115 High Street in Oxford. Wyatt would become a keen supporter of J.M.W. Turner and the pre-Raphaelites. Focusing first on picture-frame making, Wyatt gradually started to deal with pictures and prints before publishing prints himself. He made a name for himself as a picture dealer and print publisher.[290] Ryman would follow a similar trajectory. The pre-Raphaelite artist John Everett Millais was a regular visitor to Wyatt's shop and Wyatt commissioned some of his work. Turner painted two oils for Wyatt, including the well-known 'High Street Oxford' (1810), which is now worth an estimated £3.5 million. A curator of the Duke of Marlborough's collections at Blenheim Palace, justice of the peace, alderman and local councillor, Wyatt was also at one time Mayor of Oxford.[291]

In January 1819, Thomas Wyatt, a baker of High Street, Oxford, married Ann Ryman, a younger sister of James Ryman. Thomas was a brother of James Wyatt. The close connection between the Wyatt and Ryman families appears to have worked to the advantage of James Ryman. The ties James Wyatt had established with the art world probably provided important opportunities for the younger and less-experienced James Ryman. Interestingly, Ryman has been referred to as Wyatt's successor, and so it is quite possible that Wyatt had looked upon Ryman as his protégé.[292] Wyatt himself, however, had a son, James Wyatt junior, who also became a picture dealer.

It was only in the late 1830s that Ryman made a major breakthrough in the art world, and this was probably due to Wyatt's close connections with Turner. Ryman had exhibited the works of various artists in his shop. His only major venture as a publisher was a set of illustrations of Oxford produced in the 1830s. This included thirty-eight plates dedicated to

Queen Adelaide and a number of engravings and reproduced watercolours.[293] However, in 1839, Turner agreed to paint for Ryman the work which became known as 'Oxford from North Hinksey'.

Turner knew Oxford very well. In his childhood he had often stayed with his uncle who had lived at Sunningwell, not far from Oxford.[294] According to one account, Turner had visited Oxford in 1834 at the request of Ryman, who was interested in Turner producing a watercolour of Oxford. This apparently eventually resulted in the painting of 'Oxford from North Hinksey'.[295] This story has been disputed, though, as it seems that Turner and Ryman only became properly acquainted in the late 1830s. What is certain, is that Ryman commissioned Turner to produce the painting which would later be engraved on steel by Edward Goodall and then published by Ryman as a print in 1841.[296]

'Oxford from North Hinksey' was painted by Turner in 1839 on the first floor of Ryman's shop on the High Street. The famous watercolour – now displayed in the Manchester Art Gallery – has a view of the gleaming spires of Oxford in the distance, although Tom Tower and Christ Church College's cathedral are in shade. In the foreground, women are reaping corn, a farmer is on horseback and two members of the college are approaching dressed in their gowns and wearing mortarboards. The finished work was presented as a gift by Turner to Ryman, who was then 'fortunate' to sell the painting for eight hundred guineas.[297] According to one account, Ryman dated his success in business from the selling of Turner's watercolour.[298]

This generosity from Turner must have certainly helped Ryman in his career. The cash from the sale of Turner's work – which sold for substantially more than the Chandos Portrait – would have enabled Ryman to expand his business. The money may also have allowed Ryman to purchase the Summerhill estate. His ties with Turner would have also opened doors for Ryman to establish other contacts in the art world. Ryman would have had the opportunity to shift the focus of his work and concentrate more on becoming an art dealer.

It is not clear when Ryman was first commissioned by the Countess of Jersey to help expand her art collection, but presumably he had been employed by the Countess for some time before the auction at Stowe in 1848. Ryman must certainly have benefitted financially, and socially, by working for such a wealthy and influential woman. The daughter of the tenth Earl of Westmoreland, Lady Sarah Fane, had married George Child-Villiers, the fifth Earl of Jersey, in 1804. The Countess was one of the patronesses of Almack's Assembly Rooms at St James. At the time, this was one of the most exclusive social clubs in England. Obviously a woman of boundless energy, the Countess was the mother of seven children and had a reputation as a lady of fashion as well as being a socialite. She had several sobriquets including 'Sally Jersey', 'Queen Sarah' and 'Silence', because she apparently never stopped talking. A close friend of Benjamin Disraeli, the character Zenobia in Disraeli's *Endymion* was modelled on the Countess. She lived part of her life not far from Oxford at Middleton Park in Middleton Storey in Oxfordshire, where her husband trained racehorses. Her annual income was estimated to amount to £60,000. In comparison, the Duke of Devonshire, one of the largest landowners in the country, had a yearly income of £50,000. As well as being a famous political hostess, the Countess was a senior partner in the banking firm Child & Co. She was the only offspring of Robert Child, the principal shareholder in the banking business.[299]

At the Stowe auction Ryman had purchased for the Countess the much acclaimed and so-called 'Jersey Portrait'. This was thought to be a painting by Holbein of Queen Mary in a black dress with richly ornamented sleeves. Critics later believed that the painting was one of Lady Jane Grey, or possibly of Catherine Parr, one of the wives of King Henry VIII.[300] Ryman also bought for the Countess a toilet table and matching toilet glass of silver which had once belonged to the Villiers family.[301] In March 1854 Ryman published a work in lithograph of a miniature oil painting of the Countess of Jersey produced twenty years earlier by the artist James Holmes.[302]

The art critic and writer John Ruskin was also an associate of James Ryman. A possible – but unproven – encounter between Ruskin and Turner in Ryman's shop on the High Street in Oxford has been relayed by several commentators. Ruskin was a student at Christ Church College in Oxford between 1837 and 1840. Instead of participating in sports with his fellow students, Ruskin preferred to spend his leisure time in Ryman's shop which was full of prints and drawing of Turner's works. Ryman allowed the young Ruskin to go to the back of his shop where the student made sketches of Turner's pictures. Supposedly, one day Turner visited the shop and observed Ruskin at work. Questioning Ryman who the student was, Turner apparently declared: 'The young man draws very nicely'. Ryman formally introduced the two and a close relationship between Turner and Ruskin thus commenced. However, Ruskin himself did not refer to such a meeting in his writings.[303] He did admit, though, that he was once ashamed to be seen with both his father and mother in Ryman's shop. Unusually, Ruskin's mother was present in Oxford throughout her son's studies, and Ruskin's father often came down to Oxford on weekends.[304]

Ryman's close ties with the Arundel Society would have also helped him to expand his network among art circles. The Society was founded in 1848 by the Earl of Arundel, a well-known patron of the arts. The aim of the Society was to promote an interest and knowledge of the works of the old Italian, Flemish and German painters, and the Italian sculptors of the Middle Ages and the Renaissance. Members of the Society included aristocrats, politicians and religious leaders. In 1849, James Ryman was listed as one of the original thirteen agents of the Arundel Society. After his death, Ryman's company continued to work as an agent of the Society until 1895.[305]

Sir William Henry Gregory, the Anglo-Irish writer and art critic, and at one time a Governor of Ceylon, was a member of the Arundel Society and knew Ryman well. According to Gregory, Ryman was instrumental in purifying 'undergraduate taste' by exhibiting and selling line engravings of the old Italian masters. Gregory purchased from Ryman a print by Richomme of Raffnelle's *Triumph of Galatea*. Ryman had said to Gregory: 'Put that up, sir, in your sitting room, and I'll engage that at the end of the week there will be neither racehorses nor ballet dancers in its company'. Following Ryman's advice, Gregory acquired more line engravings and this enhanced his love of paintings and art.[306]

Ryman's shop on the High Street became an essential port of call for local and visiting artists intellectuals and passing dilettante. The mathematician Charles Dodgson (Lewis Carroll) frequented the shop to view exhibits and procure prints. Many an hour could be spent rummaging through the prints and other items that Ryman had on display in his shop.

Ryman's success in the art world may also be attributed to how he was able to adapt skilfully to the changing times. The 1830s had been the golden age of reproduction engraving with new methods of printing technology enhancing the quality of engravings. Dealers made substantial profits from improved engravings which were sold to an increasingly wider clientele. Art dealers worked at the interface between the art world and the general public. They received generous commissions and mark-ups. In the 1840s and 1850s the newly enriched middle classes were eager to splash out their money on engravings and paintings.[307] At this time, the average annual income of the top twenty publishers and print sellers in London amounted to about £16,000.[308] Ryman may not have earned such high sums, but close to London, and with a ready market of university staff and students keen to purchase prints and other works, Ryman's shop clearly provided a focal point for interested local consumers and patrons of art.

But by the 1850s, the days of engravings attracting a mass market were numbered. The quality of engravings was deteriorating through the employment of less skilled engravers. In an attempt to address this issue the Printsellers' Association had been founded in London in 1847. Ryman was one of its two vice-presidents – a clear indication of the standing Ryman had already achieved in the print-selling world.[309] The Printsellers' Association was in effect a self-regulatory body. Only prints supposedly of a high enough quality were approved and stamped by the Association and were then able to be sold on the market.

The impact of photography should also not be underestimated. Photographs were rapidly improving in quality and these would soon drive out of business many of those engaged in the laborious and time-consuming work of engraving original paintings. Ryman was one of the pioneers in exhibiting photographs in his shop. By late 1855, Ryman was displaying photographs taken by Roger Fenton of scenes from the war in the Crimea. These included the famous photograph of the *Valley of the Shadow of Death* 'thickly strewn with spent balls and broken shells'. The exhibition drew many visitors to Ryman's shop, including officers who had fought in the Crimean War.[310]

James Ryman had moved into Summerhill some time before 1846. In that year, the vestry minutes of St John the Baptist Church in Summertown, dated 16 July, referred to Ryman being present when the accounts of the churchwardens over the past year were discussed. This seems to imply that Ryman may have already been resident in the village for some time. He regularly attended other meetings of the church, including one as churchwarden in April 1850. Two months earlier Ryman had chaired a meeting in which parishioners discussed choosing a suitably qualified person to serve as Parish Constable.[311] According to J.F. Ryman Hall, a nephew of Frank Ryman Hall, who later took up residence at Summerhill, James Ryman had decided to live in Summertown after his first visit to the then village.[312] However, Ryman also continued to spend a period of time living above his shop on the High Street.

Under Ryman's occupancy, Summerhill was renamed Summerhill Villa. It became a place of beauty rather than utility. The main building has been described as 'a rather grand Italianate villa, ashlar, with a tower'.[313] No longer required to service the interests of a butcher, the estate was attractively redesigned. The slaughterhouse, for example, would have definitely been removed. Summerhill Villa and its gardens became, in effect, a bold statement of prestige, attainment and social status.

The concept of the villa – a large house with extensive gardens – may be traced back to the Roman Empire. Interest in building villas had been renewed by wealthy landowners and businessmen in the late eighteenth century. Located close to the city or town, these became the second homes for the moneyed classes. From their villas, the owners, such as Owen Grimbly, could commute to their place of work by carriage.[314] The design of the garden attached to these new homes was dictated by the architecture of the building. Hearing 'the singing of birds in their season', the inhabitants of the villa could feel that they were living in the countryside while still residing close to neighbours and near to the facilities and amenities offered by the town or city.[315]

The mid-nineteenth century witnessed a period of so-called 'villa mania'. Much smaller detached and even semi-detached houses, adjoining a patch of lawn, shrubbery or trees, were labelled villas by their proud owners. With ongoing suburban development, these 'villas' were presented as attractive alternatives to terraced housing.[316] With this popularisation of the 'villa', the term became unfashionable. It was 'one of a growing number of suburban affectations that attracted mockery'.[317] The owners of larger properties abandoned the term 'villa' in preference for 'house' or 'lodge'. Summerhill Villa itself would in time become known again simply as Summerhill.

Under Ryman's occupancy, with the land no longer needed to raise livestock to be slaughtered, the grounds around the main building at Summerhill were radically transformed. An exotic garden was created at the side and at the back of the house. Along the border with 'Middle Way' there was a paddock known as 'Mr Ryman's fields'.[318] Ryman acquired more land. The pleasure grounds extended over eleven acres and were enclosed by today's Squitchey Lane, Middle Way, Banbury Road and Hobson Road.[319] Various parish functions were held in the gardens of Summerhill. Activities were organised for the children from the local Blue Coats' schools. The annual show of the Summertown Horticultural Society was held in the grounds. Refreshments were provided, a bazaar was laid out and a band performed for the local parishioners. All proceeds raised went to grateful local charities.

Harry Charles Ingle, later Mayor of Oxford, and the son of the master of the local school by the Parish Church on 'Middle Way', has described in some detail his personal memories of the excitement young children experienced when visiting Ryman's pleasure grounds in the 1870s. School treats were held there each year at the end of July. Mr and Mrs Ryman made it their practice to personally welcome the children. The grounds were full of 'wonderful adornments and statues'. There was a large sunk lawn, avenues of trees, four fields and an aviary with birds 'of painted plumage gay'. Near the lawn was a summer house which resembled a Greek temple. Its roof was of yellow glass and its walls were coloured blue and decked with white plaques depicting scenes from Ancient Greece. 'Most enchanting' was a fountain in which the children were encouraged to catch tadpoles with their cups. When it was time for tea a large school band bell rang and the children quickly settled on the sunken lawn. Cakes and cans of tea were served by 'pretty maidens from the house'. On a specially prepared table were dishes piled high with 'chumps of cake' and 'slices of bread and jam'.[320]

New houses and buildings were also constructed on the Summerhill estate in Ryman's time as the grounds expanded. The property known as 'The Firs' was acquired by the estate and was then sold to a civil engineer by the early 1900s. The Grange, a Swiss-like chalet with five bedrooms, which was also known as Ryman's Folly, was erected on the estate most probably in the late 1870s by the well-known architect and surveyor Frederick Codd. The British Gothic Revival architect had fallen into debt and was bankrupt by 1876.[321] Ryman may have helped to revive his career. Codd himself lived in Ryman's Folly with his family for several years.[322] Near Codd's residence, and also on the estate, were nine small houses, called Russell Place, which in 1881 were occupied by general labourers, bootmakers, a stone mason, a coachman and a railway signalman. There was also Summerhill Villa Lodge, presumably at the front of the estate, which housed another coachman – perhaps Ryman's personal chauffeur – and his family.

Ryman's property in Summertown was listed in the national Return of Owners of Land which was carried out in 1873. In effect a modern Domesday Book, the Return listed the names of the owners of holdings of over one acre together with the estimated yearly rental of these holdings.

According to the Return, Ryman owned over thirteen acres of land in Summertown which had a gross estimated rental in excess of £330.[323]

Ryman preferred to engage in charity work rather than enter local politics. An obituary in a local newspaper stated that Ryman had been a person of 'very simple and unassuming habits'. It was noted that he was 'an unostentatious benefactor to many good works'. Ryman had rejected numerous offers to participate in municipal contests and had declined to seek civil honours.[324] However, he was a known supporter of the Conservative party. In spite of the nonconformist background of his wife, Ryman was for many years a churchwarden and manager of the church school on Church Street in Summertown.[325] He gave as a gift to St John the Baptist Church a 'fine organ' built by Messrs Willis of London.[326]

In an eventful life Ryman had also suffered his share of misfortune. In 1854 he had suffered a 'serious accident' in his gig. He had been travelling to Summerhill in a pony chaise when the animal suddenly took fright and Ryman's gig crashed into another carriage going in the same direction. Thrown out of the gig, Ryman had a shoulder dislocated and sustained severe head injuries. At the time it was feared that he would not recover.[327] Ryman must have made a quite remarkable recovery for a man then approaching sixty years. Less than a year later a fire caused 'considerable damage' to paintings and engravings at Ryman's residence on the High Street. Luckily, Ryman was not at home and it was the quick actions of his housekeeper who called help from neighbours which prevented the fire from spreading and destroying the property.[328]

Ryman eventually passed away in Summertown aged eighty-six. He left a personal estate worth just under

£20,000. In his will it was noted that he held leasehold properties from St John's College in north Oxford and owned freehold cottages, a paddock and premises in Kidlington.[329] Ryman also was the owner of 10 The Terrace at fashionable Park Town.[330] Having no children of his own, his nephews, to whom he had 'entrusted the management of his business' for 'some years', were the main beneficiaries of his will.[331] However, the terms of Ryman's will were also quite controversial, and this would have a significant impact on the life of his nephew, Frank Ryman Hall, the next resident of Summerhill.

Frank Ryman Hall (1839–1925): The Disadvantaged Nephew

Although not on the same scale as the grand auction at Stowe House, the sale of the paintings, drawings and professional engravings at Summerhill after the death of James Ryman was nevertheless impressive. Commencing on 3 May 1881, the sale extended over four days. Much of the bidding took place in The Turner Room, but the 'gems' of the collection were sold in The Drawing Room – presumably the most imposing room in Summerhill. There was a 'splendid collection' on display, and the auction was well-attended, with some dealers having travelled a considerable distance. Works for sale included paintings by Overbeck, Raffaelle, Landseer, Rembrandt, Zuccarelli, Turner, Hogarth, Rubens, Vandyke, Carreggio and Titian, among others. The auctioneer declared that it was imperative that the whole of the lots should be sold in accordance with the terms of the will of James Ryman.[332]

Other items were also auctioned. These included 'two very handsome and beautifully in-laid large Chinese cabinets', and several sideboards, other cabinets, tables, chairs and 'richly carved' old furniture. Also for sale were no less than three pianofortes and about four hundred volumes of books 'mostly in handsome bindings and very rare editions'.[333] It seemed that almost all of Ryman's life collection was being offered for sale.

One of the principal purchasers in the sale was James Ryman's nephew, Frank Ryman Hall. For example, Ryman Hall acquired the oil painting by Tweedie of the late Bishop of Oxford (Dr Wilberforce) for thirty-nine guineas. He also procured one of the 'gems' of the sale. This was the set of the twelve original paintings by Johann Friedrich Overbeck titled 'The Passion of our Lord'. The late Sir Robert Peel, the former Prime Minister, had previously attempted to buy the set in order for the paintings to be exhibited at the National Gallery. A romantic painter of Christian religious subjects, Overbeck was one of the key members of the Nazarene Movement. The set was purchased by Ryman Hall for the sum of 235 guineas. This was evidently the most expensive item sold at the Summerhill auction. Clearly having a penchant for Overbeck, Ryman Hall also bought two other original drawings by the German painter from his uncle's collection for seventy-two guineas.[334]

The sale at Summerhill followed the instructions specified by James Ryman in his will. These terms came into effect after the death at Summerhill of Ryman's wife in December 1880. The trustees and heirs were expected to sell all the residue of Ryman's estate and its effects, both real and personal, including the furniture, Overbeck's drawings and Turner's engravings held at Summerhill, and to hold the proceeds upon Trust.[335]

The terms of the will of James Ryman were somewhat complicated. According to the original version of the will prepared in October 1874, his three nephews, Frank and Edwin (Ryman) Hall, and William Richards would take over the running of the print-selling business on the High Street in Oxford. Two years later a codicil was inserted which stipulated that with the death of Richards, Ryman's great-nephew William (Emanuel) Richards Junior would take over his father's share of the business. The original will of James Ryman had also stated that after the death of his wife, Summerhill, with all its gardens and closes and other freehold houses, cottages, land and estate at Summertown, would be inherited by Frank and his heirs forever. The codicil added in 1876 amended this and noted that Summerhill would be inherited by Frank for life, and after the death of Frank and his wife, Sarah, the property would pass to William Richards Junior and his heirs forever. Frank Ryman Hall was named one of the three trustees of the will.[336]

It is not clear why the terms of the will of James Ryman were adjusted to benefit William Richards Junior at the expense of Frank Ryman Hall. Had there being a falling-out between James Ryman and Frank Ryman Hall? And, as Fasnacht pointed out, although Ryman may have left Ryman Hall the estate at Summertown for life, he had not provided his nephew with the means to maintain the property.[337] Indeed, Ryman Hall was even forced to spend considerable sums of money to ensure that at least some of his uncle's works remained at Summerhill. In fact, in his later years Frank Ryman Hall would be plagued by various financial issues and problems, and this would compel him to mortgage the estate at Summerhill.

Frank was the second son of Thomas Hall, who in 1832 married Maria Ryman, another sister of James Ryman. The Halls were a family of nonconformists from Reading who worked as innkeepers. Thomas Hall was at one time a publican, but he also had an interest in printing and worked as a compositor tasked with the responsibility to arrange type for printing. Probably under the influence of his brother-in-law, Thomas later concentrated on establishing a printing business. His three sons, Frank, Edwin Alder and James Thomas, also worked in the printing profession.

James Thomas was employed by his father at Hall and Son, Printers, based at Queen Street in the centre of Oxford. In 1881, as a master printer, he had six men and two boys working under him. Edwin Alder and Frank, however, both worked with James Ryman, and were 'adopted' by their uncle. In March 1881 Edwin Alder announced that by deed poll he had assumed the name Ryman as a surname and prefix to Hall, and so henceforth he would be known as Edwin A. Ryman-Hall.[338] Fifteen years later Edwin had pulled out of the partnership with Frank and William Richards Junior at Ryman and Co and then relocated to Wales with his wife.[339]

It is not known when Frank changed his name to Ryman Hall – apparently without the hyphen. At the time of his wedding in 1869 to Sarah Golding, Frank was referred to by a local newspaper as Frank Ryman Hall.[340] James Ryman was one of the witnesses to this marriage. Sarah was the only daughter of the late John Goundry of Oxford. The Goundrys were a family of maltsters and brewers. Sarah's first husband, James Golding, who died in 1862, had worked as a servant at one of the colleges in Oxford. Sarah and James had one child, Alice Marian Golding, who would live for many years with Frank and Sarah at Summerhill until Frank's death.

In Frank's obituary, it was noted that in his youth he was an assistant in the print-selling and art-dealing business of his uncle. Frank was apparently a 'well-known authority on works of art' and 'had great taste and judgement as a connoisseur'.[341] However, there are few other references in the media to Frank's work in the art world. One newspaper article published in 1854, though, did praise an engraving produced by Frank from a drawing made by a Daguerreotype taken by Bracher of Oxford. Frank's engraving was 'pronounced by his family and friends to be a most perfect likeness'.[342] The photographer, Edward Bracher, who specialised on portraits and landscapes, lived and worked at 26 High Street in Oxford between 1852 and 1863.

In contrast to his uncle, Frank concentrated more on his civic duties in his later years. As a City Councillor, he represented the Conservative party in the North Ward of Oxford in the 1880s and 1890s. He became a magistrate in 1885 and served as a justice of the peace for forty years. His obituary stated that he was 'certainly one of the most assiduous in his duties' and attended the courts 'with a regularity remarkable in one of his advanced years' until he eventually fell ill.[343] Frank led an active and full life. President of the Oxford Photographic Society, a member of the Oxfordshire county cricket club and the Oxford Angling Society, and a senior member of the Alfred Lodge of Freemasons, he also served as a manager of Summertown schools for fifty years.

Like his uncle, Frank was well-known for his charitable works. The Summerhill estate continued to be used as a venue for school fairs and other community events, and also hosted the annual cricket match between the choir and Sunday School of the local church.[344] Following in the footsteps of his uncle, Frank also served as treasurer of the Oxford Blue Coat Boys School.[345]

Financial problems dogged Frank Ryman Hall in his later years. Extensive work on renovating and further developing the estate at Summerhill must have proved costly. It has been suggested that Summerhill – then also known as 313 Banbury Road – probably had more money spent on it than any other house in Summertown.[346] In the final two decades of the nineteenth century work was carried out, for example, to extend the north-west side of the main building at Summerhill.[347] Interestingly, Summerhill was not connected with the water mains until 1913, and so the occupants, or rather the servants, had to make do with the tiresome task of drawing water from wells on the land. The main house had no bathrooms, but all bedrooms were fitted with marble mantlepieces.[348]

Frank Ryman Hall was forced to pay the cost of road repairs at Summerhill and elsewhere in Summertown. Serious attempts were made in the final quarter of the nineteenth century to tackle the problems of flooding and drainage in Oxford. A Public Health Act was passed in 1875 to improve sanitation. This gave powers to a new Urban Sanitary Authority.[349] The Turnpike Trusts for Banbury Road and Woodstock Road were wound up in 1876 and 1878. The Oxford Highways Board was given responsibility for improving these roads. Its remit included parts of Summertown. A start was made to clean up the roads and install surface water drains, but local ratepayers complained about the expense.[350]

After becoming part of the Oxford City area in 1889, more concerted efforts were made to upgrade road infrastructure in Summertown. In a report issued in 1890, the City Engineer to the Public Improvements Committee announced that property owners would be served notice with regard to further works that needed to be carried out concerning sewerage, drainage and roadmaking. The report provided full details of roads in Summertown which were in a 'bad state' and were 'almost impassable in wet weather'. There was no proper system of sewers and drains. Roads, coated with mud, were too elevated. Much of the road surface had to be removed so that houses did not lie below the level of the footpath. Some roads required widening. Each householder was obliged to pay five per cent of all costs.[351]

In March 1892 the local media noted that Ryman Hall had been summoned to court for the non-payment of certain sums due to be paid to the Urban Sanitary Authority with reference to road repairs in Summertown. A total of £114 6s 3d still needed to be paid for work done on George Street (i.e. Middle Way) adjoining Summerhill, and a further £10 5s 8d for improvements to Church Street given that Ryman Hall was the manager of the school located there.[352] Property owners had been given one month to undertake the work required for sewerage, draining, curbing, paving and channelling. Not surprisingly, this work was not carried out by the homeowners and so responsibility fell on the Corporation, which then charged the owners the appropriate costs. A discount was offered if payments were made within one month. In total, Frank Ryman Hall had been charged £677 2s 5d and £55 1s 1d for the upgrading of George Street and Church Street (today's Rogers Street). Ryman Hall was summoned to court over a dispute concerning whether his previous payments had made him eligible to receive the discount. Ultimately, an arrangement was agreed by the mayor and other judges in which interest was charged on the sum which Ryman Hall had not paid on time.[353]

In his will, prepared in June 1923, Frank Ryman Hall stated how in 1891–2 he had paid the Corporation of Oxford £698 18s 7d out of his own personal estate for 'roadmaking and otherwise' on the Summerhill estate which he had never claimed and recovered from the estate of James Ryman. He therefore instructed his executors to claim and recover this amount from the estate so that it would become part of his residuary estate.[354] The amounts involved here, although obviously not trifling, would not have bankrupted Ryman Hall. They were, though, symptomatic of what appeared to be a general financial mismanagement. Ryman Hall's initial refusal to complete the full payments had resulted in a court case which must have been embarrassing for a longstanding justice of the peace. However, it seems that his reputation, although tarnished, was not severely damaged. But, soon after, mounting financial difficulties forced Ryman Hall to mortgage the Summerhill estate.

The deeds of 73 Middle Way reveal that in the period between 1895 and 1925 a total of seventeen declarations and agreements were concluded concerning the mortgaging of the estate. In what appeared to be almost a who's who of Oxford, the various parties to these agreements who were prepared to lend backing to Ryman Hall included several well-known local individuals and families. These were the people with whom Ryman Hall would have worked and socialised. The Eaglestons had an established ironmongering business in the city. The Wootten-Woottens, Gilletts and Braithwaites were all prominent banking families. Sir Walter Gray, a fellow local Conservative, was also a neighbour who lived for a period at Summertown Lodge/Villa. Gray was recognised as 'the father of Oxford Conservatism'.[355] Prior to Gray, Oxford was largely a bastion of Liberalism. A former railway porter, Gray had made his personal fortune by cleverly investing in property developments in north Oxford.

Frank Ryman Hall was not directly involved in the mortgaging process. He handed responsibility to William Emanuel Richards (i.e. William Richards junior), the great-nephew of James Ryman, and to William's wife, Thirza. As noted above, according to a codicil inserted into the will of James Ryman in 1876, after the death of Frank Ryman Hall and his wife, the estate at Summerhill would be inherited by William Emanuel Richards and his heirs forever. Ryman Hall had no children. It seemed then, that by the mid-1890s Richards had taken over the financial management of Summerhill as well as helping to run the shop on the High Street. Frank Ryman Hall had perhaps wisely relinquished financial control of his various assets. William Emanuel Richards died in 1914. In his will he bequeathed all his real and personal estate – which valued over £12,000 – to Thirza, 'including the property coming to me under the will of my late uncle James Ryman unto my Trustees'.[356] After his death, William Emanuel's son, John William Richards, also a print seller, took responsibility for mortgaging Summerhill together with Thirza. John William Richards, who for a time had a fine art and picture-framing shop in Swansea, had married Mary Winifred Boffin, the daughter of Alfred Boffin. The Boffins were a pillar of the Methodist community in Oxford and Alfred ran a highly successful baking and confectionary business.[357]

The Richards-Ryman family connection can be traced back to the marriage in 1818 of Mary Ryman, another sister of James Ryman, to Emmanuel Richards, a carpenter. Born in 1849, William Emanuel Richards was the grandson of Emmanuel Richards. He had started to work in Ryman's shop in 1864 as an assistant to the gilding department. After the death of James Ryman, William Emanuel became a partner in Ryman & Co. In 1909 the firm relocated to 23 High Street after Brasenose College demolished the premises at 24/25 High Street. A business known as Ryman and Co. would continue to maintain a presence on the High Street until 1968.[358] The Ryman family itself, though, was no longer running the firm after 1913. In that year William Emanuel sold the company to his manager, Charles Henry Walker.[359]

Frank Ryman Hall's wife, Sarah, passed away in June 1909 when Frank, for health reasons, was absent on a tour. In a touching gesture, the children of the local school in Summertown had lined each side of Church Street as the cortege departed on its final journey to Holywell cemetery in the city centre.[360] Frank lived at Summerhill with his stepdaughter, Alice Marian Golding, for a further sixteen years until he died on the estate in April 1925. In his obituary, he was referred to as a 'well-known Oxford man' who had lived in Oxford all his life apart from periods of extensive foreign travel. His funeral drew a large crowd and was attended by the mayor, the sheriff and the chief inspector of the local police.[361]

According to the will of Frank Ryman Hall, the gross value of his estate amounted to approximately £2,212. This was far less than the value of the estate his uncle had bequeathed forty-five years previously. Frank's stepdaughter, and the local businessman and alderman, Francis Twining, were listed as the main beneficiaries of Ryman Hall's estate.[362] Originally a grocer, Twining had been a neighbour and good friend of Frank Ryman Hall, living at Summertown House on the eastern side of Banbury Road in Summertown. Thirza Richards and her son, John William Richards, quickly decided to sell the property at Summerhill. By the order of the Trustees of William Emanuel Richards, the house and land was to be sold.[363] Alice Marian Golding left Oxford to live with her brother in Hampton Hill, Middlesex, where she died in 1935.

The sale of antique and modern household furniture belonging to Summerhill was sold at an auction on 6 May 1925. Other properties connected to Frank Ryman Hall were also placed on sale. These included two leasehold residences on Woodstock Road, four freehold residences within Summertown, a well-stocked orchard and freehold building land in the north of Summertown.[364] In contrast to his uncle, Ryman Hall may have experienced financial problems and losses in his later years, but the size of his estate at his death was not inconsiderable.

The builders, Aubrey and Harry Capel, acquired Summerhill through a conveyance drawn up in November 1925. After being in the possession of the Ryman and Ryman Hall families for almost eighty years, the estate at Summerhill was about to be broken up.

Conclusion

Summerhill flourished in what was a golden age under the ownership of James Ryman. The estate and its beautifully laid out gardens became a centre of attraction for the Summertown community. The slaughterhouse and other facilities associated with the butchering profession had been dismantled. No longer primarily a place of utility for its owners, the estate was now fully appreciated for its aesthetic value. It was a treasured retreat from the hustle and bustle of the city, and the confined living area above the picture-frame shop on the High Street where the Rymans still resided from time to time. While Summertown itself was becoming increasingly congested, Summerhill and its pleasure grounds offered a welcome and refreshing open space for its inhabitants and local parishioners to enjoy. It is possible that Ruskin himself may have spent some of his leisure time strolling through the garden together with Ryman.

The golden age came to an end with the death of the famous picture-frame maker. The new owner, Frank Ryman Hall, struggled to maintain the upkeep of the estate. To be fair to Frank, he had not been helped by the legacy left to him by his uncle. It must have been somewhat perplexing for Ryman Hall to be forced to purchase art treasures accumulated by his uncle to ensure that they remained on the estate. In contrast to his uncle, Ryman Hall took much more seriously his civic responsibilities and this probably facilitated his mingling and mixing with the local high society. This stood him in good stead when in the last three decades of his life he was obliged to mortgage Summerhill in order to continue to live there. With the passing of Frank Ryman Hall, Thirza Richards and her son, John William, were not prepared to continue to cling hold of the estate, even though John William may have had the financial means to do so given his marriage to the Boffin family.

The new owners, who briefly took possession of Summerhill, were of a different stock. The Capels came from the local village of Cumnor, and some members of the family were quite poor. However, being of humble origin, and rapidly working his way up the social ladder, the life of the publican and then builder, Noah Capel, the father of Aubrey and Harry Capel, was not entirely dissimilar from the upbringing and career of James Ryman.

SIX

PUBLICANS AND BUILDERS

'Risk is the companion of fortune'

(Jeffrey Fry)

Introduction

The Capels have left a major imprint on the development of north Oxford and Summertown. The partially tree-fringed avenue Capel Close runs for a short distance between Middle Way and Banbury Road in a straight line north to south. The back entrance to what remains of the original Summerhill estate, which at the time of writing was an international school, may be accessed from the east side of Capel Close. After purchasing Summerhill and the grounds encompassing it in 1925, the Capels made preparations to build new housing and lobby for the laying of connecting roads across the former estate, including what would become Capel Close. One of the last substantial areas of greenery in Summertown would disappear following the break-up of the Summerhill estate. Aubrey and Harry Capel, two sons of Noah Capel, the founder of the family's construction business, were responsible for working on the development of infrastructure for new houses in the area, which included what would become 73 Middle Way.

The burgeoning increase in population in Oxford in the latter half of the nineteenth century had offered welcome opportunities for those involved in the building trade. In 1851, a population of less than 29,000 lived in around 5,100 houses in the city. Fifty years later, almost 50,000 inhabitants were accommodated in nearly 10,500 houses.[365] The building business, however, had its risks, especially for smaller, family-run firms. Available capital was essential as builders had to spend money on each house they constructed. Loans were provided by landowners, solicitors, banks, developers and investment companies. Builders had to quickly sell or let the properties they had built in order to secure a return or profit which they could then use to construct further housing. They might also be forced to resort to mortgaging property in order to finance their future work. Ultimately, revenue could be earned by builders provided that there were enough interested buyers to sustain the housing market.

Smaller building firms were thus heavily dependent on credit. Eager to sell the properties they had built, builders often added extra attractions such as stained glass on front doors, marbled fireplaces, cupboards or tiled halls to induce potential buyers to part with their cash.[366] The concept of 'speculative builder' could be applied to many in the trade who were compelled to take risks in the hope of making at least some profit by meeting anticipated demand for housing.[367]

The term was also used in a more derogatory sense at the time to include someone – 'a kind of nondescript' – who opted to be engaged in the building trade after having previously unsuccessfully worked in other businesses. The speculative builder could be 'a man who has tried many things but succeeded in nothing'.[368] Some speculative builders acquired a dubious reputation. They were looked upon as people eager to make quick money. Not always regarded as proper builders, they were often accused of constructing shoddy dwellings – 'He found a solitude and leaves a slum'.[369]

In practice, the term 'speculative builder' covered a wide range of functions and involved individuals who had different degrees of financial independence. At one end of the spectrum were those wealthy businessmen who were to all intents and purposes financiers. Towards the other end of the scale were those individuals who had little capital or those who were starting to develop family companies and who were prepared to take considerable risks to attempt to expand their operations.[370] Initially, the Capels were to be found in this lower range of speculative builders.

In the nineteenth century, many small construction firms could briefly pop up and quickly collapse to be replaced by other similarly doomed ventures. Fortunately, in Oxford there was a practice of landowners accepting the deferring of payments. Builders were not usually required to pay up front the whole purchase price of plots. It was customary for them to pay immediately one eighth of the total cost and cover the remainder over five to eight years at an interest rate of five per cent.[371] This eased to some extent the financial pressure on new speculative builders.

There was a serious decline in the housing market in Oxford in the early 1880s. A spate of overbuilding had resulted in houses standing empty with no one ready to buy them. This led to the collapse of the Oxford Building and Investment Company (OBIC) in 1883. The OBIC had brought together lenders and borrowers and provided investment required for suburban development. Many small investors deposited their savings in the OBIC which then offered capital to builders.[372] Loans were supposed to be paid back in instalments, but pressured by speculative builders the OBIC became the victim of excessive advances.[373]

However, the housing market in Oxford quickly recovered. In north Oxford, the major landowner St John's College encouraged the construction in the 1890s of large houses with front gardens on the Bardwell estate. There was another wave of housing construction immediately north of the estate in the early 1920s.[374] Following the demise of the OBIC, a key role was played by developers who acted as middlemen between builders and buyers/lessees, arranging finances for loans and mortgages. Walter Gray, the friend of Frank Ryman Hall, was arguably the most successful developer and financier in this period, and it was largely through his support that more housing was built off the Woodstock and Banbury Roads.[375] Other suburbs were developed, including Cowley and west Oxford. Smaller firms specialised in building in areas of the city which they knew well. Such firms were often dependent on the health, sound judgement and good luck of one individual. East Oxford was especially attractive for family-run building businesses given the small size of available plots, fewer restrictions on building and the largely freehold nature of the property.[376] Tradesmen and artisans were also prepared to purchase housing on low-lying land even though it was prone to flooding.

The Capels may then be categorised as speculative builders, although they were clearly not of the so-called 'nondescript' kind. Their workmanship must also have been of a recognised and accepted standard, otherwise the family business would not have been able to develop. Capital was not always readily at hand and members of the family business did on occasion face bankruptcy. Originally concentrating on building properties in Cowley, and also in west Oxford, Noah Capel and his sons later focused on profiting from the housing boom in north Oxford and in Summertown. The Capels appeared to be endowed with a natural entrepreneurial spirit. They were originally carpenters and wheelwrights based in the then Berkshire village of Cumnor, just outside Oxford. The founder of the family's building company, and the lynchpin for its success or failure in its formative years, Noah Capel seemed to inherit in particular many of the qualities of his uncle, Charles Capel. As a publican, Charles had been determined to enhance his earnings by seeking to exploit the interest in the village of Cumnor triggered by the publication of Walter Scott's novel, *Kenilworth*.

Charles Capel (1810–1878): A Would-be Giles Gosling?

Completed in 1820, *Kenilworth* was inspired by the events surrounding the suspicious death of Amy Dudley, the only daughter of Sir John Robsart, at Cumnor Place in Cumnor in 1560. The twenty-eight-year-old was discovered dead at the foot of the staircase in the house which was at the time owned by the son of George Owen, the physician. Was she pushed, or did Amy commit suicide? It was quite possible that she was murdered. Amy's husband, Robert Dudley, the later Earl of Leicester, was one of the favourites of Queen Elizabeth I, and it was rumoured that Dudley wanted his wife out of the way so that he could then marry the monarch. Amy's ghost had to be exorcised by nine Oxford clergymen, who 'drowned' the spectre in a nearby pool, after which the water in the pool apparently never froze over.[377] Scott's novel, which was not at all historically accurate, centred around a meeting between the Queen and Dudley at Kenilworth Castle in 1575.

The first chapter of the novel describes the village of Cumnor and its well-stocked famous public house, 'the bonny Black Bear', with its portly, genial host, Giles Gosling. The Black Bear was depicted as 'an excellent inn of the old stamp'. Its landlord was blessed with 'a cellar of sound liquor, a ready wit, and a pretty daughter'. The reputation of Gosling was such that to go to Cumnor 'without wetting a cup' at the Black Bear 'would have been to avouch one's-self utterly indifferent to reputation as a traveller'.[378]

Originally published anonymously, once the identity of the much-acclaimed author was known in 1827, locals and visitors from further afield flocked to Cumnor to try to locate a public house and its publican, which may have inspired Scott to write of the bonny Black Bear and the hospitable Giles Gosling. Many students from the university were devotees of Scott, and in a kind of pilgrimage they made the trip up

Cumnor Hill to tour the village and drink in its watering holes. The quaint hamlet with its several thatched dwellings was not readily accessible, and by the 1850s it seemed that the magic of Scott's novel had started to wane. While employed as a consul in Liverpool between 1853 and 1857, the American novelist Nathaniel Hawthorne spent his leisure time visiting different parts of the country and he wrote about English life and scenery. Entering Cumnor, Hawthorne noted that the secluded and remote village, not connected to the railway network, had 'retained more of a sylvan character' than other English country towns. Hawthorne encountered no travellers in the village.[379] It seemed, then, that there was a limited window of opportunity – for a few decades at most from the late 1820s – to exploit Scott's *Kenilworth* and thereby reap possible financial benefits, and that is what the local publican, Charles Capel, consciously set out to do.

The Capels had long been resident in Cumnor. There was a whiff of scandal associated with William Capel, a grandfather of Charles. Serving as parish clerk, while employed as a carpenter, evidently William had attempted to hold on to some documents from the parish chest in the vestry. The significance of this action is not apparent, but it was noted for posterity in the parish records and so was presumably of some importance at the time. Charles Capel was the son of Charles Capel senior, another carpenter, who died shortly before the birth of his son.[380]

In 1814 Mary, the mother of Charles Capel junior, remarried. Seven years later, according to the village census, the fifty-five-year-old Mary was living with her much younger husband, the twenty-eight-year-old William Barrett, at The Vine Inn in Cumnor. Barrett had established himself as the landlord of the inn.[381] The Vine Inn dated back to the sixteenth century, and so may have existed at the time of Amy Dudley's unfortunate death. Unlike other drinking establishments in Cumnor, The Vine Inn was strategically located on the village High Street, opposite the church and close to the vicarage. The public house was known as the 'provider of ale for the ringers' of the church bells. It seemed that Barrett was also aware of the possible significance of Scott's work. By 1827 The Vine Inn had been renamed and was then known as The Bear and Ragged Staff.[382] This was a reference to the crest of the Earls of Warwick, which had also been adopted by Robert Dudley, the younger brother of Ambrose Dudley, the Earl of Warwick. Sometime in the 1830s Charles Capel took over the management of The Bear and Ragged Staff and consciously attempted to drum up more trade by seeking to establish more connections with Scott's bonny Black Bear. Charles had mixed success.

One publication in 1847 noted that 'honest' Charles Capel, the host of The Bear and Ragged Staff, was but 'a degenerate successor of portly Giles'.[383] A much more favourable account of Charles Capel, published in 1846, was provided by two travellers. The author and illustrator Alfred Henry Forrester (who used the pseudonym Alfred Crowquill) and Francis Paul Palmer, a writer of stories for children, depicted Charles as 'a sample of good nature, and a specimen of Oxfordshire strength and comeliness'. Running a 'snug tavern', with a sweet-smelling and amply stocked cellar, Charles was described as 'a rare good host, in plain fashion, for men after our own unceremonious ways'.[384] A local newspaper article printed three years earlier had noted how The Bear and Ragged Staff was identical to the jolly Black Bear in 'all its primate glory' and that the hospitality of the landlord was 'equally as warm and comforting as Giles Gosling'.[385]

Charles Capel endeavoured to promote his public house by putting up a sign board which referred to Giles Gosling. The sign board on display in 1843 depicted a bear and had the names of Giles Gosling and Charles Capel written on it, but it was in a dilapidated condition and was in danger of falling to pieces.[386] Forrester and Palmer advised Charles Capel to put up a new sign board. The old sign board was brought down and put on a table inside the inn for the travellers to make a toast. Capel told his guests that after Scott had come to the village some scholars had encouraged him to put up a sign depicting a bear. In reality, though, Scott had never visited Cumnor. The bear displayed on the sign bore little resemblance to an actual bear, and Capel confessed that he had never seen a bear himself. Forrester and Palmer advised 'friend Capel' to have a better sign sculptured in stone, 'and then you and your Bear will last in men's minds for years to come'. Charles Capel eagerly agreed, and his two guests then drew on paper what the new sign board should display. Upon seeing the drawing, Capel 'had fits of ecstasy'.[387]

It is not known if Charles Capel followed these instructions to the letter. What is clear is that The Bear and Ragged Staff was closed and demolished in the early 1850s. This followed complaints from the young vicar, the Reverend Charles Frederick Octavius Spencer, a graduate from Cambridge University who was not a local, about the noise emanating from the public house. The bar room had become 'objectionable' to the vicar, and as one visitor remarked, the public house was destroyed by 'an impious act of vandalism'.[388] Charles Capel moved to a nearby residence where his relatives lived on

Appleton Road and transferred his licence there together with the name of the inn and its sign board. A ceremony was held on 11 October 1847 to reopen the public house with its sign board.[389] The Bear and Ragged Staff is still serving customers today from its location on Appleton Road.

The forced closure of the original The Bear and Ragged Staff may have sapped energy and enthusiasm from Charles Capel. By the mid-1850s he had handed over his licence to Charles Godfrey and instead turned his attention to farming on an eighty-five-acre piece of land at nearby Chawley Lane. However, Charles Capel appeared to miss working as a publican and by the early 1860s he had become the landlord of The Three Cups Inn on Queen Street in the centre of Oxford. In his final years, after becoming briefly bankrupt, Charles managed a hotel in Sandown on the Isle of Wight and then ran The Wheatsheaf Inn in Basingstoke, where he died in 1878. He was buried in the graveyard of St Michael's Church in Cumnor.

Noah Capel, having been raised in the house which would become the new The Bear and Ragged Staff, would have known his uncle well. Following in the footsteps of Charles, Noah would try his hand at working as a publican. But ultimately, it would be in the building trade where Noah would display his own particular brand of entrepreneurial skills and know-how.

Noah Capel (1845–1937): Master Builder from Cumnor

It seems that several generations of the Capel family had been living in the house which would become The Bear and

Ragged Staff. St John's College had acquired ownership of the property in the sixteenth century. It had previously belonged to the manorial court of nearby Eaton. The college then leased out the house to gentlemen of means. But by the late eighteenth century, the dwelling had become the home and workplace for artisans. There was a workshop, garden and a yard at the back of the building. The frontage of the property, though, was still impressive. On their visit to Cumnor, Forrester and Palmer delayed their journey for a while to take note of 'the ancient ivied cottage with its ornamented casements'.[390]

The carpenter, John Capel (1793–1853), the father of Noah, was resident in the cottage before his brother transferred his business. The initials 'J.C.', which John Capel carved on one of the side doors, are still visible today. Before the arrival of Charles Capel, one commentator noted that in the 1840s the dwelling was 'a low thatched cottage, snug and neat', which was maintained by a 'certain old Mr Capel', who was 'a perfect incarnation of good-nature and a good specimen of Berkshire health and strength'[391] – words which interestingly appeared to echo some of the comments made by Forrester and Crowquill with regard to Charles Capel. John Capel passed away in 1853. Married three times, John had at least sixteen children. In his will he gave instructions for the house, shop, yard and garden to be let until the lease expired in 1864.[392] Charles Godfrey presumably then became tenant, with Charles Capel vacating the property to relocate to his farm. However, John's widow, Ann, together with her children, including Noah, remained at the rear of the property. The 1861 census referred to Ann as a seamstress. Noah and his brothers Samuel and George were listed as agricultural labourers. The Capels were a close-knit family. The carpenter Thomas Capel, a stepbrother of Noah's, was living next door.

In 1870 Noah Capel married Eliza Ritchings (1846–1910), the daughter of Alfred Ritchings, a master stone mason and builder from Longworth in Berkshire. Alfred died only a few days after his daughter's wedding. Evidently, Alfred had experimented with working with a type of artificial stone. The window surrounds and mullions of Warren Cottage – the house he built in Longworth – were reportedly made of this artificial stone.[393] It is quite possible that Alfred introduced Noah to the building trade. By 1871, Noah was a bricklayer living on Cowley Road in Cowley, together with Eliza and his daughter, Isabel, born in 1868. It is not clear if Isabel was the daughter of Noah and Eliza.

According to the 1881 census, Noah Capel, living at St John's Cottage on St Mary's Road in Cowley, was a master builder, employing six men. By the end of the year, though, he was facing bankruptcy. With the commencement of liquidation proceedings, a local decorator acted as Noah's trustee.[394] This was at a time when the housing market in Oxford was starting to decline and Noah Capel had apparently suffered the fate of other small-scale speculative builders working in the city.

Noah had also been working as a publican – following the example of his uncle – and he may for a period have simultaneously worked as a pub landlord and builder. His record as a publican was somewhat blemished. In July 1878 he was employed as the landlord of the Duke of Edinburgh on the High Street in St Clement's. Noah Capel was fined 10s and also charged 6s in costs because he had supplied beer to a customer who was drunk. Noah's licence would also not be extended.[395] Five years later, he was working as the publican at the Exeter Hall on Oxford Road in Cowley. Again, Noah was summoned for permitting drunkenness on his premises and was fined and forced to pay costs, and the conviction was to be recorded on his licence.[396]

Recovering from his bankruptcy, by the early 1890s Noah Capel was back to house building and played a role in the expansion of the suburb of Cowley where he and his family lived. Between 1851 and 1901 the housing stock of east Oxford, including the Cowley district, had increased sixfold from almost six hundred to over 3,600 houses.[397] Builders were attracted by the cheaper land and prospective tenants were drawn to the area because of the lower rents and rates. Much of this development was unplanned and was often dependent on the whim of wealthy landowners. One such landowner was Daniel Clarke, a gentleman from High Wycombe. In the late 1880s Clarke purchased eleven and a half acres of land on the south-west side of Oxford Road in Cowley, a little beyond Cowley Marsh. In May 1893 Clarke sold a piece of this acreage to Noah Capel, with space reserved for a forty-foot-wide road which would be known as New Road (today's Littlehay Road). The sale came with certain conditions. Each house to be built on the land would have a minimum value of £150. Until the houses were constructed, the land could only be used as an orchard, garden or meadow.[398] This suggested that the area to be developed was still largely rural. Noah Capel also apparently speculated on building property on land in west Oxford in Botley on and near to Elms Road.[399]

It was in north Oxford, though, that Noah Capel finally established himself as a successful house builder. Between 1892 and 1930 he and his sons – through the company known as Noah Capel and Sons – were responsible for the construction of at least eighteen substantial properties off the Woodstock and Banbury Roads. Noah Capel was involved in the development of the Bardwell estate on land leased by St John's College.[400] The college would have only been prepared to engage builders who had acquired a reputation for previous good workmanship. By 1901 Noah had relocated to the area and was living at St John's Cottage on Bardwell Road – the same name he had given to his residence in Cowley. He built several properties on the eastern side of Chalfont Road, which lay in a kind of intermediate zone between the grand houses on Woodstock Road and the much smaller homes for artisans on Hayfield Road. One of the residents on the western side of Chalfont Road complained to St John's College about the noise stemming from the pigs which were being reared and slaughtered in the adjoining garden of a house on Hayfield Road.[401] The owners of the properties built by Noah Capel on the more prestigious side of Chalfont Road were well-known names in Oxford. The confectioner Alfred Boffin, a stalwart of the Methodist community and the father-in-law of the print seller John William Richards, owned the house at 24 Chalfont Road. Another Methodist, James Nix, who would become the Chief Clerk of the Oxford Post Office, owned the houses built by Capel at 18 and 20 Chalfont Road. Boffin and Nix were attracted to the area because of the nearby Wesleyan Chapel. In the 1880s the two had successfully campaigned to have the chapel built.[402]

Noah Capel appeared to have a meteoric rise up the social ladder in Oxford. Living among the affluent on Bardwell Road marked a considerable advance from mixing with the tradesmen in Cowley. The Oxford Preparatory School, also known as Lynam's (the later Dragon School), had relocated to Bardwell Road in 1894. A number of its pupils were destined to attend schools such as Rugby, Harrow and Eton. The Capels were now moving in different social circles. In August 1902 the press reported a 'very interesting wedding' at St Margaret's Church in Oxford. Clarissa, the third daughter of Noah, married Arthur Richmond of Barnsley. After the ceremony, the couple went to the Isle of Wight to spend their honeymoon.[403] By 1903, the company Noah Capel and Sons was established at 279 Banbury Road. The Capels were expanding their business and were starting to specialise in house building in the Summertown area. One of Noah's sons, Reginald Philip Capel (1886–1961), gradually took over the running of the family firm. A prominent freemason, and a member of various clubs in Oxford, Reginald served as mayor of the city in the mid-1940s. In his will, he left effects totalling over £70,000.[404]

In spite of the success of the family business, another of Noah's sons, Frederick (1878–1946), faced bankruptcy in 1925. A builder himself, it seemed that Frederick had chosen to work independent of the family firm. He suffered a loss of about £800 on a contract for construction work at Radley College in 1923. Frederick had over-extended himself and was unable to repay his creditors.[405] He was perhaps not the most financially astute member of the family. Frederick confessed that he did not keep proper records and had no books disclosing his trade receipts and payments. He admitted 'that he was not in a big way of business'. Details emerged that he had previously run into financial trouble in 1912 when he then had debts amounting to £600.[406] Here was an example of a speculative builder who had miscalculated and had taken unnecessary risks and was then confronted with the consequences of his actions.

Noah Capel himself was fortunate to survive two serious traffic accidents. In 1902 his horse trap crashed into a car on Cumnor Hill. Severely bruised, Noah was taken to the Radcliffe Infirmary, where he remained in a comatose condition for some time with serious head injuries.[407] Eight years later, Noah was steering his horse trap on the road to Summertown when the horse suddenly bolted and he was thrown from the trap. His son Reginald took him to the nearby Radcliffe Infirmary, where Noah was treated for concussion, scalp wounds and an ankle injury.[408]

Clearly, Noah Capel had created a successful family firm in what was the high-risk business of housing construction in Oxford. Overcoming initial mishaps and ill fortune, he had created a company which his sons could use as a springboard to launch and expand their own careers. Noah eventually passed away in September 1937. In his will he left effects of almost £10,800 to be equally divided between all of his children. Two of his sons, Aubrey and Harry, were made executors of the will.[409]

Aubrey Capel (1877–1948): Builder and War Veteran

Much of the information I gathered about Aubrey Capel came from an interesting communication with one of his grandsons, also called Aubrey. I learned details of Aubrey's experience in the First World War and the specific circumstances in which he had encountered his future second wife. This information would have been impossible to obtain by simply studying newspaper archives and generally available family history records. Aubrey's grandson also recounted how his grandfather had worked for a period in New York, where he was involved in the construction of some of the skyscrapers there. Unfortunately, I have not been able to unearth evidence of Aubrey's activities in the United States.

According to his grandson, Aubrey Capel turned up to volunteer to serve with the forces in the First World War together with his car, which would be converted to serve as a motor ambulance.[410] His military record shows that he enlisted in February 1915, where he referred to himself as a 'motor driver'. This was eleven months before conscription was introduced in Britain by the Military Service Act. Within five months Aubrey had disembarked at Rouen as a part of the British Expeditionary Force. In January 1916 he was posted to Mondicourt in northern France, where from March 1916 he started to serve with the Third Motor Ambulance Convoy (MAC), which was connected to the Seventh Corps of the Third Army.

The principal task of the MACs was to evacuate the sick and wounded from the war front. Each convoy consisted of fifty motor ambulance cars, three lorries, two motor cars and one motorcycle. The shelling and destruction of roads meant that the motorised convoys could not always reach the front, and so horse-driven carriages were also employed. The work was both difficult and dangerous.

The Third MAC played a role in the bloody Battle of the Somme, which was fought between July and November 1916. Troops from the 56th Division were briefly based in Mondicourt before engaging with the German Second Army at the Gommecourt Salient on 1 July. In what came to be regarded as a military debacle, the British suffered five thousand casualties at Gommecourt. Troops wounded at the Battle of the Somme were loaded onto ambulance trains at Doullens, which lay some fifteen kilometres from the railhead at Mondicourt.

In 1916 British officers had taken over the so-called Red House in the village of Mondicourt. Their troops were billeted elsewhere in the village. A makeshift hospital had been set up in the so-named White House in Mondicourt. The Third MAC established a depot in the village.[411] Aubrey Capel firstly drove a Daimler ambulance car between March 1916 and January 1917. He was then at the wheel of a Daimler lorry.

His grandson recounted how Aubrey met his future second wife while serving at Mondicourt. Not content with the food which was being served to the troops, Aubrey Capel asked the local village postmaster where he could find a proper meal in the village. The postmaster said that his daughter, Simone, could cook for him. A relationship between Aubrey and Simone developed and the couple married on 24 July 1918 while the war was still continuing. Marie Simone Henriette Mesmacre, born in 1893, had lived on Grand Rue in the centre of Mondicourt with her parents. Simone had at least three siblings – two brothers and a sister. According to Aubrey's grandson, the marriage was not well received by some members of the family. Unable to forgive Simone for marrying an Englishman, several family members refused to speak to her again.[412]

One of Aubrey's brothers who also fought in the First World War was less fortunate. Alexander Capel was killed in action fighting with the First Battalion of the Grenadier

Guards on the Western Front on 1 December 1917. Alexander was a casualty in the First Battle of Cambrai – a tank battle in part – when the Germans had launched a ferocious counterattack against British forces. Alexander's name is commemorated on the Cambrai Memorial at Louverval in northern France. He left behind a grieving widow.

This was not the first time that Aubrey had volunteered to help the British armed forces. In 1900 and 1901 he had also served in southern Africa with the Imperial Yeomanry in the Second Boer War. The British had suffered a string of military defeats against the Boers in so-called Black Week in December 1899. In response, the British authorities created a volunteer, irregular cavalry regiment known as the Imperial Yeomanry. The 59th Oxfordshire Company, also called the Queen's Own Oxfordshire Hussars, was formed in early 1900 to be a part of the Imperial Yeomanry. Lord Valentia, the commanding office of the Queen's Own Oxfordshire Hussars, had requested volunteers to form a company of 120 men. But two companies were formed because so many volunteers came forward.[413] Aubrey Capel was one of these volunteers.

Aubrey received several medals for his service to the Imperial Yeomanry. The 59th Oxfordshire Company was largely involved in scouting missions and patrols and occasional skirmishes, and did not take part in major battles in the Second Boer War.[414] However, Aubrey may have participated in the action at Modderfontein in late January 1901, when units of the Imperial Yeomanry held off for a few days an attack by around three thousand Boers.[415] Aubrey was not wounded while serving in southern Africa and he was commended for his 'very good conduct'. He was finally discharged on 22 June 1901 after serving for one year and one hundred days.

Apart from his military service, like father like son Aubrey Capel worked first as a bricklayer and a publican before becoming established in the building trade. He spent much of his life living and working in the Boars Hill district of Oxford. Aubrey would have benefitted from his father's connections in the housing market, but it seems that he operated independently or in partnership with his elder brother, Harry, rather than working full time for Noah Capel and Sons.

When Aubrey enlisted to fight in the Second Boer War in 1900 he had declared that he was employed as a bricklayer. In 1903 he was working as a brickmaker at the brick and tile works at Chawley just outside Oxford.[416] The Kimmeridge clay in the area was easy to dig and was ideal to produce bricks, tiles and pipes. The Earl of Abingdon had taken control of the brick and tile works in 1877 and invested substantially in the business. A new rail line was connected to the works and a state-of-the-art Hoffman continuous kiln was installed. Chawley bricks were hard and water-resistant. Some of the bricks were handmade and quite expensive.[417] Aubrey was not the only member of the Capel family employed at the brick and tile works. In 1901 the sixteen-year-old Arthur, the son of Noah's brother, George, was working as a sawyer at the works.

In 1905 Aubrey Capel married a widow who was twenty years his senior called Martha Stone. Martha (1857–1912) was the daughter of Frederick and Sarah Cotmore. The Cotmores were well-known at Boars Hill as market gardeners. Before his death in 1878, Frederick was also the innkeeper at The Fox in Boars Hill.[418] The family had a cottage in the area on Cotmore's Hill. According to the reminiscences of a local, the Cotmores owned a piece of land which displayed 'the finest show of wallflowers'.[419] The Cotmores lived in Boars Hill before it was made famous by the poets Arthur Hugh Clough and Matthew Arnold. The originally largely unwooded area was celebrated for its spectacular views of the dreaming spires of Oxford before poets, academics and businessmen discovered the site and planted trees and shrubs to decorate the spacious gardens of their newly erected grand houses.

Martha Cotmore had previously married a local farmer, Thomas Stone, who also came from a well-established family in the neighbourhood. Martha may have emigrated to New Zealand with Thomas, who died at Parnell near Auckland in 1894. In the 1901 census Martha was listed as living at Boars Hill and helping to manage The Fox together with her mother. Sarah Cotmore died in 1902, but Martha maintained the running of the public house and after her marriage to Aubrey, the couple continued to manage The Fox until Martha's death in 1912. Aubrey and Martha had no children. In her will, Martha left an estate with a gross value of over £1,428. Most of her property, including presumably The Fox, was bequeathed to her husband.[420] Although his building work had started to expand, Aubrey Capel continued to live at The Fox and was still registered, for example, as a licensed victualler in the electoral roll in 1927.

According to his grandson, while living and working at Boars Hill Aubrey also did considerable work on the side for Randal Thomas Mowbray, the 8th Earl of Berkeley.[421] This must have been before 1916 when the earl relocated to inherit his family's estate at Berkeley Castle in Gloucestershire. Between 1897 and 1916 the earl was resident at Foxcombe Hall on Boars Hill. It was in this country house with its tower and Italian-style garden, that the earl built his own personal laboratory. Elected to the Royal Society in 1908, the earl was a distinguished physicist engaged in cutting-edge research on thermodynamics. However, it seems that the earl had less time and interest in the day-to-day management and running of Foxcombe Hall, and so apparently Aubrey often helped out with odd jobs and settling the bills.

Obviously benefitting from their father's success in building housing in north Oxford, in the 1900s Aubrey and his brothers, Frederick and Harry, became heavily involved in the development of Summertown. The grocer, Francis Twining – destined to become one of the main beneficiaries in Frank Ryman Hall's will – had bought a large area of land east of the Banbury Road in Summertown in the early 1900s. Houses along two new streets – Lonsdale Road and Portland Road – were erected on fields which had previously belonged to Hawkswell Farm. The farm, which had once been owned by Walter Gray, had been purchased by Twining in 1900. The grocer was determined to ensure that houses should be built to a standard which would attract the lower middle class. Each house, therefore, should not cost less than £250. The semi-detached houses on Lonsdale Road were built on plots which usually cost about £75. At least twenty-five houses on Lonsdale Road and twenty-six houses on Portland Road were built by the three Capel brothers. Aubrey, for example, built 57 Lonsdale Road on a plot bought in 1906 and sold it to a commercial traveller in 1920.[422]

Together with his wife, Ada, Harry Capel moved into a house he had built on Portland Road. He named the house 'Billericay'. In 1901, prior to his marriage to Ada Jeffries, as a bricklayer Harry had lodged in a house in Billericay in Essex. His wife-to-be came from the same Essex town. In the First World War Harry served in the Machine Gun Corps of the Queen's Own Oxfordshire Hussars – Aubrey's former company. After the war, in the 1920s Harry was also responsible for building houses on Victoria Road and Hamilton Road which were also east of Banbury Road in Summertown. He also constructed the nearby King's Cross Road Garage and its store.[423] Harry appeared to have more connections with Noah Capel and Sons than his brother Aubrey. Before the death of his father, Harry died at the company's address at 279 Banbury Road in March 1931.

The Capel family were the principal purchasers in the sale of the Summerhill estate on 10 June 1925. Although Noah Capel was named as one of the buyers, it was quite likely that given his advanced years Noah had allocated most of the responsibility to his sons to make the purchases. The estate was divided into nine lots. The first lot covered the main building at Summerhill and its immediate grounds. The second lot encompassed the extensive gardens across the whole estate. The other lots involved The Grange and its outbuildings, the five cottages which fronted Banbury Road known as Russell Place, three other dwellings facing Albert Road (today's Hobson Road), and one property immediately to the west of George Street (Middle Way).[424]

Lot One – the residence itself and one and a half acres attached to it – was purchased by the Capels for £2,550. The property, developed and expanded by James Ryman and Frank Ryman Hall, had three bedrooms and three dressing rooms. Each of the bedrooms had fireplaces and marble mantles. There was also a drawing room, a breakfast room, a study and kitchen facilities. Details were also provided of

1. Godstow Abbey (Courtesy of Simon Burchill, Wikimedia Commons)

2. The Countess of Yarmouth, Amelie von Wallmoden, Mistress of King George II
(Wikimedia Commons)

*3. Henry John North,
Woodstock-based solicitor
(Courtesy of the Oxfordshire
Museums Service)*

*4. Sir Samuel Romilly,
lawyer representing
Henry John North
(Wikimedia Commons)*

5. 'Oxford from North Hinksey'. Copy of etching and engraving by Edward Goodall (Creative Commons). The original painting by J.M.W. Turner was presented by Turner himself to James Ryman, art dealer.

6. *James Ryman outside Summerhill (Courtesy of the Oxfordshire History Centre)*

7. *Wedding of Aubrey Capel and Simone Henriette Mesmacre, Mondicourt, France, 24 July 1918 (Courtesy of Aubrey J. Capel)*

8. Elaine Garnett, daughter of Harry and Alvina Garnett, c. 1937
(Courtesy of Elaine Pearce)

9. Juanita Christina Lecky-Thompson and her children, c. 1912
(Courtesy of Roy Lecky-Thompson)

10. Florence and William Lecky-Thompson, on the left of the photograph, at the wedding of a relative, 1960
(Courtesy of Roy Lecky-Thompson)

11. Gareth and Nazan Winrow outside 73 Middle Way

12. Middle Way today

the outside area. It was noted that the immediate grounds included an aviary, a fountain, a conservatory, a palm house, a summer house, a tennis court and ornamental stone figures. There were also 'shaded walks and arbours' and 'a large assortment of choice forest trees of mature growth'. The grounds were entered by carriage through a pair of folding gates.[425] Clearly, much had changed on the property since the two butchers were in residence. The Summerhill estate had been beautified. It embraced a large garden area which had been carefully tended and which was in tune with what had become in effect a gentleman's impressive suburban villa.

Noah Capel paid £5,000 for the second lot, which covered eight and a half acres of land around the property which was ready to be built on. This freehold building land was listed as 'The Summerhill Building Estate'. It was noted that this land was ripe for immediate development. The land had frontages to Banbury Road and to George Street and Albert Road. A suggested scheme for development referred to the possibility of building two new connecting roads across the estate along which houses could be built.[426]

Aubrey Capel purchased for himself one of the five freehold cottages of Russell Place. Most of these cottages were sold to sitting tenants for prices ranging between £147 and £164.[427] Continuing to reside on Boars Hill, Aubrey Capel did not live at the cottage at 305 Banbury Road. Presumably, he let out the property. In 1939 a sheet metal worker from a motor works was living in the house with his wife.

Two years after the auction, plans made by the Capels for the development of the former Summerhill estate were approved by Oxford City Council. Two new roads were to be built. Summerhill Road would connect George Street with Banbury Road, and Capel Close would be built to run parallel to George Street. The go-ahead was given to build sixty-four new houses on the former Summerhill estate.[428] One of these houses would become 73 Middle Way. Harry Capel had proposed the names of the two roads and a meeting of The Highways Committee in March 1928 gave its approval.[429] The name Capel would henceforth always be associated with the development of Summertown. However, Aubrey and Harry Capel did not actually build 73 Middle Way. They contracted out the construction of the house to another local building firm – Hinkins and Frewin.

Conclusion

Aubrey Capel eventually moved out from The Fox after building his own house, 'Overdowns', on Boars Hill. Together with his two sons he established his own building company – A.J. Capel and Sons. The Capel family had come a long way from working as wheelwrights, carpenters and publicans in Cumnor. It appeared that in general the Capels had mastered the practice of speculative building. Plots were acquired on prized land, houses swiftly built and the profits speedily made use of to build more properties and generate further revenues. Given the family's acquired knowledge of house building in north Oxford and in Summertown, it came as no surprise that the Capels became the chief beneficiaries of the break-up and sale of the Summerhill estate. What remained of the original Summerhill estate – the main house and immediate grounds around it – would be quickly sold by the Capels to the successful master tailor, Horace William Adamson.

SEVEN

TAILORS AND GUNMAKERS

'Without labour, nothing prospers'

(Sophocles)

Introduction

With the sale of the Summerhill estate in 1925, what had been the original building of Summerhill and the grounds immediately attached to it no longer immediately bordered George Street (Middle Way). This chapter, therefore, is a sort of digression in that it is not strictly connected to the history of 73 Middle Way. However, having traced in some detail the origins of the estate and the lives of its various owners, it would be remiss not to follow up on what became of Summerhill.

A look at what happened to Summerhill after its purchase and then immediate sale by the Capels is also of interest because of the acquisition of the property by a married couple who came from two important Oxford families. Horace William Adamson came from a family of tailors who had founded a highly successful business on the High Street in Oxford. Nellie Julie Venables was the granddaughter of a gunmaker who had also set up and developed a lucrative trade in the city centre. The student body of the university and the local gentry were important clientele for the numerous tailors and several gunmakers based in Oxford. The Adamson and Venables families were examples of successful upward social mobility. Both families were outsiders who had arrived in Oxford at the start of the Victorian era. They would both eventually prosper, although the Adamsons initially suffered financial difficulties.

In the interwar period, Horace William Adamson became a well-known member of the so-called Oxford Town Set – a group of high-flying businessmen and professionals who played an active role in the local community. This was a time when Oxford was rapidly changing and industrialising with the launching and then expansion of Morris Motors in Cowley. Horace William had close ties with William Richard Morris (the later Lord Nuffield), the founder of Morris Motors.

Summertown continued to evolve between the two World Wars. In 1929 the boundary of the Oxford municipality was once again redrawn to include a large area to the immediate north of Summertown. Three years later, the parish of Summertown was also expanded to cover a section of this area and thereby incorporate the district known as Cutteslowe. Longstanding residents of Summertown were adamant that Cutteslowe had nothing to do with the real Summertown.[430]

Even today this sentiment persists among some members of the community, although, as previously observed, the original Cutteslowe estate had covered the whole area. The inclusion of Cutteslowe almost immediately led to problems with heightened tensions and social friction on the margins of Summertown as a result of the building of the so-called Cutteslowe Walls.

In 1931 the City Corporation had started to build a new housing estate in Cutteslowe. Two years later, a private enterprise, the Urban Housing Company, led by the developer Clive Saxton, decided to build a separate and adjoining housing estate on land it had purchased from the City Corporation. The properties built by the Urban Housing Company were considerably more expensive than the council housing erected by the City Corporation in Cutteslowe. Stories began to circulate that slum clearance families were being relocated to this new cheaper council housing. Saxton was alarmed, fearing that his houses would not sell if they were built next door to 'slum-dwellers'. This resulted in the Urban Housing Company erecting two walls to separate their houses from the new council properties. Over two metres in height, the walls were topped with rotating and lethal iron spikes. Because of the walls, the tenants of the council housing were forced to take a lengthy detour to reach Banbury Road and then access the shops in Summertown. The erection of the Cutteslowe Walls sparked fury and outrage among some local residents. Several attempts were made to demolish the walls, but they would only be finally dismantled in 1959.[431]

In vain, the City Corporation had alleged that only twenty-eight of the 298 houses on the new council estate were occupied by people rehoused from slum clearance areas. A surveyor who went to visit these new residents had attempted to ease tensions by noting that they seemed to him to be proper and respectable people – like 'good-class cottage people' rather than former slum occupiers.[432] The Urban Housing Company was not convinced. The story of the Cutteslowe Walls was a sorry episode which could in no way be justified. It illustrated the worst aspects of social and class division in Oxford at that time.

The Adamsons: A Family of Tailors

The tailoring profession in Oxford is a longstanding and respected one. Oxford had one of the earliest Weavers' Guilds and it was probably in existence shortly after the Norman Conquest.[433] In 1621 it was estimated by the guild that the tailoring profession supported the livelihoods of around five hundred people in and around the city. Even back then, tailors in Oxford were expected to be employed in shops rather than go round touting for business or working directly from home. Great importance was placed on the relationship between the master tailor and his young apprentices.[434] Of the 678 apprentices enrolled in Oxford in the period between 1770 and 1795, almost one fifth were connected to the tailoring trade. The profession, though, started to gradually lose its pre-eminent position, and so by 1901 only 443 men and boys were involved in the trade in Oxford, in contrast to 639 who were employed in the printing industry.[435] Nevertheless, especially given the presence of a significant student body and their continuing need for academic gowns and other forms of dress, there would always be a ready market in Oxford for a hardworking and honest tailor.

Horatio George Adamson (1811–1885), the grandfather of Horace William Adamson, had briefly established for himself a tailor's shop on the Oxford High Street[436] before then becoming a cowkeeper in London. Horatio was born and raised in the capital. However, at the time of his marriage to Harriet Barton in Oxford in 1838, it was noted that he was then a parishioner of St Mary the Virgin in the same city. Presumably, Horatio was working in Oxford around the time of his marriage. Why he would then choose to relocate and change profession is not known, but by the mid-1840s he was working again as a tailor in London. In 1852, though, Horatio George Adamson, the linen draper, hosier and dealer of shoes, was suddenly declared bankrupt.[437] In what was a drastic and life-changing move, Horatio then moved again, this time to the city of Cork in Ireland.

In the mid-nineteenth century, Cork had become a key centre for the manufacture of cloth, cotton and wool, and was a major port for transatlantic trade. By 1855 Horatio had established a drapery business at 86 Grand Parade.[438] This was one of the main commercial thoroughfares at the heart of the city. Two years later, he had set up shop at 12 Patrick Street (also known as St Patrick Street) in the city centre, conveniently close to the railway and to the steamboats.[439] His business seemed to thrive, and Horatio became a well-known member of the local community. He served as a member of the Grand Jury in the Quarter Sessions in Cork and he was a supporter of the local Conservative party. Horatio was one of the ratepayers who signed a petition in 1856 which called on the Mayor of Cork to convene a public meeting to ensure that the residents should continue to receive gas at a reasonable price.[440]

By the early 1860s, Horatio had returned to Oxford. He was initiated as a member of the freemasons at the Alfred Lodge in Oxford in June 1861. On 24 May 1862, with much fanfare, his drapery business at 28 High Street was opened.[441] Over the following decades, the Adamson family on several occasions moved their shop to different locations on the High Street. However, in January 1870 Horatio was again a victim of bankruptcy. He owed almost £300 to the London-based wholesale dealers Spencer, Turner and Boldero.[442] Addressing the Court of Bankruptcy in London in March 1870, Horatio declared that his annual expenditure over the last two years had amounted to £300. His fifty-three unsecured creditors were scattered throughout the country, but they were mainly based in cities such as Oxford and Bristol. Horatio announced that he had not been previously insolvent or bankrupt – a blatant mistruth! After the termination of the proceedings, Horatio was returned his gold watch which he had earlier been forced to hand over, together with £4 as the remainder of his estate.[443]

Horatio George Adamson quickly recovered from his latest financial problems, and his High Street shop became a major attraction for students eager to keep up with the latest fashions. Alfred Richard Allinson of Lincoln College admitted that he was drawn to Adamsons to purchase spotted items which were all the rage at the time. He bought, for example, a spotted Brussels scarf which cost 7s 6d. The Newcastle-Upon-Tyne born student later became a well-known academic, author and translator. Charles Read Seymour of Merton College procured an Ottoman blue spot long scarf from Adamsons for the same price. He also bought from Adamsons a fancy black diagonal cloth D.B. morning coat, a black and white mixed diagonal cloth waistcoat, and a pair of fancy grey stripe Angola trousers.[444] Seymour later played cricket for Hampshire.

In the 1870s, Adamsons was one of the few shops in Oxford which pioneered payments in cash rather than continuing to rely on a system based on credit. Credit was widely used in business in the nineteenth century to ensure that orders were not interrupted and trade could continue to grow. As the Commissioners on Bankruptcy and Insolvency succinctly noted in 1840: 'Credit must be, or commerce cannot be'. Here, a tacit agreement was struck between salesmen and consumers. However, debts spiralled out of control, and tradesmen in Oxford were pilloried by the press for allowing this to happen in the hope that credit could attract and retain more customers. In the second half of the nineteenth century, the problem was compounded by the fact that students from diverse social backgrounds were entering the university. Concerns were raised that these students might be less familiar with the credit system and so debts could proliferate. Pressure increased for the increased use in shops of cash sales at fixed prices.[445]

Cash payments had been previously trialled by two Oxford firms in the 1850s, and in 1876 Adamsons in a circular they published sought to revive the practice. A local newspaper noted how the credit system had become a real 'evil' for students in Oxford with 'a number of heedless, if not absolutely reckless, young men, who often buy their experience in the very dearest market'. Other 'leading traders' were strongly encouraged to follow the example set by Adamsons.[446] It had been thought that the 'ready money system' would fail to work in Oxford, unlike its success in London, given the better class of trade in the university city. However, it was decided to give the system a 'fair trial'. Goods were to be marked in prices which were at least thirty per cent less than the ordinary credit price.[447] It was ironic that Adamsons would be leading the way here given the recent financial problems of Horatio. Adamsons was clearly a business on the up.

By the time of Horatio's death in 1885, Adamsons had expanded its business to include a branch on Cavendish Square in London, and an agency on the Rue des Capucines in Paris. The firm had acquired a niche in catering for the market in Oxford by specialising in providing gowns and other items of academic attire. Adamsons became the official academic dress supplier to the University of Oxford. In his will, Horatio left a personal estate of over £1,175. Of this amount, £600 was to be divided equally between his five sons. The residue of the estate was given to William Charles (c.1842–1927), the sole executor of the will. William was to inherit the family business.[448] The oldest son, Horatio George junior, had chosen a different career path and was working as an auctioneer.[449]

In contrast to the first years of his father's working life, William Charles Adamson and his family enjoyed a relatively comfortable standard of living. In the late 1870s William Charles had purchased a quite substantial property known as Highfield Cottage in Headington, just outside Oxford. This five-bedroomed dwelling had a large garden attached to it. Highfield Cottage seemed to be a country retreat for William Charles, who spent much of his time living directly above his shop on the High Street. According to the 1881 census, the family had a live-in servant at the cottage who was described as a porter. The family were no longer residing at Highfield Cottage by the time of the next census ten years later.[450]

The tailoring business continued to prosper under the helmsmanship of William. In 1891 the firm moved to much larger premises at 102 and 103 High Street, with an attached outlet at 1, 2 and 3 Oriel Street. Oriel College leased the property for an initial period of fourteen years at a rent of over £380. The new 'capacious' premises in the Grade II listed buildings were fitted with all the modern conveniences – a hot water system and baths, electric bells, and a fresh lick of paint.[451] This was a strategic location on the High Street which had previously been occupied by the much-celebrated Spiers & Son, dealers in fancy goods and a favourite among students such as Oscar Wilde. Spiers & Son had fallen victim to the new fad of collecting photographic souvenirs.[452] In contrast, Adamsons continued to move with the times, and trade in London was also flourishing. In 1898 the inhouse magazine for tailors noted how Messr's Adamson & Co. had 'invaded the metropolis and established a branch of their business in Saville-Row'.[453] Six years later William Adamson and Sons announced that they would begin production of ladies' costumes, coats and riding habits, etc. Assurances were given that 'only male workers will be employed in all the branches, thus ensuring genuine Tailor-made Garments throughout'.[454]

In 1874 William Charles Adamson married Julia Seager, the daughter of a London-based tailor. The couple had four children – three boys and one girl. Not content with solely running the family business, William also ran a small farm at Long Hedge (Five Mile Drive) in Wolvercote in north Oxford. He was initiated to the Alfred Lodge of freemasons in Oxford in January 1883. William also represented the Liberals as a councillor in the East Ward of Oxford. In 1891, William triumphed in what appeared to be a bruising election battle for the East Ward against Colonel Swinhoe, a military gentleman new to Oxford who stood for the Conservatives. In the campaign, Swinhoe noted how his rival had alleged that there had been a 'very great improvement in the cleaning of the streets'. The colonel added, to laughter and applause, that he couldn't help but think that Adamson had 'been dreaming of the trim villas and beautiful roads of the north where he lived'.[455] In the election, Adamson polled 855 votes compared to 828 votes cast for Swinhoe.[456]

In February 1927 William Charles Adamson, after a short illness, passed away at his home on 165 Banbury Road – not far from his son's residence at Summerhill. According to his newspaper obituary, 'the well known tailor of High Street' had been in business for sixty years.[457] In his final years, William had served as the governing director of Adamsons Ltd. In his will, he left an estate valued at over £41,411. All the shares in Adamsons Ltd and the dividends accruing at his death were to be equally apportioned between his son Horace William, and his daughter, Beatrice. The other two sons, Bertie and Reginald, were each allocated £1,000. Horace, who had been effectively running the family business for a number of years, was appointed one of the three executors and trustees in the will.[458]

The Venables Family: Oxford Gunmakers

University students and local gentlemen provided a ready market for gunmakers based in Oxford. Sporting guns were also popular with those members of the monied classes who spent their leisure time shooting game. As early as 1620 a Richard Mellor was known to be working as a gunsmith in

Oxford. Gunmakers had established a firm presence in the city by the time of the Civil War when Charles I was encamped in his headquarters in Oxford. Seventeen gunmakers arrived from London to produce weaponry such as breechloaders and repeating guns for Prince Rupert and the Royalist Army. Several families set up apprenticeships and maintained their gunmaking businesses in Oxford with a specialisation in fashioning multi-barrelled weapons. Arguably the best known of these families were the Uptons, who provided three generations of gunsmiths in the seventeenth and eighteenth centuries. By the nineteenth century, many gunmaking businesses concentrated more on finishing, repairing and retailing guns instead of producing them.[459]

The Venables family emulated the Uptons and provided several generations of gunmakers working in Oxford. John Venables (1809–1882) was the son of an innkeeper from Cantley near Doncaster. He was the uncle of William Richard Gowers, the famous neurologist and author of the two-volume work *Manual of Diseases in the Nervous System*. After the death of his father, as a child William spent a number of years in Oxford with his uncle in St Aldates, opposite Christ Church College School, which William attended as a student. There is no evidence to suggest that William did not get on well with his uncle, but these were unhappy years for a young child who missed his mother (John's sister, Ann), who was forced to live in Doncaster to look after her own ailing mother.[460]

John Venables built up a reputation as a gunmaker, who, unlike many of his local competitors, made his own percussion pocket pistols and bore muzzle-loading percussion sporting and hunting rifles. In 1844 he established himself at 21 St Aldates when he took over the business and unfinished part of the stock-in-trade of the late William Field, gunmaker. With a recommendation from Field's widow, Venables informed members of the university and the gentry of the city and county that he had upwards of twenty years' experience in some of the finest shops in the kingdom and had spent the last ten years working in Oxford.[461] Seventeen years later, he had relocated to 99 St Aldates when he acquired the premises and the whole of the stock-in-trade of the late Mr Pether, gunmaker.[462] By this time Venables also owned the rifle range at Iffley Butt which was used for practice shooting by the Oxford City Rifle Volunteer Corps.[463] Apparently a marksman himself, presumably Venables, spent time honing his own shooting skills at Iffley Butt.

Venables became a prominent member of the local community. He became well known for his extensive charity work, particularly with regard to the Oxford Friendly Institution which he had helped found in 1840. The Institution provided invaluable financial and medical support for workers when they were sick or had suffered a bereavement. The charity had been founded 'chiefly through the foresight, energy and benevolence' of Venables, assisted by a few other prominent citizens.[464] The Institution collapsed due to a lack of subscriptions only a few months after the death of Venables.[465] It appeared then that Venables had been the chief driving force behind the Institution. As a Liberal, he was also actively involved in local politics and served as Sheriff of Oxford in 1867. Venables represented the South Ward of Oxford – an area he must have known well, living at The Elms on 158 Abingdon Road. He would have most probably become Mayor of Oxford the following year if it had not been for the case of a Mr J. Watson, who, facing financial difficulties, was forced under harsh circumstances to abandon his farm. In protest at this ruling an exasperated and furious John Venables declared that he would never again enter the Council Chamber.[466] He kept to his word.

After his death, John's son, Sidney, took over the family business. Sidney Venables (1838–1913) married Emma Allen (1842–1889) at Yardley Parish Church in Birmingham in September 1865. The Allens were another established family of gunmakers. Birmingham was also an important centre of gunmaking, providing, for example, cheap muskets to the Hudson Bay Company which were exchanged in trade with the natives to obtain furs. There was, though, a much darker side to the work of the Birmingham gunsmiths. Their inexpensive flintlock muskets were sold to African 'kings' who used them to coerce and round up slaves to be shipped across the Atlantic. By 1828 Emma's father, George, had become known in Birmingham as a gun lock maker. George later established himself in the city as a gun and pistol maker.[467]

Sidney and Emma had two sons, Sidney George and John Richmond, who would not surprisingly both become gunmakers. A third son, Richard, was referred to as a gentleman in his father's will. There was also a daughter, Nellie Julie. Sidney left an estate worth almost £12,700.[468]

Horace William Adamson (1874–1952) and Nellie Julie Venables (1873–1949): Families United

In the mid-1920s the Welsh businessman Miles Thomas (who would later be known as Sir Miles Thomas) arrived in Oxford to join Morris Motors. The car works set up in Cowley was in the process of expansion. In 1920 Morris

Motors produced less than two thousand cars. Five years later, over fifty-five thousand vehicles were produced. Oxford had finally industrialised. The company had come a long way since William Richard Morris (the later Lord Nuffield) had started up his cycle-repair business on the High Street and then entered the car-hire trade in a small building at Longwall Street before starting to produce cars in Cowley in 1912. One year later Morris had introduced the first motor bus in Oxford. These gradually replaced the out-of-date and by that time universally derided horse-drawn trams.[469] The city was making up for lost time and was swiftly modernising its transport network. Thomas would soon begin work at the Pressed Steel Company which was established in 1926 by the side of the car works to manufacture car bodies. He later became Managing Director of Morris Motors before being appointed Chairman of the British Overseas Airways Corporation.

Adapting to life in Oxford, Thomas noted in his autobiography that two of the 'outstanding personalities' in the 'Town' Set in Oxford were Horace William Adamson and his son Max, 'who looked after a flourishing business'. Their business turned out 'good products', with the Adamsons 'being fully familiar with the pageantry of the various University gowns and robes'. According to Thomas, they also extended 'fantastic credits'. Horace had said that if one allowed the 'averagely impecunious undergraduate credit', once he started a business and earned money he would pay off his debts 'and would also feel duty bound to remain a customer'.[470] Clearly, in contrast to his grandfather, Horace remained firmly attached to the entrenched use of the credit system.

Reminiscing about his time as an Oxford undergraduate in the years shortly before the First World War, Desmond

Young, the later distinguished army officer, newspaper publisher and writer, noted that William Richard Morris was a 'great friend' of Horace Adamson. Young had first encountered the future Lord Nuffield when he had 'garaged' his motorcycle at the premises of Morris at Longwall Street. Morris had introduced Young to Horace, who had made an immediate impression on the student because of 'his perfect tweeds'. Young confessed that he realised that his 'own wardrobe was painfully provincial'. This was swiftly corrected by Adamson, although at the time no mention was made of money. It would have been embarrassing to raise the issue.[471] Adamson and Morris were thus friends long before the car dealer became in effect a national treasure. In those years they would have been neighbours with Morris living with his wife at 280 Iffley Road in Oxford, and Adamson with his wife and ailing father-in-law resident in nearby Donnington Lodge on the same road.

By the 1920s, society in Oxford was more than simply a stage where the 'bright young things' immortalised by the writings of Evelyn Waugh and others frolicked. Thousands of workers were attracted to Oxford to work in the car industry. The distinction between town and gown was sharpened. The luminaries of the so-called Town Set were invariably those successful local businessmen and professionals who could provide important services and at times benefit from the presence of the large student body in the city. Horace William Adamson and his wife, Nellie Julie, came from two families which had firmly established themselves in this Town Set.

The Town Set identified by Thomas also appeared to be firmly interested in outdoor activities. Both Horace and Max 'were very keen on field sports'. Through 'the kindness of Horace', Thomas was invited to join the Hinton Shooting Syndicate. The extensive farmland and open spaces beyond Oxford offered ample opportunities for shooting parties. Horace hence shared his wife's family's close interest in guns. Other members of the Hinton Shooting Syndicate, according to Thomas, included Mr Dulake, the estate agent, Horace Fisher, a lawyer, and one or two doctors.[472] Shooting was actually deeply ingrained in the family life of the Adamsons. As a teenager in Ireland, Horace's father had quite seriously injured himself when his gun had gone off accidentally while he was snipe shooting.[473]

Horace William Adamson's admission to the Alfred Lodge of freemasons in Oxford in April 1909 would have made it easier for the master tailor to develop contacts with other like-minded successful tradesmen and business professionals. Both George Herbert Dulake and Horace James Fisher had at one time offices in Cornmarket in the heart of Oxford. They also had large residences on Woodstock Road and Banbury Road and were in effect near neighbours of Horace and Nellie after they moved to Summerhill around 1925. Arguably, Dulake, Fisher and Adamson were therefore members of what was a Summertown social set. Social divisions in Oxford at this time were not solely based on town and gown distinctions.

The contrast between the lives led by the industrial workers quartered in Cowley and those who resided in their imposing houses and gardens in north Oxford and Summertown could not have been starker. One commentator at the time noted how bus conductors on the Banbury Road route were given breaks by operating instead on the Cowley run to enable them to recover from the verbal abuse they encountered from some of the north Oxford/Summertown residents. Evidently, there were 'more black looks' on the buses on Banbury Road than on any other bus route in the country. The unfortunate bus conductors had to contend with elderly ladies, 'fractious dons' and 'self-conscious businessmen' who were seemingly connected with the mushrooming car industry in Oxford.[474]

Concerning the Adamsons in particular, father and son appeared to make quite a splash. John Ainsworth Morgan, a visiting American student then in his mid-twenties, wrote about his experiences in Oxford in the 1920s. In one of his chapters, Morgan gave a lively account of each shop one would encounter while strolling down the High Street. Adamsons was located next to Chaundy's, 'the famous book seller'. A caustic remark was made about the use of credit by the Adamsons. Every undergraduate 'is politely reminded that he owes Adamson's Limited a sum, and is also reminded that he has a limited time in which to pay it'. Morgan observed that after seeing the 'many creations and recreations in men's wearing apparel' of Mr Adamson (Horace), 'you readily understand how Mr Adamson junior can afford to sport a large Sunbeam car and a Beau Brummel air'.[475] Max was obviously perceived as a socialite and a leader in fashion.

Life in the fast lane did not come risk-free. In 1925 Max was involved in what became known as the 'Lodge Hill Tragedy'. A motor vehicle driven by Max crashed on the Oxford-Abingdon road after attempting to swerve away from an incoming van. Unfortunately, one of the passengers, the dancer Miss Diana Seal, died at the scene while Max was admitted to hospital in a 'critical condition'. The case eventually came to court and Max gave evidence and was exonerated of all blame.[476] In his later years, Max joined the Royal Artillery and fought in the campaign in North Africa in the Second World War.

Horace William married Nellie Julie in a ceremony at Iffley Church in Oxford in September 1901. Ten years later, the couple, together with the then eight-year-old Max, were living with Nellie Julie's father at Donnington Lodge. Nellie's devotion to her father was acknowledged by Sidney Venables in the will he prepared in July 1911, two years before his death. All the furniture and household effects, plates, linen and pictures, etc, were handed down to Nellie in consideration of her having left her home to live with and keep house for her father.[477] In her youth, Nellie had been a singer who performed in local charity concerts. In 1895, for example, she had participated in a function in Summertown to raise money for local parishioners in need. The local press enthused how she had 'displayed artistic abilities of no mean order'.[478]

The family business under the management of Horace did indeed flourish. Until August 1916, Adamson & Co. entailed a partnership between William Charles Adamson and two of his sons, Bertie and Horace. The company was dissolved by mutual consent from 31 August, and in future it was to be carried on by William Charles and Horace.[479] Abandoning the tailoring trade, Bertie enlisted in the war effort and then embarked on a successful career in the Royal Air Force. It would seem that from 1916 onwards Horace increasingly took control of the family business. Adjusting to the times, the firm was then advertising itself as specialist military tailors. Later, by the mid-1920s, the company had a branch in Cambridge as well as on Sackville Street in Piccadilly in London.[480]

Under Horace's watch, in 1920 Adamsons gained important publicity and presumably a lucrative contract when Oxford University decided to admit female undergraduates. It was only in October of that year that women were finally granted full membership of the university and were given the right to read for a degree. Previously, although some women had been studying at the university since the late 1880s, they had not been permitted to graduate. In July 1920, the university authorities agreed to the future academic dress for the 'sweet girl-graduate'. The gown was to be identical to the short gown worn by the male undergraduate commoner. The head dress, however, was to consist of a soft cloth cap, square at the top, with a flap at the back which would usually be buttoned up at the side like a sports cap to protect the young ladies from inclement weather. Messrs Adamsons Ltd took the credit for this 'simple and charming design'.[481] Evidently, this headgear closely resembled that worn by students at Oxford in the sixteenth century. Women were not allowed to wear mortarboards until the late 1970s.

After purchasing Summerhill in 1925, Horace and Nellie remained there in residence in Summertown – from time to time with Max – until their deaths. The 'big house' still had a large garden. In the 1940s the then schoolgirls, Shirley and Daphne Beesley, who lived on the nearby Summerhill Road, used to play in the grounds of Summerhill. Their father, William Beesley, the founder of the South Midland Motor Services, which operated a regular bus service from Oxford to London, must have known Horace Adamson quite well.[482]

Horace Adamson most probably opposed the Cutteslowe Walls which were erected only a few minutes' walk from Summerhill. In 1939, at the outset of the Second World War,

Horace was registered as an Air Raid Precaution Ambulance-First Aid Party Car driver. The Air Raid Precaution Wardens objected to the Walls which were regarded as a hindrance to their work. Citing the problems of communication, in the event of an incendiary bomb falling on the Cutteslowe estate they argued that time would be wasted in attempting to access the estate from the Banbury Road. Their complaints would be overruled.[483]

In practice, it seems that the Adamsons did not solely mingle with the Oxford Town Set. In his will, Horace rewarded his 'faithful friend' Sidney Rivett with £50. Rivett was a motor mechanic and the son of a coachman. And, in a codicil Horace added to his will, he raised the amount to be given to his housekeeper from £100 to £250. Horace passed away, nineteen days after amending his will. His wife had died three years earlier. Horace left an estate valued at over £11,000.[484]

Conclusion

Adamsons Ltd Gentlemen's Tailors of 105 High Street, Oxford, was eventually liquidated in 1972.[485] By the 1950s, Castell's had replaced Adamsons Ltd as the official academic dress supplier to the University of Oxford. Previously, in 1945, Max Adamson had acquired a share in the ownership of Castell's. Venables & Sons, Gunmakers, have also disappeared. Interestingly, though, some members of the Venables family shifted from gunmaking to the tailoring business. Dennis R. Venables, one of the grandsons of Sidney, acquired the well-known Oxford outfitters Shepherd and Woodward in the 1940s. Other members of the family later became owners of

Castell's and also Walters, another long-established tailoring business in Oxford.[486]

And what became of Summerhill? The Freemasons acquired the property after the death of Horace William Adamson. The Alfred Lodge held regular meetings there. This was particularly fitting given how several previous occupants of Summerhill, and at least three generations of the Adamsons, had belonged to the Alfred Lodge. The Freemasons made several additions to the building, including a meeting hall with a temple above, and a further temple named the Rathcreedan Temple in honour of a Provincial Grand Master, which was constructed in 1986.[487] The complex later doubled up as a conference centre and venue for weddings and other major social functions. With the construction of various annexes, the greenery immediately around the main building had gone. In 2013 Summerhill was once again put on the market. There was talk of pulling down all the buildings and constructing seventeen family houses in their place, but this was rejected by the Oxford City Council. Instead, a private school acquired the property[488] and much of the original building of Summerhill has been preserved and may still be recognised.

EIGHT

POST OFFICE WORKERS AND BANKERS

'Our aspirations are our possibilities'

(Samuel Johnson)

Introduction

In 1919 two chefs working at Keble College took over a disused bakery on the then George Street just north of the Rose and Crown public house and across from the soon-to-be demolished St John the Baptist Church. William James Oliver and Aubrey Gurden baked cakes in their spare time in the evenings. Each morning before they started work they delivered their produce by horse and cart to the Grimbly Hughes shop on Cornmarket in the centre of Oxford. Owen Grimbly, one of the shop's founding partners, had resided in Summertown Villa further up the road on

George Street. Oliver and Gurden gradually expanded their business, and they took over the Rose and Crown and then other adjoining premises on George Street. A steady flow of vans picked up packaged cakes and puddings from Oliver & Gurden's Quality House to be delivered to customers throughout the country.

At its peak, Oliver & Gurden's employed 150 staff and produced thirty tons of cake each week and five thousand jam tarts every hour. Many of their items bore the name 'Oxford' – including their famous 'Oxford cakes' – and this helped boost sales overseas. Buckingham Palace was a regular customer. Every Christmas the Queen ordered two thousand puddings, which were placed in special festive hampers and then distributed to members of the Royal Household. Oliver & Gurden's specialised in the making of high-quality cakes for weddings, birthdays and christenings.

The lower end of George Street, which had once been the centre of the village community in Summertown, was once again a hub of bustling commercial activity. In parallel with the industrialisation of Oxford, George Street now had its own flourishing local business. Oliver & Gurden's thrived for several decades, until the upmarket cake and pastry company was sold to J. Lyons & Company in 1969 and was then forced to close six years later. With their slick advertising campaigns and film promotions, Oliver & Gurden's had put George Street back on the map.[489]

The northern end of George Street was also partially transformed with the sale of the Summerhill estate in 1925 and the construction of new housing. More houses also appeared at the top of the road on Squitchey Lane after the City Council took control in 1937 over what had been a private road. Previously, the road had been known for its impressive tall trees which had lined both sides of the avenue.[490] According to the 1939 register, most of the inhabitants of George Street at that time came from the lower middle classes. There were, for example, teachers, accountants, shop assistants, motor mechanics, sign writers and decorators, printers and bankers. These were not members of the exclusive Oxford 'Town' Set. They were rather people who provided important services for the local and wider community who were able to afford the relatively inexpensive and comfortable accommodation which George Street then had to offer, and which provided an easy access to the city centre.

In line with most of Oxford, Summertown largely remained unscathed from the destruction of the Second World War. There was speculation that Hitler had wanted to make Oxford his capital of a conquered Britain. But what was not known at the time was that a prized Soviet agent had taken up residence at 50a George Street, also called Avenue Cottage. The residence belonged to Neville Laski, a judge and a prominent member of the Jewish community in Britain. Between 1942 and 1945 a certain Mrs Beurton, alias Ursula Kuczynski or 'Agent Sonya', who rented Avenue Cottage and lived there together with her English husband and children, was a familiar figure in the Summertown neighbourhood. She was often seen riding the streets on her bicycle and doing her shopping on Banbury Road. The residents of Summertown would have been shocked to learn that it was Mrs Beurton who played an instrumental role in the Soviet Union acquiring the knowledge to build the Atom Bomb. This was through Agent Sonya's regular contact with the nuclear physicist Klaus Fuchs, who was working on Britain's nascent programme to develop the bomb.[491]

George Street was renamed Middle Way in 1955. The street was often confused with another George Street in the centre of the city. The City Council decided on a new name – Twining Street. This was to honour and commemorate the Oxford-based grocer Francis Twining, the protégé of Owen Grimbly, who had been a close friend and associate of Frank Ryman Hall. Twining had served on the City Council for fifty years and had been mayor of Oxford. A generous benefactor who had played a key role in the development of Summertown in the early 1900s, Twining was seen as an example of someone who had climbed up the social ladder after first working as a humble grocer's boy and who had succeeded in life through graft and personal responsibility.[492]

However, the decision to rename George Street sparked an immediate and hostile reaction from local residents. Sixty-two people signed a petition declaring that they did not want to live on a street which would be named after a grocer. They demanded that the street should instead be named Oak Street (after Dudley's Oak) or should be called Middle Way.[493] Given that there were only around seventy-five houses on the road, a large majority of the residents opposed the City Council's decision. A don who lived on George Street at the time had written his objection in Latin, suggesting a certain snobbery.[494] But had the social status of most of the people on the street really changed since the 1939 register was completed? Whatever the case, the City Council backed down and George Street became Middle Way.

At the time of the auction of the Summerhill estate in 1925, it was suggested new houses should be erected which would have frontages to Banbury Road, George Street and Albert Road, and along two proposed new roads. With regard to the top end of George Street specifically, it was noted that houses could be built along a 660-feet stretch on the east side of the road on land which had been previously part of the pleasure gardens.[495] In August 1927 Aubrey and Harry Capel agreed to sell one hundred feet of this stretch of land for £375 to the builders and contractors Hinkins and Frewin. The contractors made a commitment to build three houses on the plot. In June 1929 the terms of this agreement were revised and Hinkins and Frewin pledged to build four houses on the site. The Capel brothers had previously been responsible for infrastructural work in the area, laying water and mains pipes and providing sewerage and surface water draining. On 7 December 1928 an agreement of conveyance was completed by Hinkins and Frewin and a Miss Eva Catley of 34 Wood Lane, Highgate, London for the sale of one of the houses on this plot. Miss Catley purchased what would become 73 George Street for £112 10s. The property had a frontage of twenty-two feet and six inches.[496] The Capels, therefore, although procuring and developing the land on which 73 George Street was built, were not responsible for constructing the house itself.

These houses were not grand villas, but they provided suitable homes for working professional people and for retirees. Immediately to the south of 73 George Street was Seton Cottage (number 71). When they were originally built the houses were given names rather than street numbers. The joint tenants of Seton Cottage were two unmarried sisters. Helena Mary and Julia Caroline Englefield lived there by their own means. Their father had been a 'fund holder' based at Notting Hill in London. At one time, Helena had worked as a sister of mercy in Edinburgh.

Attached to 73 George Street was a house (number 75) with the quaint name 'Nevermind'. This was the property of Colin William Storey Collins, a member of the Royal Air Force, who had recently married. The couple were not in the house for long, initially relocating to Cambridge. Just to the north of 'Nevermind' was the fourth house constructed by Hinkins and Frewin. 'Sandys-Col' (number 77) was occupied by Charles Robert (Bob) Hinkins, the son of Charles Hinkins senior, one of the owners of Hinkins and Frewin.

The Hinkins family were previously well-known builders living and working in Royston in Hertfordshire. William Hinkins, the grandfather of Bob, had been the main builder and plasterer of Royston. William had two claims to local fame. He had helped establish the Royston town band, which was at one time known as the Royston Teetotal Band. This was because, as one of the leading members of the Unitarian Chapel in the town, William Hinkins was a staunch supporter of the temperance movement. Charles Hinkins senior later succeeded his family as bandmaster.[497]

Charles Hinkins senior was still residing in Royston with his wife and children as late as 1911. After relocating to Oxford, the Hinkins family became prominent members of the Headington Silver Band. Bob Hinkins himself was a soprano cornet player. He helped provide jobs in his family firm for band members.[498] Bob Hinkins had just married before living in George Street, and he would continue to work in the family business, becoming eventually a building contractor manager. The newly erected and reasonably priced houses on George Street were thus suitable for young married couples.

The business partners of the Hinkins family were the Frewins. They were originally carpenters from the village of Wytham near Oxford.

Eva Catley (1875–1958): The Landlady

The clatter and rattle of luggage being pulled along pavements is an all-too-familiar sound in Oxford. A temporary home for students, a venue for conferences and a centre for English-language education, Oxford is well known as a location in which much of its population is transient. The city also attracted another transient group – young professionals seeking to establish themselves and launch their careers. For such people, Oxford was a stepping-stone and property there would be rented rather than owned. Landlords and landladies played an important role in providing accommodation for these workers arriving from different parts of the country.

Eva Catley was one of these landladies, but she herself was not born and raised in Oxford. It seems that Eva only lived briefly at 73 George Street before then renting out the property. The house remained under her name until she eventually decided to sell it in 1951. As in the past, the land and property at Middle Way was being used to provide a regular source of income for its owner. However, Eva Catley could scarcely be compared with the rich absentee landowners who had once owned Whorestone Farm.

Who were the Catleys, and what were the circumstances which had led Eva Catley to purchase 73 George Street in 1928?

The Catleys were Yorkshire through and through. They were a family which for generations had provided colliers working in the Garforth district of the county. Eva's grandfather, Edward Catley, broke with this tradition by being employed as a tailor who also ran a beer shop. In his final years he took over the licence to run the Midland (Railway) Hotel at Oulton-cum-Woodlesford near Leeds. Edward's son, Edward Catley junior (1851–1930), the father of Eva, worked as an engineer in the Post Office. Based mostly in Leeds, Edward also had a spell of employment in Islington in London. In 1911 Edward retired after forty years of service for the Post Office and had relocated back to Islington. At the time of his retirement, a local newspaper reported that between 1895 and 1903 he had been an assistant-superintendent engineer for the North-East district at the Post Office in Leeds. More recently, he had worked as superintending engineer for the North Metropolitan District.[499]

Having retired early, and after the death of his wife, Elizabeth, in 1916, Edward spent the remainder of his life living at various times with any one of his three daughters. He appeared to be especially close to Eva's sister, Mabel Catley (1878–1948). It seems that it was Edward's connection with Mabel that resulted in Eva Catley becoming owner of 73 George Street.

In 1911 Mabel Catley was employed as a nurse in a small, private nursing home. Working together with Mabel at St Faith's on Rotherfield Avenue in Bexley, Sussex, was a close friend – Maud Octavia Maynard. Maud was the daughter of a general practitioner based at Bishop Auckland in Durham. Mabel and Maud became inseparable. By the early 1920s they were living together at Rotherfield House on Chandos Road in Buckingham. The two were clearly fond of the name 'Rotherfield' – a village in Sussex. Rotherfield House was a large property with nine rooms and a spacious garden. Formerly a gentleman's villa, it now forms part of the Royal Latin School. Mabel and Maud were well known in Buckingham. The press reported how Miss Catley organised a whist drive and dance in the gardens of her residence to raise much-needed funds for the local Girl Guides and Brownies.[500]

Edward Catley also lived at Rotherfield House for several years. He appeared to play an active role in the local community. In 1920 Edward was elected churchwarden for the Buckingham Parish Church. In the same year, an 'E. Catley' was a key member of the Buckingham bowls team.[501]

The 1921 census reveals that at Rotherfield House Mabel and Maud were tending to the needs of the invalid Sarah Augusta Willis, who was the wife of a much-travelled and highly decorated major-general in the British Army. The two friends were obviously continuing their nursing work, which appeared to be a highly lucrative business. Mrs Willis passed away in January 1924. This may have encouraged Mabel, Maud and Edward to relocate to Oxford, although why they chose to move to Oxford and not elsewhere is not clear. By the mid-1920s the three were living at 'Rotherfield' (!) at 324 Woodstock Road. Maud died there in 1936. Three years later, Mabel was still living at 'Rotherfield', looking after the needs of an incapacitated son of the Chairman of the Bowring Steamship Company.

In his last years, Edward Catley divided his time between 'Rotherfield' and 73 George Street. His daughter, Eva, was living less than five minutes' walk from his property on

Woodstock Road. Presumably, Edward had assisted Eva in the purchase of the new house on George Street. Edward himself may have actually been the first person to reside at 73 George Street. The property was named 'Byway'. Perhaps it was Edward who chose this name, although the significance of this name for the Catleys is not known. Perhaps it was because of the house's location on a road which was situated between two major highways. The local directory published in 1930 noted that Edward alone lived at 'Byway'.[502] But in Edward's will, prepared in September 1929, it was stated that Edward was living at 'Byway' together with Eva, and his third daughter, Hilda. Edward died at 'Rotherfield' in December 1930. His personal estate was apportioned in equal shares among his four children.[503] His son, Cyril Kitching Catley, had started work in the Post Office following his father's footsteps, but he later made a name for himself as an actor, producer and stage manager.

Eva Catley was born in York, and, like her two sisters, remained unmarried throughout her life. She had also began her working life in the Post Office. In 1892 she was successful in an open competition to become a telegraph learner in the London postal district.[504] By 1911 Eva was employed as a shorthand typist for the submarine cable works in Islington. Ten years later, she was working as a secretary for the 'League of Roses' at the Great Northern Central Hospital (later known as The Royal Northern Hospital) on Holloway Road in London.

The League of Roses was a charity, founded in 1910, which raised money through fetes, bazaars, lectures, whist drives and other forms of entertainment. Its president at the time was Princess Helena Victoria, a granddaughter of

Queen Victoria. The organisation was composed of women, primarily drawn from the borough of Islington. Its initial aim had been to raise sufficient funds to open a surgical ward for women at the Great Northern Central Hospital.[505] This goal was achieved, and the League then broadened its work to help other parts of the hospital. In an era before the establishment of the National Health Service, hospitals like the Great Northern Central were largely run on a voluntary, self-governing basis and were greatly dependent on funds provided by charities and other donors.[506] Familiar with the borough, in the 1920s Eva would have helped to coordinate the fundraising activities of the League's several local divisions in Islington. Similar to her sister, Mabel, albeit more indirectly and through a different channel, Eva was also then working for the health sector.

Eva's London residence in 1928 at 34 Wood Lane in Highgate was a Grade II listed building. One of its previous residents who had lived there for many years was the Irish sculptor Patrick Macdonnell (1799–1870), who had been a fellow of the Royal Academy. According to the 1911 census, 34 Wood Lane was a house which had ten rooms. At that time, it was occupied by a family of four together with a live-in servant. With Mabel living comfortably at 'Rotherfield', and with the purchase of the property at 73 George Street, it would appear that the Catleys were a family which was not short of funds in the late 1920s.

In the electoral roll for 1930, Eva and Edward Catley were both registered as living at 73 George Street. But soon after her father's death, Eva decided to rent out the property and went to live with her sister, Hilda, on a poultry farm. The sisters lived together for at least fifteen years at 'The

Laurels' on York Road in what was then the Berkshire village of West Hagbourne. The village, now in Oxfordshire, was once known as Windsor Hakeborne, and was named after Walter de Windsor, the first constable of Windsor Castle, and the owner of the manor in the area at the time of the Domesday Book. According to the 1939 register, Hilda was the poultry farmer and Eva was the housekeeper and help. 'The Laurels' had been built in the late nineteenth century as an extension to Manor Farm in the village. The Catleys must have got on well with the Lay family, who were the owners of Manor Farm. The Lays were mainly involved in arable farming, although they raised cattle for their beef and kept pigs and sheep. They were also known for keeping a flock of free-range poultry, and presumably this was where Eva and Hilda made their contribution to the running of the farm.[507]

Eva spent many years of what was effectively her retirement at West Hagbourne. In the meantime, 73 George Street was rented out to various tenants. According to local directories, a Mrs Jenkins occupied the property in 1932 and 1933. It is not possible, though, to learn more about Mrs Jenkins. Neither her first name nor the initial of her first name was recorded.[508] Presumably she was widowed as she seemed to be living alone. Much more is known about the next occupants of 73 George Street – Harry and Alvina Garnett.

Harry Garnett (1908–1984): Bank Clerk from Bradford

Harry and Alvina (1910–1997) Garnett came to Oxford as newlyweds. Like the Catleys, the Garnetts were a long-established family from Yorkshire. Indeed, this Yorkshire connection may have encouraged Eva to decide to rent out her property to the young couple. The Garnetts lived at 73 George Street until 1939. A new job had prompted Harry to relocate with his wife to the Oxford area. Harry worked at the time as a clerk for Barclay's Bank. He and Alvina later returned to Yorkshire as Harry was promoted to more senior positions within the bank.

The Garnetts had been a family of agricultural labourers from Aberford in Yorkshire. Harry's grandfather, Thomas, moved from the countryside to Bradford to work there as a cotton weaver. Thomas ran into trouble with the law. He pleaded guilty to breaking and entering a jewellery shop in Bradford. He had stolen a large number of rings, earrings, broaches, necklaces and other items which amounted to over £600 in value – a very substantial sum at the time. Brought up before the Quarter Sessions in Bradford on 10 May 1875, Thomas pleaded guilty and was sentenced to eighteen months' imprisonment with hard labour.[509]

Harry's father, Henry Garnett (1878–1961), was also connected with the textile industry. In 1921 Henry was employed as a clerk with the Bradford-based J. Denison and Company, the wool and stuff export merchants. In 1903 Henry married Ruth Eaddie (1876–1950), the daughter of a coachman. Later in life, Henry worked as a grocer and sub-postmaster in Bradford. This connection with the post office, as well as the ties with Yorkshire, may have helped Harry to secure the tenancy at 73 George Street.

From quite humble origins, Harry Garnett seems to have had quite a successful career. He was educated at the prestigious Hanson Grammar School in Bradford and joined

Barclay's Bank in 1929.[510] In July 1933 Harry married Alvina Simpson at the Unitarian Chapel in Bradford. Full details of the wedding were given in the local press, including what Alvina wore for the occasion. She had on her dress a pearl pin which had been worn by her great-great-grandmother on her wedding. After the ceremony, the couple went for their honeymoon to the south of Spain, the Mediterranean Islands and Algiers.[511]

The Simpsons were practising Unitarians. Alvina's brother, Jack, sang in the choir of the Unitarian Chapel in Bradford when he was a boy.[512] As a young girl, Alvina was well known at the Chapel Lane Unitarian Sunday School in the city. The sermon she delivered as a teenager at the Sunday school's annual event celebrating the school's founding was very well received by the large congregation, according to the local newspapers. Alvina quoted Zachariah about the importance of playing fairly and not despairing if one loses – 'Because others do better than us, that is no reason for being hasty and angry'.[513]

Alvina was named after her Cornish grandmother, from the mother's side of her family. Alvina's father, Albert Samuel Simpson, born in Rhyl in north Wales, was a stone mason who lived and worked in Shipley and Bradford. In his leisure time he performed as a singer. His stage name was 'Alby Williams', and he was on the bill at concert venues throughout the country at the time of the First World War and in the 1920s. He was known affectionately as 'the eminent Welsh Tenor' and 'the singing mason'.[514]

The Garnetts moved into 73 George Street shortly after their marriage. Interestingly, their neighbour at 75 George Street was also employed at Barclay's Bank. Donald Francis

Couldrey was working in 1927 at the bank's branch on the High Street in Oxford. By 1939 he had been promoted to the position of chief clerk. Eva Catley may have been persuaded by Donald Couldrey to rent out her property to a colleague of his. The Garnetts were the first married couple to make their home at 73 George Street. In another landmark event for the house, the first child was born there in late 1937 with the arrival of Elaine Margaret Garnett.

I was finally able to track down Elaine and talk to her over the telephone.[515] Elaine provided me with more details about the Garnetts and their life in Oxford. The house on George Street was still referred to as 'Byway'. Elaine's mother used the name on her calling card which was dated from the time of her wedding. According to the rules of Barclay's Bank, Harry and Alvina could only marry after Harry had reached the age of twenty-five. Before her marriage, Alvina had worked in a department store in Bradford. Harry and Alvina had met at the Unitarian Chapel in Bradford, although the Garnetts were not particularly religious. Elaine does not recall her parents attending a church service.

The couple were very happy living on George Street. There was a grandfather clock in the house together with a piano, which Harry played. Much of the other furniture was handmade in Bradford. Times were hard financially, though. To save money, Alvina did a lot of walking. Harry often cycled. He named his trusty bicycle 'Miracle'.

By 1939 the Garnett family had moved to a large flat on Cowley Road in Oxford, and Harry and Alvina had two more children. In the war, Harry enlisted in the navy but broke his foot while exercising in the gym. Returning to Oxford, he worked for a spell at the High Street branch of

Barclay's in Oxford and the family moved again, this time to the centre of the city. Eventually, in 1948, the Garnetts left Oxford to return to Yorkshire. Harry became a chief clerk at several branches of Barclay's Bank in Bradford, before becoming an assistant manager of a branch in Leeds. After working for over four years in Leeds, he was then appointed Manager of the Bingley Branch of Barclay's Bank.[516] Harry later worked in Wakefield in west Yorkshire, where he passed away in 1984. Alvina died thirteen years later.

Elaine herself was educated at Headington Girls' School in Oxford. She became a schoolteacher and started working in a secondary school in Bingley. There she met David Berry, who was employed as the arts' teacher. The two married, had several children and worked in various parts of the country. After David's death, Elaine later remarried.

Chatting with Elaine I was able to gain a clearer impression of what it must have been like for a young couple living on George Street in the interwar period. Conditions were difficult for the Garnetts. Money was scarce, but they were still able to enjoy their family life.

Edward George Leslie Hone (1911–1988): Bank Clerk and Chorister

The next residents of 73 George Street were Edward George Leslie Hone and his wife, Winifred. Edward's grandfather, also called Edward (1859–1925), was a larger-than-life figure. 'Teddy Hone' was the son of a labourer from Shepperton in Middlesex and was educated at Winchester Training College. After being employed by several schools, in 1887 he was appointed Headmaster of the Winchester Cathedral

School, and he held this position for many years. An accomplished singer himself, Edward performed as a tenor for the Winchester Choral Society.[517] The boy choristers lived with the Hone family at Colebrook House – a spacious building dating back to the sixteenth century and located next to the Cathedral. Colebrook House doubled as a school and a home. A bespectacled and 'a heavily built bearded man', very similar to King Edward VII in appearance, although rather vain given how he regularly dyed his beard, Edward Hone was a fierce disciplinarian. The chorister boys were very much afraid of the cane, which Edward kept in his desk in the school room and which 'was in fairly constant use'. Life was tough at Colebrook House. Money was often in short supply and there was not always enough food to properly feed the family and the chorister boys.[518]

Phyllis Dorothy James, better known as P.D. James, the celebrated crime writer, was one of Edward Hone's grandchildren. Born in Jericho in Oxford, P.D. James was often taken by her mother to Winchester to stay with her grandparents at Colebrook House. The house was adorned with a William and Mary façade. In the hidden garden at the back, water from the mill stream and a smaller tributary bubbled and tinkled. According to P.D. James, 'it was a beautiful place in which to be brought up'. She recalled how her grandfather was a 'conscientious school master' who did his best.[519] Her mother, Dorothy May Amelia, often helped Edward Hone by giving scripture and confirmation lessons to the choristers and acting in effect as a matron together with her sister, Marjorie.[520]

Another of Edward Hone's grandchildren would also become well known. Ethel Betty Hone, the daughter of

Leslie and Ella Hone, was a frequent visitor to Colebrook House in her youth. In 1958 she married her second husband, Christopher Cadbury, who was a company director at the famous chocolate company. Ethel, better known as Betty Cadbury, would become a household name through her impressive collection of dolls, doll houses and other toys. Exploring the lives of people who made and played with the toys, she believed that every toy had a story to tell.[521]

Edward George Leslie Hone was the brother of Betty Cadbury. Leslie Hone, the father of Betty and Edward George Leslie, was at one time a chorister himself at the Winchester Cathedral School, together with three of his four brothers. Leslie later worked as a surveyor for the County Council in Winchester and married the daughter of a florist. Edward George Leslie continued in the family tradition and was a probationer chorister, occasionally filling in when other choristers were absent. 'Birds-nesting' was a favourite activity of the chorister boys which was not condoned by Edward Hone. Edward George Leslie recalled how he himself was once stuck up a tree for hours when endeavouring to investigate a particular nest. Directly below him, and presumably aware of his grandson's presence, Edward Hone settled himself in his deck chair to watch a cricket match, leaving the young and probably terrified Edward George Leslie trapped in the branches above.[522]

In spite of their different backgrounds, Edward George Leslie Hone and Harry Garnett had several things in common. Both moved to Oxford because of their careers in banking. It appears, though, that Edward George Leslie did not work for Barclay's. In 1972 he was listed as an employee of the National Westminster Bank.[523] Presumably, Eva Catley was comfortable with having bank clerks as her tenants. Both Edward George Leslie and Harry were newly married when they started their lives at 73 George Street. Edward George Leslie was apparently already living in Oxford – perhaps on George Street – when he married Winifred Frances Pound (1914–1998) in Portsmouth on 3 June 1939.[524] Winifred was the daughter of a railway engine fitter.

What happened to the Hones in the war years is unclear. In the 1945 electoral register only Winifred was recorded as living at 73 George Street. But by 1949, an E.G.L. Hone was also present at the address.[525] Two years later, the Hones had departed and Edward George Leslie took up posts in banking in Alton in Hampshire, in Ledbury and then at Bideford. He died at Weymouth and in his will left all his estate to his wife. There was no mention of any children in the will.[526]

Conclusion

In July 1951 Eva Catley completed the sale of 73 George Street to William and Florence Lecky-Thompson. Eva was at the time the resident of a nursing home in Islington. She had returned to the neighbourhood where she had previously lived and worked for many years. William Lecky-Thompson was listed in the deeds as an assistant schoolmaster. The Lecky-Thompsons had been living at Boars Hill, near Oxford. The signing of the conveyance was witnessed by the retired civil servant S.A. Maybury-Lewis, who was living at 9 Summerhill Road in Summertown. It will be seen that Maybury-Lewis played a key role in the decision of the Lecky-Thompsons to move to George Street. Eva passed away in the nursing home seven years later. In her will, she left three quarters of her estate and all her jewellery, clothing and other household items to her sister, Hilda.[527]

The house at 73 George Street, known for several years as 'Byway', had provided one of the final resting places for Edward Catley. After Edward's death, his daughter, Eva, opted to vacate the property and chose to live in the country with her sister Hilda rather than live near to another sibling, Mabel. With the possible exception of Eva's brother, the Catleys had appeared to be a very close-knit family.

Over an eighteen-year period 73 George Street was rented out to two families who had ties to the banking profession. The Garnetts and Hones, with their hopes and aspirations, appeared to be typical of many other households who lived on George Street in the interwar period. With Eva's death, the house at George Street came into the possession of a family who came from a completely different background. The house was no longer rented out but was a home for the new owners, with Florence Lecky-Thompson living for forty years in what would become 73 Middle Way.

NINE

POLICE OFFICERS IN BURMA AND BANDMASTERS OF MAHARAJAHS

'Chance encounters are what keep us going'

(Haruki Murakami)

Introduction

The Japanese bombers attacked Rangoon (Yangon) before lunch on Christmas Day 1941. Instinctively, the Donnison family and their friends and servants rushed out to the garden. This was the second air raid launched by the Japanese following an initial attack on the port two days earlier. Over two thousand civilians were killed in the two bombardments and the docks in Rangoon were largely destroyed. Only days after the surprise attack on Pearl Harbor on 7 December, the Japanese had launched a ground invasion of Burma (Myanmar), which was at that time no longer a part of British India but was a separate colony. The invaders were keen to disrupt aid and weapons which were being delivered to the Chinese nationalists fighting the Japanese along the Burma road.

Immediately following the second air raid Flo (Florence Elizabeth Lecky-Thompson) asked her hosts, Vernon and Ruth Donnison, if she should attempt to leave the country with her two young children and escape to Calcutta (Kolkata) where her sister lived. Flo's parents, who were visiting at the time, and her husband, William, were included in the discussion. William was then a senior police official working in Burma. The Lecky-Thompsons had been good friends with the Donnisons for several years, with William often working under Vernon. Employed as Judicial Secretary, Vernon Donnison was a leading official in the local administration who had direct access to the Governor of Burma. Concluding their talks, both family and friends decided that it was too dangerous for Flo to stay and it was agreed that she should leave as soon as possible with her two children and take with her the daughter of the Donnisons. Suitcases were promptly loaded into the car, which was stationed under the porch ready for immediate departure.

Over the next days Flo endeavoured four times to fly out of the country with the children, but on each occasion there were no empty seats on the planes. On 30 December the phone rang and an increasingly desperate Flo was told that a flying boat had just touched down on the Rangoon River. The aircraft was due to leave for Calcutta at dawn the next morning. The flying boat had transported senior military officers to Rangoon, and Flo was informed that if the officers had not completed their work by the next morning the aircraft would depart with empty seats. On this occasion luck was on the side of Flo, and she was able to leave Burma with the three children on one of the last flights out of Rangoon. This was after the Japanese had targeted and put out of action the local airport at Mingaladon. After staying with her sister in Calcutta for a few days, Flo took the children to Darjeeling. Flo and her two children lived in a cottage in Darjeeling for about a year.[528] In the meantime, the situation in Burma quickly deteriorated. The British were forced to start the partial evacuation of Rangoon on 20 February 1941 as Japanese forces swept rapidly northwards.

William's later escape from Burma would be far more harrowing and dramatic. The Lecky-Thompsons were fortunate to survive. No longer able to escape by ship or plane, many died in the jungle or in the mountain passes as they attempted to flee overland from the Japanese and reach the safety of India. At the end of the Second World War, having served in the British Army in the Burma Reserve of Officers, William Lecky-Thompson was promoted to the honorary rank of Lieutenant-Colonel and was then discharged and retired. The Lecky-Thompsons left the Indian subcontinent and returned to England, where they lived for a few years on Boars Hill near Oxford, before relocating to live at 73 George Street. Summertown became their home, and after her husband's death Flo continued to live until 1991 at what had become 73 Middle Way.

William Lecky-Thompson ('Father T') (1864–1942) and Juanita Christina Jameson ('Mother T') (1872–1950)

Lecky-Thompson is quite an unusual surname and so it was not too difficult for me to track down living relatives of the William Lecky-Thompson who lived in Summertown. I was able to communicate with two nephews of William. Tom Lecky-Thompson was the son of William's brother, Thomas, from Thomas's first marriage. Roy Lecky-Thompson was born after Thomas had remarried after his divorce. Tom is a well-known figure. He was a squadron leader and test pilot who flew the fastest time in his Harrier jet in the 1969 Transatlantic Air Race from London to New York.

I was fortunate to learn quite a lot about the Lecky-Thompsons from the two nephews that could not be found in any records. For example, I was told how William Lecky-Thompson was known as 'Leck' by family and friends. And William's parents were referred to by family members as 'Father T' and 'Mother T'. Tom, who was then a young child, recounted how he had escaped the Japanese in Burma. Over three months he and others with him had covered 1,400 kilometres first via lorry, then using donkeys and finally walking. The children were told how to dodge Japanese bullets by running in zig-zags. Roy provided me with more recent details of the lives of the Lecky-Thompsons in Oxford. He kindly provided me with a long transcript of a fascinating interview given by his aunt Flo. Other family members offered invaluable information. Interestingly, though, they knew little of the earlier history of the Lecky-Thompson family.

The early history of the family is particularly difficult to trace. Certainly they were quite poor. A William Thompson was born on 16 February 1864 in North Town, Cookham, in Berkshire. On the birth certificate, it was noted that William's father, Thomas Thompson (full name, Thomas William Thompson), was a journeyman shoemaker. William Thompson's mother, Lucretia, was previously known as Lucretia Barnes.[529] On 3 April 1865 in Holborn, Lucretia married Thomas Lecky, who was another shoemaker. At the time of this wedding, Lucretia was listed as a spinster and it was noted that her father was Richard Rose. The surname Lecky-Thompson would be derived from the surnames of Lucretia's two husbands.

A number of questions are raised here which may never be satisfactorily resolved. Certainly, relatives of the families involved remain puzzled. Did Thomas William Thompson die before Lucretia remarried? In 1891 a fifty-eight-year-old Thomas William Thompson was an inmate at the Cookham workhouse, but he was listed as a commercial traveller. And why did Lucretia in 1865 refer to herself as a spinster, rather than a widow, and give her surname as Rose rather than Barnes? It does seem that Lucretia's father was Richard Rose, a shoemaker from Bristol. One of Lucretia's brothers became quite famous. A Frederick Edward Rose climbed to the ranks of sergeant major in the second battalion of the Northumberland Fusiliers and was stationed in Mauritius, southern Africa and Ireland. In an account of his life, Frederick noted how in August 1858 he had gone to see his married sister in Slough.[530] In 1857 Thomas William Thompson had married Lucretia at Eton and then the couple had moved to live together in Slough. This again begs the question, why did Lucretia previously call herself Lucretia Barnes?

William Thompson, the father of Flo's husband, would adopt the surname of his mother's second husband and was hence known for a time as William Lecky (also spelt as Leckey or Licky to add to the confusion). However, by the time he arrived in Burma in the late 1880s, William was referring to himself as William Lecky-Thompson. William's two brothers opted for different surnames. His eldest brother, Andrew, later called himself Andrew Thompson-Lecky. Another brother, Thomas James, who emigrated to Canada, kept the surname Leckey/Lecky.

According to the 1861 census, Thomas William Thompson, the husband of Lucretia and future father of William, was living in Cookham with his wife and young family. It was noted that Thomas William Thompson was born in New York, near Earsdon in Northumberland in 1831. He may well have come from a coal miner's family. The Algernon Colliery was the main source of employment for the inhabitants of New York, a small pit village. Thomas Lecky, Lucretia's second husband, also came from a humble background. At the time of their marriage in 1865 they were living in Tyndall's Buildings in a very impoverished area of London by Gray's Inn Lane in Holborn. Formerly known as Spread Eagle Court, Tyndall's Buildings were notorious for criminality and prostitution. Pigs were kept inside the properties.[531] A court of twenty-two houses, the basement storey of almost all the dwellings was 'filled with fetid refuse'. According to George Godwin, the editor of the magazine *The Builder*, commenting at the end of the 1850s, 'it seemed scarcely possible that human beings could live' in Tyndall's Buildings.[532]

It is not known when Thomas Lecky died. More information, though, is available on Lucretia. In her later years she was in and out of St Luke's workhouse on City Road in Holborn. Destitute and alone, and suffering from pneumonia, she passed away in the workhouse in April 1910.

Given this background, the career of William Lecky-Thompson senior – who would come to be known as 'Father T' – was quite remarkable. According to the 1881 census, William was based on the navy's training ship *Arethusa*, which was moored at the dock on the Thames in Greenhithe near Dartford in Kent. The last major ship in the Royal Navy to enter a naval engagement under sail power only – in the Crimean War in 1854 – the fifty-gun frigate was decommissioned and became a training vessel in 1874. Owned by the charity, the Shaftesbury Homes, the *Arethusa* provided a refuge for up to 250 children who had been sleeping rough on the streets of London and offered them an education and training so that they could have a career in the Royal Navy or Merchant Navy.[533] This suggested that William may have left home and spent a period of time living on the streets before being offered shelter. Interestingly, William's brother, Andrew, had entered the navy and between 1873 and 1876 had served in the coastguard. However, in the summer of 1876 it was reported that an Andrew Lecky from Slough had deserted from the navy.[534] It seemed, though, that William's brother was not too adversely affected by this experience, and by 1888 he was a married man and father working as a 'general dealer' in Westminster.

In contrast to his brother, William appeared to have taken to the navy. As a 'boy', he was one of the crew of the sea clipper and cargo vessel *The Forward Ho*, which embarked from London on 30 April 1881 to sail to the port of Kanagawa in Japan.[535] After arriving in Japan, on 19 October 1881 the ship left the port of Kobe with a cargo of ballast and set course for Portland, Oregon, in the US. Nine days later the ship struck rocks and was wrecked off the Japanese coast. Fortunately, the crew were saved and *The Forward Ho* was set on shore by the current in a dead calm.[536]

By 1888, William Lecky-Thompson had joined the civil police in Burma, which was then a province of British India. After the Third Anglo-Burmese War was concluded in 1885, Burma was formally annexed as a British colony in 1886. Apparently, at the time a number of young men were attracted to working for the police in Burma. Kipling's poem 'Mandalay' had conjured up romantic and exotic images of the Orient, but in reality, conditions in Burma were grim and dreary. In contrast to the rest of India, there were no hill stations in those early days in which the young men could entertain themselves and let off steam.[537] According to the civil servant Sir Herbert Thirkell White: 'The story of the Burma Civil Police is one of time deferred, and of weary plodding through many dismal years'.[538]

For William Lecky-Thompson, however, a career in the Burma Civil Police offered an opportunity to see the world and to escape from the poverty which his parents had experienced and of which he had been a victim in his early years. It seems that he benefitted from a fast-track entry to the police branch of the Indian Civil Service. In the pacification of Burma, which continued for several years after annexation, when the British were engaged in putting down riots and local rebellions, the work of the civil police in Burma supposedly should have focused on intelligence, detection and investigation.[539] However, in the early summer of 1888, police inspector Thompson was involved in 'a sharp engagement with a small body of police' in Minhla, a town in southern-central Burma on the right bank of the River Irrawaddy. Around this time a W.L. Thompson, Inspector of Police, has passed a departmental examination in Law.[540] In August 1888, Lecky-Thompson was appointed Assistant Superintendent of Police, Second Class, in the district of Thayetmyo, close to Minhla.[541]

Over the next years William Lecky-Thompson held a number of posts in the Burma Civil Police based in different parts of the colony. In 1895, for example, he was based in Sagadaung in the Ruby Mines District. British companies became involved in the exploitation of the rich mines. The work of a police officer in Burma was not easy. In 1905 Lecky-Thompson was reprimanded for being drunk, and two years earlier in a letter from the Office of the Commissioner of Irrawaddy it was suggested that he should be transferred to another post because of friction with another police officer.[542]

In May 1890 in Thayetmyo, William Lecky-Thompson, Assistant Superintendent of Police, married Juanita Christina Jameson, the daughter of A. Leonida Jameson. According to the marriage certificate, Juanita Christina was born in Constantinople in 1872. There is some debate among family members with regard to Juanita Christina's background and the circumstances in which she may have met her husband-to-be. It seems that the family name may have been Anglicised from Ionescu to Jameson. There is also speculation that Juanita Christina was the daughter of a Romanian diplomatic official, possibly an ambassador.[543] It was only in 1878 that Romania was recognised as an independent state separate from the Ottoman Empire. Other relatives have suggested that A. Leonida Jameson had worked as a linguist and was born around 1845. There was clearly an Ottoman connection of some sort to the Jameson/Ionescu family, but the precise nature of this linkage may never be known.

The couple had a large number of children – at least seven boys and one girl. The two eldest boys died in action fighting in the Indian Army in Mesopotamia in the First World War. Several of the other boys also became police officers in Burma. Their first child, Leonida George, was baptised in Clerkenwell in London in October 1897. Presumably, William Lecky-Thompson had returned to England for a spell of leave. It is not known if he visited his mother, who was most probably living near Clerkenwell at the time.

'Mother T', as Juanita Christina was known by family members, was a very quiet, gentle and steady lady according to her grandson, Tom Lecky-Thompson. This was in stark contrast to William, who was known as a strict disciplinarian. No one was allowed to sit at the dining table until Mother T had settled herself down.[544] Apparently, in her later years she divorced William after her husband retired and had insisted that she and the children should live with him at his coconut plantation. Juanita Christina refused, insisting that they should instead move to Rangoon, where the children could receive a proper education. She taught English to Chinese residents in Rangoon.[545]

With the Japanese invasion of Burma, Juanita Christina somehow managed to escape the country and spent her final years in Calcutta, where she died in 1950. William Lecky-Thompson was much less fortunate. Choosing to remain on his plantation, it seems that he was summarily executed by the Japanese in 1942 for refusing to take down the Union Jack.[546]

William Lecky-Thompson ('Leck') (1900–1965) and Florence Elizabeth Bocker ('Flo') (1909–2001): Lives in Burma and India

After the departure of his wife and children from Rangoon by flying boat at the end of December 1941, William Lecky-Thompson junior – 'Leck' – remained in Burma for several more months. The story goes that he later drove northwards by car from Rangoon to Mandalay as the Japanese advanced across Burma. There, he handed his vehicle over to a local police officer, and then commenced on a long trek which would eventually take him to India.[547]

What is definitely known is that by June 1942 William was to be found at the remote outpost of Shinbwiyang in northern Burma. This 'extremely primitive village', with little food and no proper sanitation, and rife with disease, had become the principal junction for a flood of evacuees who were desperate to escape from the approaching Japanese army. In the words of one commentator, the village became 'a veritable charnel house'.[548] A young political officer, Cornelius North, was in command of the outpost. He was assisted by about half a dozen men, one of whom was William Lecky-Thompson.

Panic had set in among the British civilians trapped in Burma after the Japanese had bombed the aerodrome at Myitkyina in the north of the country on 6 May 1942.[549] The day before, Sir Reginald Dorman-Smith, the Governor General of Burma, had flown out from the airport on a specially chartered plane. The last escape route via air was no longer possible. Thousands of refugees had streamed to Myitkyina in the hope of using the airport. Their only remaining option was to walk northwards to Shinbwiyang and from there attempt to escape by moving across the Hukawng Valley and the Pangsau Pass to India.

William Lecky-Thompson and his colleagues may have been assisting North at Shinbwiyang for several weeks. At first the situation was largely under control. Food and medicines were dropped by air, and the weather remained fine. But the weather turned on 17 May with the start of persistent very heavy rain. On 5 June, Lecky-Thompson and a few officials, and a significant number of evacuees, decided to leave the village and attempt to reach India by moving through the Hukawng Valley. This was in spite of being instructed to remain at Shinbwiyang until the rains ended. Over the next three weeks the party struggled through dense jungle and steep hill climbs, and had to cross swollen and fast-moving streams and rivers. The treacherous current of the Namyang River could only be negotiated with the help of sturdy Indians, who made use of large bamboo poles which the evacuees wading across the river could cling on to. Over three days, about 2,500 refugees were able to cross the Namyang. But many others perished on the journey.

On 25 June the party, including Lecky-Thompson, arrived safely at the refugee camp at Margherita in Assam, India. When Flo later saw her husband she could barely recognise him. Dressed in khaki, 'he was all skin and bone'.

William Lecky-Thompson junior's career in the Burma Civil Police had followed in the footsteps of his father. He was awarded a scholarship by the Diocesan Boys' School in Rangoon – presumably the Anglican school of St John's. According to a local newspaper report, when he graduated it was noted that '...he will be remembered as one of [the] sweetest singers the Diocesan Boys' High School has ever had'.[550] Too young to experience combat in the First World War, in September 1918 he was admitted to the Indian Army Reserve of Officers as a second lieutenant.[551] Lecky-Thompson got a commission with the second battalion of the 95th Russell Infantry.[552] The battalion was stationed for a period on the North West Frontier before being disbanded in February 1921.

On 10 September 1921 'Leck' joined the Burma Civil Police as an assistant district superintendent.[553] In the interwar period he held a number of posts in the police in different parts of the country. Rising through the ranks, by 1938 Lecky-Thompson was stationed in Rangoon, where he received a medal for his work in supervising the distribution of food for the army and police.[554] Earlier, in December 1929, at Lashio in Burma, he had married Florence Elizabeth Bocker, the daughter of the civil engineer Alfred Charles Bocker (1877–1963). The couple would have two children – Joan Elizabeth, born in 1932, and Michael William, born in 1937.

The Bockers were a distinguished family of Prussian heritage who had lived in India for several generations. How they chose to become officers in the British Army in India is not clear. The family's Prussian origins would only become problematic in the 1930s after Hitler assumed power. According to Flo's son, Michael, the German connection was then carefully suppressed and not spoken about.[555]

According to the family, Lieutenant Bocker of the British Army, who famously pursued the Rani of Jhansi in 1858, was a relative of Flo's. The story of the pursuit of Lakshmi Bai, the wife of the Maharajah Gangadhar Rao and the Rani of Jhansi, has become a treasured part of Indian folklore. A fierce warrior in her own right, Lakshmi Bai dressed herself as a man when she was engaged in combat. In the wake of the failed Uprising of 1857, in April 1858 Lakshmi Bai had escaped from the fort at Jhansi, which was being besieged by the British. Her small entourage was vigorously chased by Bocker and his party. At one time Bocker believed that he was about to apprehend Lakshmi Bai only to find her tent empty, apart from the remains of her breakfast. Bocker was forced to abandon the pursuit after becoming seriously wounded. Thus, 'a brave and experienced Englishman like Bocker', was 'trounced' by a supposed 'weak Brahmin woman' who had displayed 'supernatural courage'.[556]

What is definitely known is that the Bockers became bandmasters to Maharajahs in India. Flo's great-grandfather, Johann Heinrich Conrad Bocker (1811–1877), was born in Prussia. Serving in the British Army in India, he became the bandmaster to Sawai Ram Singh II, the famous Maharajah of Jaipur. The reform-minded Ram Singh II, celebrated for his love of photography, was also a connoisseur of music. With the encouragement of the Maharajah, and with the support of Johann Heinrich Conrad, the world-famous brass band of Jaipur was founded. Every Monday evening after sunset, under the direction of its bandmaster, the brass band held a concert in Jaipur Gardens. Concerts were also organised in the Maharajah's palace. In the words of one newspaper columnist, the Maharajah took considerable pride in the brass band, which 'was quite unequalled as a native one, and did great credit to Mr Bocker, the Band Master'.[557]

Robert Max Bocker (1841–1911), Flo's grandfather, who was also born in Prussia, took over as bandmaster for the

Maharajah of Jaipur after his father's death in 1877. In turn, Robert's son, Robert William Conrad Bocker (1865–1932) (Flo's uncle), became the next bandmaster for the Maharajah of Jaipur. When he was previously employed as music master for the Indian state of Kapurthala, Robert William had a book published titled *The Rudiments of European Music* which was translated into Hindustani.[558] The Bockers clearly had a major impact on the development of brass bands in Jaipur and elsewhere in British India.

Flo's father, Alfred Charles Bocker, thus broke with family tradition by becoming a civil engineer and working for the Public Works Department in Burma. He married Olivia Gertrude Connor in Tavoy in Bengal in June 1908. Their first child, Florence Elizabeth, was born one year later. A quite small lady, Olivia was given the nickname 'Birdie' because of her beautiful voice.[559] She passed away in 1919, a victim of the Spanish Flu. Alfred Charles promptly remarried, his second wife being Olivia's sister, Grace.

As a child, Flo was a boarder at the Diocesan Girl's School in Darjeeling. It would take a whole week for Flo to travel from her home in Taung-Gye (Taunggyi) in Burma to arrive at the school, the trip entailing two train journeys and a passage by boat from Rangoon to Calcutta.[560] The school was run by nuns and had been established in the early 1880s by the Clewer sisters. The three sisters had left England to set up originally a nursing home in Calcutta, but their work soon expanded to include the founding of other hospitals and schools throughout India.

Flo had met her husband-to-be at Taung-Gye, a town south of Mandalay, where William was then working for the police. Although William was ten years older, this was not a problem according to Flo. They met each time Flo returned home on holiday and often played tennis together. The romance blossomed and they soon married. Flo had particular fond memories of their time together in the Mergui Archipelago in southern Burma. As one of the perks of the job, Leck had a 'lovely police launch' which had two cabins. They enjoyed cruising around the islands, although they also experienced 'terrible rough journeys' at the time of the monsoons. At Mergui the Lecky-Thompsons met the Donnison family. Flo paints a picture of almost an idyllic lifestyle in Burma in the 1930s, although she does mention that Leck was at one time compelled to go to Pegu (Bago) to deal with the riots there.[561] This was probably a reference to the disturbances triggered in 1931 by local support for Hsaya San – a disrobed monk who declared that he was the heir to the Burmese monarchy.

The relatively sheltered life that the Lecky-Thompsons were able to lead would come to an abrupt halt with the Japanese attacks on Burma. The Lecky-Thompsons would eventually be united in India after Leck's dramatic trek across the Burmese jungle. It was in India that the couple met by chance an Englishman, who was employed there as a civil engineer. That fateful encounter would eventually result several years later in Flo and Leck taking up residence at 73 George Street.

The Lecky-Thompsons in Oxford

Arguably, the heyday of the imposing Grand Hotel in Simla was in the late nineteenth century when the establishment was run by Signor Federico Peliti. The Italian entrepreneur and confectioner had taken control of Bentinck Castle, the former summer house of the Governor General of India. Under Peliti's management, the hotel perched high on a hill and commanding scenic views, became popular for its Western-style cakes, chocolates and pastries. It was also a location for idle gossip and a flirtatious rendezvous being one of the few places in the Indian hill station where women often outnumbered men. Kipling's early stories depict the goings-on and romantic encounters at the Grand Hotel. A fire destroyed much of the hotel in 1922, and although it was rebuilt the splendour and grandeur of the original establishment could not be replicated.

It was in the Grand Hotel in the early 1940s, after Leck had recovered from his traumatic experiences in the Burmese jungle, that the Lecky-Thompsons met Sydney Maybury-Lewis. William Lecky-Thompson was working with the government-in-exile of Burma which was then quartered in Simla. Maybury-Lewis, late of the Indian Service of Engineers (Sind), had retired in September 1941.[562] His son, David Maybury-Lewis, who became a well-known and much-published anthropologist and ethnologist, later described how his father was simply known as 'Maybury' to friends and family. He was 'a formidable civil engineer' who led teams of engineers and workers to construct barrages and dams throughout British India.[563]

According to the recollections of Flo, Mr Maybury-Lewis came to sit at their table in the Grand Hotel. They would then dine together regularly. The Lecky-Thompsons became 'very friendly' with the retired civil engineer who for some reason continued to linger in Simla. Maybury-Lewis finally left India and arrived in Liverpool in June 1944. Flo would return to England with her two children in October 1944, leaving Leck in India. She would not see her husband for at least the next two years. The Lecky-Thompsons assumed that they would not meet Maybury-Lewis again.[564]

What exactly Leck did in the years 1942–1947 is unclear. In September 1942 district superintendent William Lecky-Thompson was listed as working as a 'special officer under the Defence Department' for the Government of Burma at Simla.[565] In January 1947 it was announced that William Lecky-Thompson, a member of the Army of Burma Reserve Officers, had relinquished his office. He had been awarded the honorary rank of lieutenant-colonel in March 1946 when ill health had apparently forced him to retire from active duty.[566] Clearly, he had carried out important duties for the Government and Army of Burma. There is speculation that Leck may have fought on the Arikan front in India. According to the family, he was forced to quickly leave Burma when the nationalists were about to seize power and declare independence.[567]

By 1947 Flo and Leck had reunited and they lived for several years on Cumnor Road in the village of Wootton on Boars Hill near Oxford. But why had the Lecky-Thompsons decided to buy their 'little house' in Wootton?

The Lecky-Thompsons knew Oxford and its neighbourhood well. Leck's sister, Ruby, had left Burma and relocated to the city with her husband, Arthur, after suffering an illness. When Leck had a spell of leave in 1933, the Lecky-Thompsons came to Oxford and visited Ruby at her house on 6 St Margaret's Road. Ruby passed away in 1937. Before living at Wootton, and while Leck was still in India, Flo had lived with Vernon Donnison's mother at the residence known as The Dilbeys near Didcot in Oxfordshire. In the months before the war ended, The Dilbeys, in its rural setting, had offered Flo a safe refuge.

Oxford was also attractive to the Lecky-Thompsons because the schools in the area offered the prospect of providing a good education for their children. Michael would be enrolled in St Edward's School in Summertown. William's brother, Thomas, who had also served in the Burma Civil Police, decided to settle in the Oxford area with his wife Mary, after visiting the Lecky-Thompsons in Wootton.

One day Flo and Leck were in Gloucester Green in central Oxford after completing their shopping. By chance they bumped into a familiar figure. 'Good Heavens,' exclaimed Sydney Maybury-Lewis. After Flo and Leck explained how they had moved to Wootton, Maybury-Lewis invited the couple to visit him in his home at Summerhill Road in Summertown. This would also be an opportunity for Flo and Leck to meet for the first time Constance, the wife of Maybury-Lewis. The two couples got on famously. We had a 'lovely time', recalled Flo. They would go together, carrying lanterns and carol singing in Summertown. This was followed by consuming delicious mince pies and drinking punch at the house of Sydney and Constance. It was no surprise then that when the house at 73 George Street – literally a stone's throw away from the residence of the Maybury-Lewises – came on the market, the Lecky-Thompsons grabbed the opportunity to be close to their good friends.[568]

An insight into life at 73 George Street/Middle Way is provided by Roy Lecky-Thompson. Roy's parents, Thomas and Mary, made the journey each month by bus from Abingdon to Summertown. The grown-ups were dressed in sober suits.

An elaborate tea ceremony took place. Tea was served in fine china teacups accompanied with Battenberg cake. The adults would sit primly and chat in the living room while Roy played by himself with his toy cars. The kitchen and living room were especially cold, Roy recalls. The wall of the dining room was partially filled with the painting of a railway station made by Flo and Lecky's son, Michael. The garden outside was neatly tended and there was ample space there for a child to play. Mr Bocker (Alfred) lived in the house for a time in the 1950s. Roy remembers him as 'a charming old man'.[569]

Their neighbours at 71George Street/Middle Way were the Hartwells. The then Cynthia Hartwell was living there with her mother. She also regularly had tea with the Lecky-Thompsons. Leck loved to recount to Cynthia stories – many of them quite colourful – of his life as a police officer in Burma.[570]

Leck struggled to adapt to life in Oxford. By 1951 he had secured a position as an assistant schoolmaster. It seems that he worked at New College School in the centre of Oxford. The school, which had been originally founded to provide education for choristers of the chapel of New College, received boys aged between four and thirteen. Apparently, Leck encountered difficulties teaching. He was later employed for a spell at the old paper mill which has now been demolished in nearby Wolvercote. His health began to deteriorate. He started to lose his memory. In his final years Leck found happiness travelling around the Oxford area on a motorbike with his old friend, Aidan Kenneth Thompson. The two had known each other from Burma, where Thompson had worked for the Burma Frontier Service. Aidan would drive up from Beckenham in Kent to pick up his friend. Flo recalls how her husband often asked where Aidan was and when would they next meet.[571] William Lecky-Thompson passed away at Warneford hospital in Oxford in May 1965.

After her husband's death Flo lived for a further twenty-six years at 73 Middle Way. People who knew her well spoke of how she was so active and sociable. A keen bridge and scrabble player, she loved going for long walks. She was well known for preparing an excellent egg curry topped with a mango pickle.[572] Her neighbour remembered how Flo kept an immaculate house. She did not talk much about her past life in Burma but did speak ruefully about how she had been forced to leave everything behind in order to flee from the Japanese.[573]

Flo's prowess at tennis was legendary. She often took the children to play on the courts at Alexandra Park which was situated just off Middle Way. In her three-quarter-length dress she would glide around the court. Not particularly strong, she played with real grace and had excellent technique according to Tom Lecky-Thompson.[574] Flo had obviously continued to hone her skills since playing her first tennis matches in Burma with her future husband.

Flo agreed to the sale of 73 Middle Way in May 1991. The property was sold to Stratford Stanley Caldecott and his wife, Leonie Ann. In her last years, Flo continued to live in Summertown residing in a care home on Osberton Road, which was only a short walk from 73 Middle Way.

Conclusion

With the Lecky-Thompsons, for the first time 73 George Street/Middle Way had become a permanent home. This was a family which for several generations had lived overseas. The house on Middle Way became, in effect, a comfortable and safe refuge for a family which had witnessed suffering and which had experienced their own personal upheavals. Not surprisingly, perhaps, the promise of good schooling for their children appeared to be a significant factor in the Lecky-Thompsons opting to locate to the Oxford area. The fortuitous encounter with Maybury-Lewis resulted in Flo and Leck deciding to finally settle in Summertown. Unknowingly perhaps, William Lecky-Thompson had returned to a neighbourhood which was located not that far from where his grandfather had lived as a young child.

TEN
CONCLUSION

'Mid pleasures and palaces though we may roam
Be it ever so humble, there's no place like home'

(John Howard Payne)

This book has shown that it is possible to learn a little about the lives of the people who previously owned or occupied the land and the house which is now 73 Middle Way. Landowners and land speculators, lawyers and art dealers, bank clerks and butchers, and people from other assorted backgrounds, have all at one time had a personal interest and a stake in the property. Like other properties, it has witnessed its share of joys and upheavals, and successes and failures. For those interested in house histories, the house itself is quite modern, built less than one hundred years ago. But the land on which it stands in its prime location has been the subject in the past of much heated contestation.

The area was for many years open farmland, but much has changed over the last two centuries. James Lambourne would certainly struggle to recognise the Summertown of today. Whorestone Farm and the later extensive and exotic gardens of Summerhill Villa have disappeared to be replaced by a housing estate. And what was previously an isolated village has been gradually enveloped by the expanding city of Oxford. Once little more than a simple track, Middle Way itself has become a relatively busy thoroughfare, particularly when parents go through the twice-daily rituals of the school run and young teenagers race to school on their bikes.

After Flo Lecky-Thompson, the Caldecotts lived for five years at 73 Middle Way together with their three daughters. The son of a father who was a publisher and editor, and a mother who was a poet and novelist, Stratford Caldecott (1953–2014) at one time worked in the publishing business. He later became an author and editor who specialised in exploring the Christian themes in the works of J.R.R. Tolkien. Described as a 'giant in the Catholic world', he was appointed G.K. Chesterton Research Fellow at St Benet's Hall in Oxford. Working with his wife, Leonie, herself an author, journalist and playwright, he founded the Centre for Faith and Culture in Oxford in 1994, while living in Summertown. 'Strat', as he was known to family and close friends, had met his future wife when they were both students at Oxford.[575]

Stratford Caldecott must have known Tolkien's daughter, Priscilla, who lived only three doors down from the Caldecotts on Middle Way. He was buried at Wolvercote cemetery in Oxford, close to Tolkien's grave. The cemetery had been full, but fate would have it that space was freed when a tree near

Tolkien's resting place was vandalised. Caldecott was thus able to be buried near to the man who had inspired him in his work.[576]

The next residents at 73 Middle Way were Paul and Catherine Matthews and their family. They lived in the house for the next twenty-two years. Paul was a Professor of Neurology whose interests included research into dementia. Awarded an OBE for his services to neuroscience and made a Fellow of St Edmund Hall in Oxford by Special Election, Paul became Head of Department of Brain Sciences in the Faculty of Medicine of Imperial College, London.[577] The Thespian theme continued with Catherine Matthews, who was also a playwright. The Oxford Playwrights Group regularly held meetings at 73 Middle Way, and actors came to rehearse there.

Catherine Matthews told me that when she first viewed the house when they were considering whether to purchase it, she was immediately struck by how it was packed with books filling every available place. Her attention was also drawn to the two large trees which were visible from the back of the property. The house had 'a dear little brick path at the front' which sadly had to go when they made a parking space for their car. Catherine recalled how the property 'always had a very nice feel to it', and they 'were very fond of it'.[578] Paul and Catherine made extensions to the property. The loft was converted, an extension was added to the rear of the house and finally a conservatory was attached to the rear extension.

My wife and I, together with our two cats, moved into 73 Middle Way in 2018, having previously lived for a few years just down the road on South Parade. We are able to enjoy our own small patch of Ryman's former pleasure grounds with a magnificent garden at the back and the frontage with its splendid, small crab apple tree. The house has become our home.

Meanwhile, Summertown continues to evolve. A well-intentioned report by a local pressure group published in 1971 noted that Summertown was 'desperately in need of a comprehensive development plan'. The report recommended that the current community should be retained, its existing scale respected, and 'the trees, shrubs and hedgerows' should be 'accommodated'. It advocated that Summertown 'should become a form of conservation area'.[579] But, with Summertown throughout its history being a case in point, communities may adapt to shifting times.

Indeed, much has altered since I first came to live in Summertown as a student in the early 1980s. I lived in a household with a group of other students right on the Banbury Road just a couple of minutes' walk from The Dewdrop Inn. We lived together with our landlord, a Mr Cave – a redoubtable retired lecturer of the Oxford School of Architecture and a prominent member of the local community. My memories of Summertown as a student are admittedly somewhat blurred. For instance, I can't recall if I ever walked along Middle Way. Other than the pub, there was the nearby Co-op which came in very handy for buying groceries and there was an Italian restaurant across the road – long since closed – where we would go to if we needed to celebrate.

Returning to the area almost forty years later – and, thereby, supplementing the pool of retired academics resident in the area – today's Summertown feels much more vibrant and multicultural than the early 1980s. There also seems to be a wider cross-section of different age groups. Some of the shops and other outlets have disappeared. For example, in the last few years most of the local bank branches have closed. It was an especially sad day when the bookshop on the corner of South Parade and Banbury Road was forced to shut its doors. But in its place, a lively coffee house with an al fresco vibe opened, offering the locals a convenient site to congregate, muse and watch the world pass by, while a new bookshop surfaced further down the main road. At the time of writing, there were worrying reports that the local Co-op was threatened with closure. Although he may not have exactly approved, thankfully the building housing The Dewdrop Inn still remains from John Badcock's time – for now at least.

ENDNOTES

1 *Summertown & St Margaret's Neighbourhood Plan*, https://summertownstmargaretsforum.org.uk/our-plan (accessed 12 February 2022), p.59.
2 *Ibid.*
3 Kinchin, *Seven Roads in Summertown*, p.169.
4 Sinclair, *Portrait of Oxford*, p.53.
5 Angela Swann, 'Summertown named as one of best places in UK for commuters to live', *Oxford Mail*, 9 October 2016.
6 McGuiness, *Real Oxford*, p.151.
7 *Ibid.*, p.149.
8 *Ibid.*
9 Hibbert and Hibbert (eds.), *The Encyclopaedia of Oxford*, p.284.
10 Snow, *Oxford Observed*, pp.157–8.
11 Lively, *The House in Norham Gardens*, p.2.
12 Ruskin, *Fors Clavigera*, p.218.
13 Symonds, *The Changing Faces of North Oxford: Book One*, pp.11–2.
14 *Ibid.*, p.24.
15 Dibden, *Dirty Tricks*, pp.11–9.
16 Winrow, *Whispers Across Continents.*
17 Stevenson and Salter, *The Early History of St. John's College*, pp.508–9.
18 Fasnacht, *Summertown Since 1820*, p.6.
19 Hinchcliffe, *North Oxford*, p.6.
20 Fasnacht, *Summertown Since 1820*, pp.11–12.

21 Morris, *Oxford*, p.20.
22 Badcock, *The Making of a Regency Village*, pp.35–6.
23 Fasnacht, *A History of the City*, p.189.
24 Marshall, *Memorials of Westcott Barton*, pp.19, 22 and 56–7; and Baggs et al., 'Parishes: Westcott Barton', *A History of the County of Oxford*.
25 National Archives, Kew, TS 25/3/63.
26 Wharton, *The History and Antiquities of Kiddington*, p.19.
27 Knapp, *A History of the Chief English Families*, p.42. In 1683 George Knapp had married Mary Bolton (née Buswell), 'the widow of Wootton'.
28 Will of Robert Buswell of Kiddington.
29 National Archives, Kew, TS 25/3/63. For more information on the Reverend Thomas Wisdom(e) see, Geare, *Farnham*, pp.45, 69 and 80. After marrying Fanny Howlett in 1802, Wisdom(e) was obliged to forfeit his Fellowship.
30 National Archives, Kew, SP 36/112/2/29.
31 Howard, *The State of the Prisons*, p.316.
32 Davies, *Stories of Oxford Castle*, pp.96–107.
33 *Ibid.*, pp.103–7.
34 Will of Thomas Terry of Dummer.
35 Collins, *Jane Austen*, p.116.
36 Rosen and Cliffe, *The Making of Chipping Norton*, pp.70 and 79.
37 Will of Thomas Wisdom of Chipping Norton.
38 National Archives, Kew, C 217/160.
39 Bodleian Library, MS. Top. Oxon. b. 111.
40 Dodson, *The Life of Sir Michael Foster*, p.31.
41 National Archives, Kew, SP 36/112/2/2.
42 National Archives, Kew, SP 36/112/2/24.
43 National Archives, Kew, SP 36/112/2/25.
44 National Archives, Kew, SP 36/112/2/22.
45 National Archives, Kew, SP 36/112/2/28.
46 National Archives, Kew, SP 36/112/2/23.
47 National Archives, Kew, SP 36/112/2/27.
48 'Keck, Anthony', *The History of Parliament*.

49 For more details of Lady Susan Keck see, Chalus, 'My Lord Sue', pp.443–59.
50 National Archives, Kew, SP 36/112/1/128.
51 Jesse, *Memoirs of the Court of England, Volume 3*, pp.421–2.
52 Smith, *Georgian Monarchy*, p.217.
53 Savage, *The Registers of Stratford on Avon*, p.252.
54 *Oxford Journal*, 23 February 1780, p.2.
55 National Archives, Kew, C 205/16/6.
56 The supposed connection to the Hanslope estate was mentioned, for example, in 'Knapp, Tyrrell (1790–1869) – People: Headington History'. Interestingly, however, the first husband of Christobella (1695–1789), one of the co-heiresses of the Hanslope estate, was a John Knapp (1699–1727). This John Knapp was a relative of the John Knapp of 'Ensham' who married Mary Bolton (née Buswell).
57 'Parishes: Hampton Poyle', *A History of the County of Oxford.*
58 *Oxford Journal*, 16 September 1786, p.3.
59 *Instructor and Select Weekly Advertiser*, 15 November 1809, p.8; and *European Magazine, and London Review*, Vol. 56, 1809, p.400.
60 'George Knapp', *Abingdon Area Archaeological and Historical Society.*
61 *Ibid.*
62 Galbraith (ed.), *The Journal of the Rev.*, p.45.
63 *Ibid.*, p.110.
64 *Ibid.*, pp.212–3.
65 Knapp, *A History of the Chief English Families*, pp.54–6.
66 *Notes and Queries*, Vol. 2, Eleventh Series, 9 July 1910, p.36.
67 'George Knapp', *Abingdon Area Archaeological and Historical Society.*
68 *Ibid.*
69 'Thomas Theophilus Metcalfe', *Abingdon Area Archaeological and Historical Society.*
70 'Edward Loveden Loveden', *Abingdon Area Archaeological and Historical Society*; Thorne, *The House of Commons*, section on Berkshire, pp.9–10.
71 'Knapp, George', *The History of Parliament.*
72 'George Knapp', *Abingdon Area Archaeological and Historical Society.*

73 Cox, *The Story of Abingdon*, p.178.
74 *Sir Francis Burdett's Plan*, Hc. Deb.
75 Knapp, *A History of the Chief English Families*, p.56.
76 'Ock Street Chapter Part 2'.
77 Mavor, *General View*, p.450.
78 'Parishes: Hampton Poyle', *A History of the County of Oxford*. Knapp secured more land with the enclosure of the fields at Hampton Poyle in 1797. The pooling of land resulted in the setting up of a 230-acre farm which came to be known as Knapp's Farm.
79 *Oxford Journal*, 10 August 1805, p.3.
80 National Archives, Kew, C 205/16/6.
81 *Ibid.*
82 *Oxford Journal*, 5 March 1774, p.3.
83 Stapleton, *Three Oxfordshire Parishes*, p.171.
84 Will of John Rowland of Water Eaton.
85 *Oxford University and City Herald*, 28 June 1817, p.3.
86 National Archives, Kew, C217/144.
87 Chance et al., 'Outlying Parts of the Liberty', *A History of the County of Oxford*.
88 Baggs et al., 'Wolvercote: Manors and Other Estates', *A History of the County of Oxford*; Salzman (ed.), 'The Domesday Survey: The Text', *A History of the County of Oxford*.
89 Chance et al., 'Outlying Parts of the Liberty', *A History of the County of Oxford*; Baggs et al., 'Wolvercote: Manors and Other Estates', *A History of the County of Oxford*.
90 Wigram, *The Cartulary of the Monastery of St. Frideswide*, p.472 – for the original text of the agreement in Latin. In 1524 Cardinal Wolsey dissolved St Frideswide Priory. The building was demolished and what later became Christ Church College Cathedral was built in its place.
91 'Dictionary of National Biography, 1885–1900/Owen, George (d.1558), https://en.wikisource.org/wiki/Dictionary_of_National_Biography,_1885-1900/Owen,_George_(d.1558) (accessed 28 November 2021).
92 'Owen, George', *The History of Parliament*.

93 Furdell, *The Royal Doctors*, pp.30–1.
94 'Owen, George', *The History of Parliament.*
95 Baggs et al., 'Wolvercote: Manors and Other Estates', *A History of the County of Oxford.*
96 'St John's College', *A History of the County of Oxford.*
97 Stevenson and Salter, *The Early History of St. John's College*, pp.194–5.
98 Childs, *Reliques of the Rives*, p.20.
99 Stevenson and Salter, *The Early History of St. John's College*, p.534.
100 Childs, *Reliques of the Rives*, p.54.
101 Bodleian Library, *MS. Charters Oxon. a.29 no.646.*
102 Rylands (ed.), *The Four Visitations of Berkshire*, p.11.
103 Thompson Cooper, 'Baskerville, Hannibal', *Dictionary of National Bibliography, 1885–1900, Vol.3*, https://en.wikisource.org/wiki/Dictionary_of_National_Biography,_1885-1900/Baskerville,_Hannibal (accessed 15 March 2022).
104 Bodleian Library, *MSS Rawl. D.859, no.56.*
105 'Peter Heylyn', *Abingdon Area Archaeological and Historical Society.*
106 Cox, *The Story of Abingdon*, p.21.
107 Chance et al., 'Outlying Parts of the Liberty', *A History of the County of Oxford*; Bodleian Library, *MS. Charters Oxon. a.30 no.675.*
108 Hearne, Doble and Rannie (eds.), *Remarks and Recollections*, p.70.
109 'New Woodstock. Borough', *The History of Parliament.*
110 'George Spencer-Churchill', *David Nash Ford's Royal Berkshire History.*
111 Ballard, *Chronicles of the Royal Borough of Woodstock*, pp.110–5; Baggs et al., 'Woodstock: Local Government', *A History of the County of Oxford.*
112 Baggs et al., 'Woodstock; Parliamentary Representation', *A History of the County of Oxford.*
113 'New Woodstock Borough', *The History of Parliament.*
114 Ballard, *Chronicles of the Royal Borough of Woodstock*, pp.126–7.
115 Baggs et al., 'Woodstock: Local Government', *A History of the County of Oxford.*
116 Ballard, *Chronicles of the Royal Borough of Woodstock*, pp.126–7.
117 Baggs et al., 'Woodstock: Local Government', *A History of the County of Oxford.*

118 *Morning Post*, 25 November 1829, p.2.
119 Information provided by Pat Crutch, local historian.
120 Baggs et al., 'Woodstock: Buildings', *A History of the County of Oxford.*
121 Roberts, *Sir William Beechey*, p.4.
122 Information provided by Carol Anderson, Cultural Services, Oxfordshire County Council.
123 Horton-Smith, *The Baily Family of Thatcham*, p.4.
124 Manning, *The Lives of the Speakers*, p.312.
125 Gretton, *The Burford Records*, pp.286–9.
126 Godfrey, 'Burford Priory', *Oxoniensia*, p.88.
127 Will of Henry John North of Woodstock.
128 *Oxford University and City Herald*, 6 January 1810, p.2.
129 *Oxford University and City Herald*, 3 February 1810, p.2.
130 I am grateful to Tommy Bull for drawing my attention to this document available under the heading of the will of Thomas Rose Wisdom (1771) on Findmypast.co.uk.
131 Information provided by Pat Crutch, local historian.
132 National Archives, Kew, C 205/16/6.
133 *Ibid.*
134 *London Courier and Evening Gazette*, 26 April 1814, p.2. I am grateful to Janine McMinn, another relative of Elizabeth Buswell, for drawing my attention to this important article.
135 *Hansard*, Volume 27, Commons Chamber, 25 April 1814 – Corruption of Blood.
136 Bodleian Library, *MS. Top. Oxon. b.111.*
137 National Archives, Kew, C 217/144.
138 *Hansard*, Volume 27, Commons Chamber, 25 April 1814 – Corruption of Blood.
139 Romilly, *The Speeches of Sir Samuel Romilly*, p.16.
140 National Archives, Kew, C 205/16/6.
141 Bodleian Library, *MS Top. Oxon. b.111.*
142 *Oxford Journal*, 7 November 1807, p.3.
143 Allen, *Morrells of Oxford*, pp.xviii and 25.
144 *Oxford Mail*, 8 July 2010.
145 *Oxford Journal*, 19 January 1836, p.21.

146 'Parishes: Shabbington', *A History of the County of Buckingham.*

147 *Oxford University and City Herald*, 23 January 1836, pp.1 and 2.

148 Badcock, *The Making of a Regency Village*, pp.67–8.

149 Morris, 'The Friars and Paradise', *Oxoniensia*, p.87.

150 Anderson, 'The Operation of the Early Nineteenth-Century', *Construction History*, pp.69–70.

151 Graham, *Wholesome Dwellings*, p.1.

152 Morris, 'The Friars and Paradise', *Oxoniensia*, p.75.

153 Hinchcliffe, *North Oxford*, p.13.

154 Morris, 'The Friars and Paradise', *Oxoniensia*, pp.86–97.

155 Hibbert and Hibbert (eds.), *The Encyclopaedia of Oxford*, p.386.

156 Osmond, 'Building on the Beaumonts', *Oxoniensia*, p.314; Hinchcliffe, *North Oxford*, pp.18–9.

157 Osmond, 'Building on the Beaumonts,' *Oxoniensia*, pp.314–5.

158 'History of the Rose & Crown Public House', https://roseandcrownoxford.com/history/ (accessed 23 November 2021).

159 Hinchcliffe, *North Oxford*, p.26.

160 *Oxford Chronicle and Reading Gazette*, 15 January 1848, p.2.

161 Baggs et al., 'North Leigh: Manor and other Estates', *A History of the County of Oxford.*

162 *Oxford University and City Herald*, 7 November 1846, p.1.

163 *Oxford University and City Herald*, 26 December 1846, p.3.

164 Badcock, *The Making of a Regency Village*, p.68.

165 The 1832 map was reproduced in Minn, 'A Manuscript History of Summertown', *Oxoniensia*, p.161. A copy of the Palin sketch may be seen in Fasnacht, *Summertown since 1820*, p.20. Unfortunately, the original version of this sketch appears to have been lost.

166 Fasnacht, *How Summertown Started*, p.iii.

167 *Oxford University and City Herald*, 3 November 1821, p.3; *Oxford University and City Herald*, 17 November 1821, p.2.

168 *Oxford University and City Herald*, 17 November 1821, p.2.

169 Fasnacht, *Summertown since 1820*, p.19.

170 *Ibid.*, p.6.

171 Badcock, *The Making of a Regency Village*, p.69.

172 Fasnacht, *Summertown since 1820*, p.52.

173 Badcock, *The Making of a Regency Village*, p.49.
174 *Ibid.*, pp.48–9.
175 Fasnacht, *Summertown since 1820*, p.57.
176 Hibbert and Hibbert (eds.), *The Encyclopaedia of Oxford*, p.257.
177 Kennedy, *The Changing Faces of Summertown*, p.29.
178 Badcock, *The Making of a Regency Village*, pp.20 and 55.
179 *Oxford Journal*, 2 April 1836, p.2.
180 Thompson, 'Life after Death', *Economic History Review*, p.58.
181 Hibbert and Hibbert (eds.), *The Encyclopaedia of Oxford*, p.37.
182 Osmond, 'Building on the Beaumonts', *Oxoniensia*, p.308.
183 *Ibid.*, pp.306, 314, 315 and 319.
184 Badcock, *The Making of a Regency Village*, p.68.
185 *Oxford Journal*, 13 February 1836, p.2.
186 *Oxford Journal*, 9 April 1803, p.1.
187 *Oxford University and City Herald*, 30 January 1836, p.1.
188 Stevens, 'Oxford's Attitude to Dissenters', *Baptist Quarterly*, pp.4–6.
189 Chance et al., 'Protestant Nonconformity and other Christian Bodies', *A History of the County of Oxford*.
190 *Oxford University and City Herald*, 27 September 1806, p.3.
191 *Oxford University and City Herald*, 4 October 1806, p.1.
192 Mead, *Whence and Whither*, p.2.
193 *Ibid.*, p.1.
194 Badcock, *The Making of a Regency Village*, pp.28 and 57.
195 Mead, *Whence and Whither*, p.1.
196 Fasnacht, *Summertown since 1820*, pp.30–1.
197 Will of William Hayes of St Giles.
198 Fasnacht, *Summertown since 1820*, p.71.
199 Symonds and Morgan, *The Origins of Oxford Street Names*, p.128
200 Fasnacht, *Summertown since 1820*, p.61.
201 Badcock, *The Making of a Regency Village*', pp.43 and 36–7.
202 John Hanson, 'James Lambourne', https://users.ox.ac.uk/~djp/cumnor/articles/hanson-lambourne.htm (accessed 2 March 2022).
203 Badcock, *The Making of a Regency Village*, p.37; Major and Murden, *A Right Royal Scandal*, pp.77–80.
204 Minn, 'A Manuscript History of Summertown', *Oxoniensia*, p.154.

205 Badcock, *The Making of a Regency Village*, p.38.
206 Fasnacht, *Summertown since 1820*, pp.7, 9 and 10.
207 Badcock, *The Making of a Regency Village*, p.18 – for an Introduction by Ruth Fasnacht.
208 Minn, 'A Manuscript History of Summertown', *Oxoniensia*, p.153.
209 *Oxford Journal*, 11 November 1820, p.3.
210 Fasnacht, *Summertown since 1820*, pp.105–7; Minn, 'A Manuscript History of Summertown', *Oxoniensia*, pp.152 and 153.
211 Fasnacht, *Summertown since 1820*, p.45.
212 Badcock, *The Making of a Regency Village*, p.22.
213 Minn, 'A Manuscript History of Summertown', *Oxoniensia*, p.152.
214 Fasnacht, *Summertown since 1820*, pp.51–2 and 69–70.
215 *Ibid.*, pp.73, 82–3 and 94. Fasnacht, though, mistakenly refers to a horse tramway running up the Banbury Road. But the first horse tramway in Oxford only began operating in 1882.
216 *Ibid.*, p.28.
217 *Ibid.*, p.97; Badcock, *The Making of a Regency Village*, pp.52–8.
218 Badcock, *The Making of a Regency Village*, p.50.
219 Minn, 'A Manuscript History of Summertown', *Oxoniensia*, p.161.
220 Fasnacht, *Summertown since 1820*, p.20.
221 Fasnacht, *A History of the City of Oxford*, p.36.
222 Hibbert and Hibbert (eds.), *The Encyclopaedia of Oxford*, pp.345 and 429.
223 *The London Gazette*, 9 October 1824, issue no. 18,069, p.1,663.
224 'Southwark Prisons', *Survey of London*.
225 Naomi Clifford, 'Life in the King's Bench Prison', 3 April 2015, https://www.naomiclifford.com/life-in-the-kings-bench-prison/ (accessed 30 November 2021).
226 *Motion for a Committee on King's Bench*, Hc. Deb.
227 *The Law Advertiser, Vol. 2, 1824*, p.332.
228 Will of Thomas Hunt, gentleman, of Oxford.
229 *Oxford University and City Herald*, 21 February 1818, p.3. I am grateful to Libby Shade for drawing my attention to this article. John Mobley was the three-times great-grandfather of Libby's husband, Frederick. More details of the Mobley family can be

found on Libby's website – https://www.shade.id.au/Mobley/Mobley4.htm (accessed 12 December 2021).

230 *Oxford Journal*, 24 July 1824, p.3.

231 *Oxford Journal*, 13 November 1824, p.3; *Oxford Journal*, 20 November 1824, p.3.

232 *Oxford University and City Herald*, 26 February 1825, p.21.

233 Hibbert and Hibbert (eds.), *The Encyclopaedia of Oxford*, p.383; 'Parishes: St. Clement's', *A History of the County of Oxford*.

234 Graham, 'The Building of Oxford Covered Market', *Oxoniensia*, pp.84 and 88–9.

235 *Oxford University and City Herald*, 24 December 1847, p.3; *Oxford University and City Herald*, 1 January 1848, p.3.

236 *Oxford University and City Herald*, 11 March 1848, p.4.

237 *Oxford Chronicle and Reading Gazette*, 27 August 1853, p.4.

238 Fasnacht, *Summertown since 1820*, p.53.

239 *Oxford University and City Herald*, 20 September 1817, p.3.

240 *Oxford University and City Herald*, 10 March 1810, p.3.

241 Will of Thomas Brain of St Giles, Oxford.

242 *Plarr's Lives of the Fellows*, Royal College of Surgeons of England – Braine, Francis Woodhouse (1837–1907) https://livesonline.rcseng.ac.uk/client/en_GB/lives/search/detailnonmodal/ent:$002f$002fSD_ASSET$002f0$002fSD_ASSET:373137/one (accessed 6 December 2021).

243 Richard de Lucy, *Encyclopaedia Britannica.*, https://britannia.com/biography/Richard-de-Lucy (accessed 2 November 2022).

244 Fairfax-Lucy, *Charlecote & the Lucys.*

245 *Hereford Journal*, 13 December 1815, p.1.

246 *Oxford University and City Herald*, 18 September 1819, p.3; *Oxford University and City Herald*, 7 May 1825, p.3.

247 Badcock, *The Making of a Regency Village*, pp.90–1.

248 *Oxford Journal*, 8 December 1832, p.2.

249 *The London Gazette*, 6 June 1856, issue no. 21,890, p.2,038.

250 *West Kent Guardian*, 8 September 1849, p.5.

251 *Morning Herald (London)*, 15 October 1844, p.1.

252 Information kindly provided by Jorge Brain, a direct descendant

of James Brain. For further details see http://familiabrain.blogspot.com/2009/05/santiago-brain.html (accessed 7 December 2021).

253 Mayo, 'Britain and Chile', *Journal of Interamerican Studies and World Affairs*, p.1,081.

254 Will of Thomas Brain of St Giles, Oxford.

255 Prince, *Kenneth Grahame*, no page given; 'The Quad of the Future', *St Edward's Chronicle*, 36, 670 (April 2016), p.4 https://archive.stedwardsoxford.org/Filename.ashx?tableName=ta_publications&columnName=filename&recordId=701 (accessed 17 December 2021).

256 Fasnacht, *Summertown since 1820*, pp.70 and 73.

257 Hinchcliffe, *North Oxford*, pp.15–16.

258 Symonds, *The Changing Faces of North Oxford*, p.6.

259 Graham, *Images of Victorian Oxford*, p.85.

260 Hinchcliffe, *North Oxford*, pp.36 and 47; Hinchcliffe, 'Landownership in the City', in Whiting (ed.), pp.87 and 93.

261 Hinchcliffe, 'Landownership in the City', in Whiting (ed.), pp.100–101.

262 Ingle, 'Summertown', OHC PA Pamphlets, p.9.

263 Graham, *The Suburbs of Victorian Oxford*, p.370.

264 Hart, 'The Horse Trams of Oxford', *Oxoniensia*, pp.222–4.

265 Graham, *Images of Victorian Oxford*, p.135.

266 Tuckwell, *Reminiscences of Oxford*, p.297.

267 Fasnacht, *Summertown since 1820*, p.95.

268 Ingle, 'Summertown', OHC PA Pamphlets, p.12.

269 Steane, *Soapsud Island*, pp.xii–xiii.

270 Badcock, *The Making of a Regency Village* – Introduction by Fasnacht, pp.20–1.

271 Fasnacht, *Summertown since 1820*, p.82.

272 Kuchta, 'Semi-Detached Empire', *Nineteenth-Century Prose*, pp.178–9.

273 Ballard, *Kingdom Come* (London: Harper Perennial, 2008).

274 Forsyth, 'Defining Suburbs', *Journal of Planning Literature*, pp.270–81.

275 Fasnacht, *Summertown since 1820*, pp.62 and 101–2.

276 Lamouria, 'Financial Revolution', *Victorian Literature and Culture*, pp.497–500.

277 Thompson, 'The End of the Great Estate', *The Economic History Review*, pp.38–9 and 47–8.
278 'Searching for Shakespeare', *National Portrait Gallery*, https://www.npg.org.uk/support/individual/face-to-face/searching-for-shakespeare (accessed 10 December 2021).
279 M.W. Westgarth, 'A Biographical Dictionary of Nineteenth Century Antique and Curiosity Dealers' Regional Furniture Society, Glasgow (2009) http://eprints.whiterose.ac.uk/42902/6/westgarth.M1.pdf (accessed 10 December 2021).
280 Forster and Duke of Buckingham and Chandos, *The Stowe Catalogue*, p.187.
281 *Oxford Chronicle and Reading Gazette*, 16 September 1848, p.3.
282 Forster and Duke of Buckingham and Chandos, *The Stowe Catalogue*, p.177.
283 *Oxford Times*, 30 October 1880, p.5.
284 *Oxford Journal*, 20 September 1890, p.6.
285 'British Picture Frame Makers 1600–1950 – J' https://www.npg.org.uk/research/conservation/directory-of-british-framemakers/ (accessed 17 December 2021).
286 See https://www.invaluable.com/auction-lot/18th-c-english-genre-oil-painting-after-george-mo-299e-c-7464deb8c9# (accessed 19 December 2021).
287 Oxford Heritage Search, 'Oxford Freeman Index 1663–1997 – ref. OPI-57272 https://apps2.oxfordshire.gov.uk/srvheritage/resultsSearch?archiveName=people (accessed 19 December 2021).
288 Harrison, *Turner's Oxford*, p.92.
289 *Oxford Journal*, 9 August 1823, p.3.
290 Harrison, *Turner's Oxford*, p.76.
291 See https://theframeblog.com/tag/james-wyatt-of-oxford (accessed 19 December 2021).
292 Rawlinson, *The Engraved Work of J.M.W. Turner*, p.37.
293 Harrison, *Turner's Oxford*, p.92.
294 *Ibid.*, p.38.
295 Shanes, *Turner's England*, p.261.
296 Harrison, *Turner's Oxford*, pp.88 and 92.

297 *Oxford Chronicle and Reading Gazette*, 2 April 1909, p.7.
298 Butler, *The College Estates and Advowsons*, p.43.
299 'Cheryl Bolen's Regency Ramblings – Almack's Patroness Sally Jersey' (2011) https://cherylsregencyramblings.wordpress.com/2011/09/11/almacks-patroness-sally-jersey (accessed 10 October 2021).
300 'The Stowe House Portrait: Lady Jane Grey Revisited: Iconography of Lady Jane Grey', https://ladyjanegreyrevisited.com/2019/04/01/the-stowe-house-portraits/ (accessed 20 December 2021).
301 Forster and Duke of Buckingham and Chandos, *The Stowe Catalogue*, p.19.
302 'National Portrait Gallery – Sarah Sophia Child-Villiers (née Fane), Countess of Jersey'.
303 Cook, *The Life of John Ruskin*, p.108, n.1: Hunt, *Pre-Raphaelitism and the Pre-Raphaelite Brotherhood*, p.323.
304 Cook, *The Life of John Ruskin*, p.53.
305 Ward, 'Quaestio Vexata', *Australian Journal of Victorian Studies*, pp.28–9.
306 Littell and Littell (eds.), *Littell's Living Age*, p.491.
307 Hamilton, *A Strange Business*, pp.4 and 203–4, 215 and 216.
308 Tedeschi, 'Where the Picture Cannot Go', *Art Institute of Chicago Museum Studies*, p.17.
309 Parkes, *Art Monopoly*, p.30.
310 *Oxford Journal*, 17 November 1855, p.5.
311 Summertown Parish Church Vestry Minutes, OHC.
312 Fasnacht, 'Summerhill', OHC PA Pamphlets.
313 Sherwood and Pevsner, *The Buildings of England*, p.333.
314 Olusoga and Backe-Hansen, *A House Through Time*, pp.160–2.
315 Loudon, *The Suburban Gardener*, pp.1 and 10.
316 Whitehead and Carr, *Twentieth-Century Suburbs*, pp.3–4.
317 Olusoga and Backe-Hansen, *A House Through Time*, p.193.
318 Fasnacht, 'Summerhill', OHC PA Pamplets.
319 Fasnacht, *Summertown since 1820*, p.54.
320 Ingle, 'Summertown', OHC PA Pamphlets, pp.32–3.
321 Hinchcliffe, 'Landownership in the City', in Whiting (ed.), pp.97–8.

322 Ingle, 'Summertown', in OHC PA Pamphlets, p.14.
323 *England and Wales Return… Oxford*, p.18.
324 *Oxford Journal*, 30 October 1880, p.5.
325 Fasnacht, *Summertown since 1820*, p.53.
326 *Oxford Journal*, 16 January 1858, p.5.
327 *Reading Mercury*, 4 February 1854, p.5.
328 *Oxford Journal*, 13 January 1855, p.5.
329 Will of James Ryman of Summertown and High Street, Oxford.
330 *Oxford Journal*, 27 August 1881.
331 *Oxford Journal*, 30 October 1880, p.5.
332 *Oxford Chronicle and Reading Gazette*, 7 May 1881, p.5.
333 *Oxford Chronicle and Reading Gazette*, 9 April 1881, p.4.
334 *Oxford Chronicle and Reading Gazette*, 7 May 1881, p.5.
335 Will of James Ryman of Summertown and High Street, Oxford.
336 *Ibid.*
337 Fasnacht, *Summertown since 1820*, p.55.
338 *Oxford Chronicle and Reading Gazette*, 9 April 1881, p.1.
339 *The London Gazette*, 7 July 1896, issue no. 26,756, p.3,936.
340 *Oxford Chronicle and Reading Gazette*, 24 July 1869, p.5.
341 *Oxford Chronicle and Reading Gazette*, 10 April 1925, p.17.
342 *Oxford University and City Herald*, 21 January 1854, p.1.
343 *Oxford Chronicle and Reading Gazette*, 10 April 1925, p.17.
344 Fasnacht, *Summertown since 1820*, pp.54–5.
345 *Oxford Chronicle and Reading Gazette*, 7 February 1891, p.5.
346 Fasnacht, 'Introduction' in Badcock, *The Making of a Regency Village*, p.24.
347 John Moore Heritage Services, 'An Archaeological Desk-Based Assessment (Including Building Assessment of Summerhill Villa, 333 Banbury Road, Oxford)' (May 2013), p.26 https://archaeologydataservice.ac.uk/archiveDS/archiveDownload?t=arch-988-1/dissemination/pdf/johnmoor1-239465_1.pdf (accessed 21 December 2021).
348 Fasnacht, *Summertown since 1820*, pp.78 and 91.
349 Howe, 'Intellect and Civic Responsibility', in Whiting (ed.), p.23.
350 Fasnacht, *Summertown since 1820*, pp.78–9.

351 *Ibid.*, pp.79–80.

352 *Oxford Journal*, 5 March 1892, p.8.

353 *Oxfordshire Weekly News*, 9 March 1892, p.7; *Oxford Chronicle and Reading Gazette*, 5 March 1892, p.7.

354 Will of Frank Ryman Hall of Summerhill.

355 Fenby, *The Other Oxford*, p.132.

356 Will of William Emanuel Richards of Oxford, print seller and picture dealer.

357 Information kindly provided by Linda Thurman, a great-granddaughter of John William Richards.

358 'Oxford History: The High', oxfordhistory.org.uk/high/tour/north/023.html (accessed 9 March 2022).

359 *Oxford Chronicle and Reading Gazette*, 1 May 1914, p.8.

360 *Oxford Times*, 26 June 1909, p.10.

361 *Oxford Chronicle and Reading Gazette*, 10 April 1925, p.17.

362 Will of Frank Ryman Hall of Summertown.

363 *Oxford Chronicle and Reading Gazette*, 5 June 1925, p.3.

364 *Oxford Chronicle and Reading Gazette*, 24 April 1925, p.2.

365 Graham, *Wholesome Dwellings*, pp.1 and 3.

366 Graham, *The Suburbs of Victorian Oxford*, pp.191–2.

367 Dyos, 'The Speculative Builders and Developers', *Victorian Studies*, p.663.

368 Graham, *The Suburbs of Victorian Oxford*, pp.226–7 – quoting *The Builder*, 3 April 1880, p.424.

369 Dyos, 'The Speculative Builders and Developers', *Victorian Studies*, p.673.

370 *Ibid.*, pp.660–1.

371 Graham, *The Suburbs of Victorian Oxford*, p.230.

372 Hinchcliffe, *North Oxford*, pp.38, 40, 54, 58 and 63.

373 Graham, *The Suburbs of Victorian Oxford*, p.236.

374 Hinchcliffe, *North Oxford*, pp.85–6 and 130 1.

375 Hinchcliffe, 'Landownership in the City', in Whiting (ed.), pp.99–100.

376 Graham, *The Suburbs of Victorian Oxford*, pp.215 and 226.

377 For details of Amy Dudley/Robsart, see the Cumnor Parish Record website at https://users.ox.ac.uk/~djp/cumnor/ (accessed 4 December 2022).

378 The text of Sir Walter Scott's *Kenilworth* is available at https://www.gutenberg.org/files/1606/1606-h/1606-h.htm (accessed 31 December 2021).

379 Hawthorne, *Our Old Home*, pp.210–1.

380 For more details about the Capel family of Cumnor, see https://users.ox.ac.uk/~djp/cumnor/families/capel.htm (accessed 31 December 2021).

381 Cumnor Tything: Census 1821 at https://users.ox.ac.uk/~djp/cumnor/index.html (accessed 31 December 2021).

382 *Oxford Journal*, 29 December 1827, p.3.

383 Thorne, *Rambles by Rivers*, p.55.

384 Palmer and Crowquill, *The Wanderings of a Pen and Pencil*, pp.151–2.

385 *Berkshire Chronicle*, 1 July 1843, p.4.

386 *Ibid.*

387 Palmer and Crowquill, *The Wanderings of a Pen and Pencil*, p.160.

388 Olcott, *The Country of Sir Walter Scott*, p.273.

389 *Oxford Chronicle and Reading Gazette*, 16 October 1847, p.2.

390 Palmer and Crowquill, *The Wanderings of a Pen and Pencil*, p.159.

391 Dallas, 'A Summer Day at Cumnor', *Once a Week*, p.324.

392 For a summary of the will, see 'Summaries of Wills' https://users.ox.ac.uk/~djp/cumnor/index.html (accessed 1 January 2022).

393 See https://ourfamilyhistory.club/alfred-richings-b-1816-d-27-oct-1870/ (accessed 1 January 2022). Further information here was kindly provided by Sheila and Paul Wheatley.

394 *The London Gazette*, 6 December 1881, issue no. 25,045, p.6,585; *The London Gazette*, 10 January 1882, issue no. 25,058, p.133.

395 *Oxford Journal*, 20 July 1878, p.8.

396 *Oxford Journal*, 24 November 1883, p.6.

397 Graham, *The Suburbs of Victorian Oxford*, p.104.

398 Graham, 'Housing Development', *Oxoniensia*, pp.151, 152 and 157.

399 https://users.ox.ac.uk/~djp/cumnor/families/capel.htm (accessed 1 January 2022).

400 Hinchcliffe, *North Oxford*, pp.219, 221, 222, 231, 234 and 242.

401 Graham, *The Suburbs of Victorian Oxford*, p.75.

402 Hinchcliffe, *North Oxford*, pp.177 and 222.

403 *Oxford Times*, 9 August 1902, p.8.

404 Reginald Philip Capel (1886–1961) – Oxford History – Mayors and Lord Mayors www.oxfordhistory.org.uk/mayors/1836_1962/capel_reginald_1944.html (accessed 2 January 2022).

405 *Oxford Chronicle and Reading Gazette*, 24 July 1925, p.10.

406 *Oxfordshire Weekly News*, 19 August 1925, p.6.

407 *Oxford Times*, 16 August 1902, p.12.

408 *Oxford Journal*, 14 September 1910, p.4.

409 Will of Noah Capel of 279 Banbury Road, Oxford.

410 Telephone interview with Aubrey J. Capel.

411 Gliddon, *Somme 1916*, no pages given.

412 Telephone interview with Aubrey J. Capel.

413 Eddershaw, *The Story of the Oxfordshire Yeomanry*, p.40.

414 *Ibid.*, pp.42–3.

415 See SA Artillery/Military Defense Security – Intelligence Politics – the Imperial Yeomanry part 2 1901 at https://saartillery.wordpress.com/archives/anglo-boer-war/the-imperial-yeomanry-part-two-1901/ (accessed 4 January 2022).

416 *Kelly's Directory of Berkshire, 1903*, p.303.

417 Dodsworth, 'The Chawley Brick and Tile Works', *Oxoniensia*, pp.350–1.

418 Details of the Cotmore family and their links to The Fox were kindly provided by Mandy Wood. Frederick and Sarah Cotmore were Mandy's four-times great-grandparents.

419 Mary Bright Rix, *Boars Hill, Oxford* https://boarshill.info/wp-content/uploads/2018/01/BoarsHillbyMaryBrightRix-1941.pdf (accessed 3 January 2022).

420 Will of Martha Capel of The Fox Inn, Foxcombe Hill, Wootton, Berkshire.

421 Telephone interview with Aubrey J. Capel.

422 Kinchin, *Seven Roads in Summertown*, pp.15–7 and 222–3.

423 *Ibid.*, pp.223, 224 and 225.

424 *Oxford Chronicle and Reading Gazette*, 12 June 1925, p.24.

425 Fasnacht, 'Summerhill', OHC PA Pamphlets; 'Particulars – Development of Summerhill Estate'.

426 OHC PA Pamphlets, 'Particulars – Development of Summerhill Estate'.

427 *Ibid.*

428 Fasnacht, *Summertown since 1820*, p.91.

429 *Oxford Chronicle and Reading Gazette*, 6 April 1928, p.7.

430 Fasnacht, *Summertown since 1820*, p.95.

431 Collison, *The Cutteslowe Walls.*

432 *Ibid*, p.77.

433 Fasnacht, *History of the City of Oxford*, p.46.

434 Sarah A. Bendall, 'The Tailoring Trade in Seventeenth-Century Oxford: Tales from the Bodleian Archive', https://sarahabendall.com/2020/04/03/the-tailoring-trade-in-seventeenth-century-oxford/ (accessed 30 March 2022).

435 Chance et al. (eds.), 'Modern Oxford', *A History of the County of Oxford.*

436 *The London Gazette*, 8 October 1852, issue no. 21,365, p.2,660.

437 *Ibid.*

438 *Cork Constitution*, 20 December 1855, p.2.

439 *Cork Advertising Gazette*, 30 September 1857, p.4.

440 *Cork Constitution*, 20 May 1856, p.1.

441 *Oxford Chronicle and Reading Gazette*, 24 July 1862, p.1.

442 *Bicester Herald*, 4 February 1870, p.1.

443 *Oxford Journal*, 26 March 1870, p.6.

444 Chaouche, *Student Consumer Culture*, p.86, n.30.

445 *Ibid.*, pp.15–7.

446 *Oxfordshire Weekly News*, 29 March 1876, p.6.

447 *Oxford Times*, 20 May 1876, p.1.

448 Will of Horatio George Adamson of 33 New Inn Hall Street, Hosier and Tailor.

449 Information kindly provided by Yvonne Tye, a direct descendant of Horatio George Adamson.

450 'Headington History – Non-Listed Buildings – 61 Old Road', headington.org.uk/history/buildings/oldroad61.htm (accessed 30 March 2022).

451 *Oxford Journal*, 17 October 1891, p.8.

452 Graham, *Oxford Heritage Walks*, pp.8–9.
453 *Tailor and Cutter*, 24 March 1898, p.24.
454 *Oxford Times*, 16 April 1904, p.12.
455 *Oxford Journal*, 31 October 1891, p.6.
456 *Oxford Chronicle and Reading Gazette*, 7 November 1891, p.8.
457 *Oxford Chronicle and Reading Gazette*, 18 February 1927, p.12.
458 Will of William Charles Adamson of 165 Banbury Road, Oxford.
459 Evans and Godwin, *The Gunmakers of Oxford*, pp.1, 2 and 14.
460 Scott, Eade and Lees, *William Richard Gowers*, p.7.
461 *Oxford University and City Herald*, 8 June 1844, p.1.
462 *Oxford University and City Herald*, 11 February 1860, p.1.
463 *Oxford Chronicle and Reading Gazette*, 28 July 1860, p.5.
464 *Oxford Journal*, 11 February 1882, p.5.
465 *Oxford Journal*, 19 August 1882, p.5.
466 *Oxford Chronicle and Reading Gazette*, 1 July 1882, p.2.
467 McKenna, *The Gunmakers of Birmingham*, p.115.
468 Will of Sidney Venables of Donnington Lodge, Iffley Road, Oxford.
469 Scargill, 'Response to Growth', in Whiting (ed.), p.111.
470 Thomas, *Out on a Wing*, p.150.
471 Young, *Try Anything Twice*, p.7.
472 Thomas, *Out on a Wing*, p.150.
473 *Cork Constitution*, 18 November 1858, p.2.
474 Sinclair, *Portrait of Oxford*, pp.58–9.
475 Morgan, *Oxford Observations*, pp.42–3.
476 *Oxford Chronicle and Reading Gazette*, 26 June 1925, p.24; *Oxford Chronicle and Reading Gazette*, 24 July 1925, pp.10–1.
477 Will of Sidney Venables of Donnington Lodge, Iffley Road, Oxford.
478 *Oxfordshire Weekly News*, 6 November 1895, p.7.
479 *The London Gazette*, 29 September 1916, issue no. 29,769, p.9,496.
480 *Oxford Chronicle and Reading Gazette*, 26 June 1925, p.24.
481 *Oxford Chronicle and Reading Gazette*, 16 July 1920, p.11.
482 Steane, *Soapsud Island*, p.5.
483 Collison, *The Cutteslowe Walls*, pp.122–6.
484 Will of Horace William Adamson of 'Summerhill', Banbury Road, Oxford.

485 *The London Gazette*, 21 September 1972, issue no. 45,782, pp.11,223–4.

486 I am grateful to Julie van Onselen for this information. Nellie Julie Venables/Adamson was her great-great-aunt.

487 Hibbert and Hibbert (eds.), *The Encyclopaedia of Oxford*, p.146.

488 *Oxford Mail*, 1 September 2014, 'd'Overbroecks College keen to make use of Oxford's Old Masonic Lodge'.

489 Fasnacht, *Summertown since 1820*, pp.64–5; John Chipperfield, 'Nine Tons of Pudding Please', *Oxford Mail*, 23 December 2013.

490 Fasnacht, *Summertown since 1820*, pp.91–2.

491 Macintyre, *Agent Sonya*, pp.232 and 240.

492 Oxford History: Mayors & Lord Mayors – Francis Twining (1848–1929), www.oxfordhistory.org.uk/mayors/1836_1962/twining_francis_1905.html (accessed 23 January 2022).

493 Hibbert and Hibbert (eds.), *The Encyclopaedia of Oxford*, p.257.

494 Symonds and Morgan, *The Origins of Oxford Street Names*, pp.27–8.

495 OHC PA Pamphlets, 'Particulars – Development of Summerhill Estate'.

496 Information from documents and deeds in the possession of the author.

497 'Royston Town Band – History' roystontownband.org.uk/history/ (accessed 2 April 2022); Alan R. Ruston, 'Unitarianism in Hertfordshire – Document History', pp.3 and 22, https://www.unitarian.org.uk/wp-content/uploads/2021/01/1979_Hertfordshire.pdf (accessed 2 April 2022).

498 'The City of Oxford Band (formerly Headington Silver Band) – Reminiscences of James Alder', https://www.cosb.co.uk (accessed 2 April 2022).

499 *Leeds Mercury*, 1 March 1911, p.3.

500 *Buckingham Advertiser and Free Press*, 4 August 1923, p.5.

501 *Buckingham Advertiser and Free Press*, 10 April 1920, p.4; *Buckingham Advertiser and Free Press*, 14 August 1920, p.4.

502 *Kelly's Directory of Oxford, 1930*, p.70.

503 Will of Edward Catley of Oxford.

504 *London Gazette*, 30 September 1892, issue no. 26,330, p.5,509.

505 Jewesbury, *The Royal Northern Hospital*, p.85.

506 Gorsky and Mohan, 'London's Voluntary Hospitals', *Nonprofit and Voluntary Sector Quarterly*, p.262.

507 West Hagbourne Village History Group, *Windsor Hakeborne*, p.169.

508 *Kelly's Directory of Oxford, 1932*, p.72; *Kelly's Directory of Oxford, 1933*, p.74.

509 *Bradford Observer*, 10 May 1875, p.2; *Leeds Times*, 15 May 1875, pp.3 and 5.

510 *Bradford Observer*, 17 July 1954, p.6.

511 *Shipley Times and Express*, 22 July 1933, p.6.

512 Information kindly provided by Christine Knowles, the daughter of Jack Simpson.

513 *Leeds Mercury*, 4 May 1925, p.5; *Lancashire Evening Post*, 4 May 1925, p.4.

514 *Airdrie and Coatbridge Advertiser*, 3 May 1919; *Boston Guardian*, 18 March 1916, p.10.

515 Telephone interview with Elaine Pearce, 18 February 2022.

516 *Bradford Observer*, 17 July 1954, p.6.

517 *Hampshire Chronicle*, 4 January 1890, p.4.

518 Crook, *A History of the Pilgrims' School*, pp.24 and 31.

519 James, *Time to be Earnest*, pp.6, 9 and 30.

520 Crook, *A History of the Pilgrims' School*, pp.27 and 29.

521 Lisle, *Life in Miniature*, no page numbers given.

522 Crook, *A History of the Pilgrims' School*, pp.29–31.

523 *Polk's World Bank Directory 1972 – International Section*, p.256.

524 *Portsmouth Evening News*, 3 June 1939, p.11.

525 *Kelly's Directory of Oxford, 1949*, p.98.

526 Will of Edward George Leslie Hone of Weymouth.

527 Will of Eva Catley of Islington.

528 These details of Flo's escape from Burma are from Donnison, *Last of the Guardians*, pp.228–9, and from the transcript of a family interview (undated) with Flo. Flo is mistakenly referred to as Fleur in the Donnison book.

529 The birth certificate was kindly provided by Barry Sheehan. Barry's

wife, Laura, is the great-granddaughter of Thomas James Lecky, who was a brother of William Thompson (i.e. William Lecky-Thompson).

530 Information provided by Keith Hollingsworth. Frederick Edward Rose was Keith's great-great-grandfather.

531 Yale University Press Official Blog, 'Dirty Old London: 30 Days of Filth: Day 28', yalebooksblog.co.uk/2014/10/06/dirty-old-london-30-days-filth-day-28 (accessed 6 February 2022).

532 Jerry White, History Extra, 'Life in 19th Century Slums: Victorian London's Homes from Hell', historyextra.com/period/Victorian/life-in-19th-century-slums-victorian-londons-homes-from-hell/ (accessed 6 February 2022).

533 'The Shaftesbury Homes and *Arethusa*', childrenshomes.org.uk/SH/ships.shtml (accessed 30 January 2022).

534 *Bicester Herald*, 28 July 1876, p.2.

535 I am grateful to Charles Brookson, the husband of Helen Granville, a granddaughter of William Lecky-Thompson junior, for providing this information.

536 *Dundee Advertiser*, 1 December 1881, p.4; *The National Magazine*, Vol. 51, 1882, p.316.

537 Hingkanonta, *The Police in Colonial Burma*, pp.2–3.

538 White, *A Civil Servant in Burma*, p.158.

539 Chrosthwaite, *The Pacification of Burma*, p.38.

540 Articles in the *Rangoon Times*, May–June 1888, courtesy of the Anglo-Burmese Library.

541 Information from the Anglo-Burmese Library.

542 *Ibid.*

543 Telephone interview with Roy Lecky-Thompson, 24 February 2021. Roy was the nephew of William Lecky-Thompson junior.

544 Telephone interview with Tom Lecky-Thompson, 4 March 2021. Tom was the son of Thomas Lecky-Thompson, a brother of William Lecky-Thompson junior.

545 Transcript of family interview (undated) with Flo (Florence Elizabeth Lecky-Thompson).

546 *Ibid.*, and telephone interview with Roy Lecky-Thompson, 24 February 2021.

547 Telephone interview with Roy Lecky-Thompson, 24 February 2021.

548 Tyson, *Forgotten Frontier*, pp.56–7.

549 The following account is taken from excerpts of B.R. Pearn's account of the civilian evacuation of Burma, a report by R.E. McGuire, the Warden of the Oil Fields at Yenangyang (both courtesy of the Anglo-Burmese Library), and Leigh, *The Collapse of British Rule in Burma*, pp.51–95.

550 Article in the *Rangoon Gazette*, 1918, courtesy of the Anglo-Burmese Library.

551 *The London Gazette*, 11 March 1919, issue no. 31,223, p.3,304.

552 Article in the *Rangoon Gazette*, 1918, courtesy of the Anglo-Burmese Library.

553 *The India Office List for 1928*, p.692.

554 Transcript of family interview (undated) with Flo.

555 Telephone interview with Roy Lecky-Thompson, 24 February 2021.

556 Rana, *Rani of Jhansi*, no page numbers given.

557 *Englishman's Overland Mail*, 6 October 1880, p.10.

558 *Civil and Military Gazette (Lahore)*, 19 September 1894, p.3.

559 Transcript of family interview (undated) with Flo.

560 *Ibid.*

561 *Ibid.*

562 *The India Office and Burma Office List for 1945*, p.252.

563 Maybury-Lewis, *Manifest Destinies*, p.226.

564 Transcript of family interview (undated) with Flo.

565 *Civil List for Burma, 1942*, courtesy of the Anglo-Burmese Library.

566 *The London Gazette*, 17 January 1947, issue no. 37,885, p.354.

567 Telephone interview with Roy Lecky-Thompson, 24 February 2021.

568 Transcript of family interview (undated) with Flo.

569 Telephone interview with Roy Lecky-Thompson, 24 February 2021.

570 Telephone interview with Cynthia Byrt, 18 February 2021.

571 Transcript of family interview (undated) with Flo.

572 Telephone interview with Roy Lecky-Thompson, 24 February 2021.

573 Telephone interview with Cynthia Byrt, 18 February 2021.

574 Telephone interview with Tom Lecky-Thompson, 4 March 2021.

575 For more details of the life of Stratford Stanley Caldecott, see, Zaleski, 'Stratford Caldecott' in Murphy (ed.), pp.273–80.

576 Zaleski, 'Stratford Caldecott (1953–2014)', *VII: Journal of the Marion E. Wade Center*, p.8.

577 'Professor Paul Matthews' https://www.seh.ox.ac.uk/people/paul-matthews (accessed 18 April 2022).

578 Communication with Catherine Matthews, 4 February 2021.

579 Berry, *Summertown*, p.7.

BIBLIOGRAPHY

Archives and Online Sources

Ancestry (ancestry.co.uk)

Findmypast (findmypast.co.uk)

General Register Office (https://www.gov.uk/general-register-office)

The London Gazette (thegazette.co.uk)

Anglo-Burmese Library

Various materials

Bodleian Library, Oxford

Indenture for the Lease of Land for One Year between Christopher Blower and John Ayleworth and Anthony Lambert, 1707, MS. Charters Oxon. a.30, no.675.

Indenture on the Sale of Land to Christopher Blower, 1659, MS. Charters Oxon. a.29, no.646.

Letter of Christopher Blower to Hannibal Baskerville, 28 May 1663, MSS Rawl. D.859, no.56.

Warrant to Make Inquisition of the Property of Elizabeth Slatter, Condemned for Murder, 1813, MS. Top. Oxon. b. 111.

National Archives, Kew

Draft Special Commissions (some with Writs of Certioriari) to Inquire into and Seize the (Effects or) Lands of Felons: Elizabeth Slatter (Murder), no date given, C 217/160.

Elizabeth Slatter, Formerly Elizabeth Wisdom, for Murder County: Oxon, 19 November 1812, C 205/16/6.

Folios 2–5. Baron Charles Clarke's Report of the Case of Elizabeth Wisdom, Sentenced to Death for Poisoning her Maid Servant Grace Hall, 21 March 1749, SP 36/112/2/2.

Folio 22. Certificate of Several Persons, Relating to the Case of Elizabeth Wisdom, a Convict at Oxford, 24 March 1749, SP 36/112/2/22.

Folio 23. Affidavit of Mary Spicer and Sarah Wilkes of Chipping Norton, Relating to Grace Hall, Deceased, and Elizabeth Wisdom, a Convict at Oxford, 24 March 1749, SP 36/112/2/23.

Folio 24. Affidavit of John Buswell, Relating to the Case of Elizabeth Wisdom, a Convict at Oxford, 24 March 1749, SP 36/112/2/24.

Folio 25. Affidavit of Mary Smith, Relating to the Case of Elizabeth Wisdom, a Convict at Oxford, 24 March 1749, SP 36/112/2/25.

Folio 27. Copy of a Letter from Mr Ryves to the Duke of Marlborough, Relating to the Case of Elizabeth Wisdom, a Convict at Oxford, 24 March 1749, SP 36/112/2/27.

Folio 28. Affidavits of Several Persons, Relating to Elizabeth Wisdom, a Convict at Oxford, 24 March 1749, SP 36/112/2/28.

Folio 29. Certificate of Reverend Mr Edmund Trott, Relating to Elizabeth Wisdom, a Convict at Oxford, 25 March 1749, SP 36/112/2/29.

Folios 128–143. Lady Susan Kirk to the Countess of Yarmouth, with Two Affidavits Relating to the Death of Grace Hall of Chipping Norton, 20 March 1749, SP 36/112/1/128.

In the Matter of Elizabeth Slatter, Order for Leave to Traverse the Inquisition found on Behalf of the Crown. Papers in Various Cases, including: Rex v Robert (17 Geo II)..., 11 August 1813, C 217/144.

Opinion of Law Officers Respecting Whorestone, a Freehold Estate in the Parish of Saint Giles, Oxford..., 29 August 1809, TS 25/3/63.

Oxfordshire History Centre

OHC PA Pamphlets. OXFO/BANB Barcode 30655395, 'Particulars – Development of the Summerhill Estate'.

OHC PA Pamphlets. OXFO/BANB Barcode 307620014, Ruth Fasnacht, 'Summerhill'.

OHC PA Pamphlets PA 200 Barcode 306552621, Harry Charles Ingle, 'Summertown'.

OHC PAR 261/2/A/1 – Summertown Parish Church – Vestry Minutes, 1841–1941.

Hansard

Volume 27: Commons Chamber, 25 April 1814 – Corruption of Blood

https://hansard.parliament.uk/Commons/1814-04-25/debates/f5d44fe9-bae7-465e-a834-e05b12eeebe5/CorruptionOfBlood?highlight=%22corruption%20of%20blood%22#contribution-bda16668-2299-49b0-a483-92e0483866ac

Documents Online

Motion for a Committee on King's Bench, Fleet and Marshalsea Prisons, Hc. Deb. 07 March 1815. Vol.30, cc 39–41, https://api.parliament.uk/historic-hansard/commons/1815/mar/07/motion-for-a-committee-on-kings-bench (accessed 11 November 2021).

Sir Francis Burdett's Plan of Parliamentary Reform, Hc. Deb. 15 June 1809. Vol.14, cc 1041–70, https://api.parliament.uk/historic-hansard/commons/1809/jun/15/sir-francis-burdetts-plan-of (accessed 11 November 2021).

Articles Online

Baggs, A.P., W.J. Blair, Eleanor Chance, Christina Colvin, Janet Cooper, C.J. Day, Nesta Selwyn and S.C. Townley, 'North Leigh: Manor and other Estates', in *A History of the County of Oxford: Volume 12, Wootton Hundred (South) including Woodstock*, eds. Alan Crossley and C.R. Elrington (London, 1990), pp.219–24. *British History Online* http://www.british-history.ac.uk/vch/oxon/vol12/pp219-224 (accessed 24 November 2021).

Baggs, A.P., W.J. Blair, Eleanor Chance, Christina Colvin, Janet Cooper, C.J. Day, Nesta Selwyn and S.C. Townley, 'Wolvercote: Manors and other Estates', in *A History of the County of Oxford: Volume 12, Wootton Hundred (South) including Woodstock*, eds. Alan Crossley and C.R. Elrington (London, 1990), pp.313–4, *British History Online* http://www.british-history.ac.uk/vch/oxon/vol12/pp313-314 (accessed 4 November 2021).

Baggs, A.P, W.J. Blair, Eleanor Chance, Christina Colvin, Janet Cooper, C.J. Day, Nesta Selwyn and S.C. Townley, 'Woodstock: Buildings', in *A History of the County of Oxford: Volume 12, Wootton Hundred (South) including Woodstock*, eds. Alan Crossley and C.R. Elrington (London, 1990), pp.342–60, *British History Online* http://www.british-history.ac.uk/vch/oxon/vol12/pp342-360 (accessed 19 November 2021).

Baggs, A.P., W.J. Blair, Eleanor Chance, Christina Colvin, Janet Cooper, C.J. Day, Nesta Selwyn and S.C. Townley, 'Woodstock: Local Government', in *A History of the County of Oxford: Volume 12, Wootton Hundred (South) including Woodstock*, eds.

Alan Crossley and C.R. Elrington (London, 1990), pp.372–400, *British History Online* http://www.british-history.ac.uk/vch/oxon/vol12/pp372-400 (accessed 19 November 2021).

Baggs, A.P., W.J. Blair, Eleanor Chance, Christina Colvin, Janet Cooper, C.J. Day, Nesta Selwyn and S.C. Townley, 'Woodstock: Parliamentary Representation', in *A History of the County of Oxford: Volume 12, Wootton Hundred (South) including Woodstock*, eds. Alan Crossley and C.R. Elrington (London, 1990), pp.400–6, *British History Online* http://www.british-history.ac.uk/vch/oxon/vol12/pp400-406 (accessed 19 November 2021).

Baggs, A.P., Christian Colvin, H.M. Colvin, Janet Cooper, C.J. Day, Nesta Selwyn and A. Tomkinson, 'Parishes: Westcott Barton', in *A History of the County of Oxford: Volume 11, Wootton Hundred (Northern Part)*, ed. Alan Crossley (London, 1983), pp.75–81. *British History Online* http://www.british-history.ac.uk/vch/oxon/vol11/pp75-81 (accessed 26 October 2021).

Chance, Eleanor, Christina Colvin, Janet Cooper, C.J. Day, T.G. Hassall, Mary Jessup and Nesta Selwyn, 'Modern Oxford', in *A History of the County of Oxford: Volume 4, the City of Oxford*, eds. Aland Crossley and C.R. Ellington (London, 1979), pp.181–259. *British History Online* http://www.british-history.ac.uk/vch/oxon/vol4/pp181-259 (accessed 8 January 2022).

Chance, Eleanor, Christina Colvin, Janet Cooper, C.J. Day, T.G. Hassall, Mary Jessup and Nesta Selwyn, 'Outlying Parts of the Liberty', in *A History of the County of Oxford: Volume 4, the City of Oxford*, eds. Alan Crossley and C.R. Elrington (London, 1979), pp.265–83. *British History Online* http://www.british-history.ac.uk/vch/oxon/vol4/pp265-283 (accessed 17 December 2021).

Chance, Eleanor, Christina Colvin, Janet Cooper, C.J. Day, T.G. Hassall, Mary Jessup and Nesta Selwyn, 'Protestant

Nonconformity and other Christian Bodies', in *A History of the County of Oxford: Volume 4, the City of Oxford*, eds. Alan Crossley and C.R. Elrington (London, 1979), pp.415–24. *British History Online* http://www.british-history.ac.uk/vch/oxon/vol4/pp415-424 (accessed 24 November 2021).

'Edward Loveden Loveden, 1750–1822 – Biography', *Abingdon Area Archaeological and Historical Society* https://www.abingdon.gov.uk/abingdon_people/edward-loveden-loveden (accessed 21 February 2022).

Evans, John and Brian Godwin, 'The Gunmakers of Oxford: Part 1' (Research Press Library) https://dokumen.tips/documents/the-gunmakers-of-oxford-research-the-gunmakers-of-oxford-a-part-1-rpl005-4-the.html (accessed 8 January 2022).

'George Knapp, 1754–1809 – Biography', *Abingdon Area Archaeological and Historical Society* https://www.abingdon.gov.uk/abingdon_people/george-knapp (accessed 9 November 2021).

'George Spencer-Churchill, Duke of Marlborough (1766–1840)', in *David Nash Ford's Royal Berkshire History* www.berkshirehistory.com/bios/gschurchill_5dofm.html (accessed 19 November 2021).

'Keck, Anthony (1708–1767), of Great Tew, Oxon', in L. Namier and J. Brooke (eds.), *The History of Parliament: the House of Commons 1754–1790* (1964) www.historyofparliamentonline.org/volume/1754-1790/member/keck-anthony-1708-67 (accessed 27 October 2021).

'Knapp, George (1754–1809), of Abingdon, Berks', in R. Thorne (ed.), *The History of Parliament: the House of Commons 1790–1820* (1986) https://www.historyofparliamentonline.org/volume/1790-1820/member/knapp-george-1754-1809 (accessed 11 November 2021).

'Knapp, Tyrrell (1790–1869) – People: Headington History', www.headington.org.uk/history/famous_people/knapp.html (accessed 9 November 2021).

'National Portrait Gallery – Sarah Sophia Child-Villiers (nee) Fane, Countess of Jersey', https://www.npg.org.uk/collections/search/person/mp02424/sarah-sophia-child-villiers-nee-fane-countess-of-jersey (accessed 23 December 2021).

'New Woodstock, Borough', in D.R. Fisher (ed.), *The History of Parliament; the House of Commons 1820–1832* (2009) www.histparl.ac.uk/volume/1820-1832/constituencies/new-woodstock (accessed 19 November 2021).

'Ock Street Chapter Part 2: A History of Ock Street to 1835', https://aaahs.org.uk/files/Ock%20Street/Ock%20Street%20after%201835%20-%20Part%202.pdf (accessed 11 November 2021).

'Owen, George (by 1499–1558), of Oxford and Godstow, Oxon, in S.T. Bindoff (ed.), *The History of Parliament: the House of Commons 1509–1588* (1982) https://www.historyofparliamentonline.org/volume/1509-1558/member/owen-george-1499-1558 (accessed 11 November 2021).

'Parishes: Hampton Poyle', in *A History of the County of Oxford: Volume 6*, ed. Mary D. Lobel (London, 1959), pp.160–8. *British History Online* http://www.british-history.ac.uk/vch/oxon/vol6/pp160-168 (accessed 9 November 2021).

'Parishes: Shabbington', in *A History of the County of Buckingham: Volume 4*, ed. William Page (London, 1927), pp.102–4. *British History Online* http://www.british-history.ac.uk/vch/bucks/vol4/pp102-104 (accessed 21 November 2021).

'Parishes: St. Clement's', in *A History of the County of Oxford: Volume 5, Bullingdon Hundred*, ed. Mary Lobel (London, 1957), pp.258–66. *British History Online* https://www.british-history.ac.uk/vch/oxon/vol5/pp258-266 (accessed 8 December 2021).

'Peter Heylyn, 1599–1662 – Biography', *Abingdon Area Archaeological and Historical Society* https://abingdon.gov.uk/abingdon_people/peter-heylyn (accessed 22 March 2022).

Salzman, L.F. (ed.), 'The Domesday Survey: The Text', in *A History of the County of Oxford: Volume 1* (London: 1939), pp.396–428. *British History Online* http://www.british-history.ac.uk/vch/oxon/vol1/pp396-428 (accessed 8 June 2022).

'Southwark Prisons', in *Survey of London: Volume 25, St. George's Fields (The Parishes of St. George the Martyr Southwark and St. Mary Newington)*, ed. Ida Darlington (London, 1955), pp.9–21. *British History Online* https://www.british-history.ac.uk/survey-London/vol25/pp9-21 (accessed 5 August 2021).

'St John's College', in *A History of the County of Oxford: Volume 3, the University of Oxford*, ed. H.E. Salter and Mary D. Lobel (London, 1954), pp.251–64. *British History Online* http://www.british-history.ac.uk/vch/oxon/vol3/pp251-264 (accessed 12 November 2021).

'Thomas Theophilus Metcalfe, 1745–1813 – Biography', *Abingdon Area Archaeological and Historical Society* https://abingdon.gov.uk/abingdon_people/thomas-theophilus-metcalfe (accessed 21 February 2022).

***Wills* (from Government Record Office unless otherwise cited)**

Will of Horatio George Adamson of 33 New Inn Hall Street, Oxford, hosier and tailor. Probate granted 4 November 1885.

Will of Horace William Adamson of 'Summerhill', Banbury Road, Oxford. Dated 20 February 1953.

Will of William Charles Adamson of 165 Banbury Road, Oxford. Probate granted 28 April 1927.

Will of Thomas Brain of St Giles, gentleman. Made 4 November

1829. Probate granted 5 April 1838. Wills.oxfordshirefhs.org.uk/az/wtext/brain_008.html (accessed 6 December 2021).
Will of Robert Buswell of Kiddington, clerk. Made 30 April 1734. Probate granted 12 April 1760. wills.oxfordshirefhs.org.uk/az/wtext/buswell_006.html (accessed 29 November 2021).
Will of Martha Capel of The Fox Inn, Foxcombe Hill, Wootton, Berkshire. Probate granted 27 June 1912.
Will of Noah Capel of 279 Banbury Road, Oxford. Probate granted 9 October 1937.
Will of Edward Catley of 324 Woodstock Road, Oxford. Probate granted 23 January 1931.
Will of Eva Catley of 6 Fairmead Road, Islington. Dated 11 July 1958.
Will of William Hayes of St Giles, gentleman. Probate granted 23 January 1821. Available in findmypast.co.uk
Will of Frank Ryman Hall of Summerhill. Made 6 June 1923. Probate granted 6 July 1925.
Will of Edward George Leslie Hone of 11 Dolphin Court, Bincleaves Road, Weymouth. Dated 26 February 1988.
Will of Thomas Hunt of Oxford, gentleman. Made 5 February 1841. Available in findmypast.co.uk
Will of Henry John North of Woodstock, solicitor. Made 25 November 1826. Probate granted 3 September 1831. Wills.oxfordshirefhs.org.uk/az/wtext/north_009.html (accessed 29 November 2021).
Will of William Emanuel Richards of Oxford, print seller and picture dealer. Probate granted 10 August 1914.
Will of John Rowland of Water Eaton, grazier. Made 12 March 1816. Available in findmypast.co.uk
Will of James Ryman of Summertown and High Street, Oxford, gentleman. Probate granted 24 March 1881. http://wills.

oxfordshirefhs.org.uk/az/wtext/ryman_022.html (accessed 23 December 2021).

Will of Thomas Terry of Dummer, clerk. Made 12 June 1715. Probate granted 19 November 1723. https://www.victoriacountyhistory.ac.uk/explore/sites/explore/files/explore_assets/2017/11/14/thomas_terry_clerk_1723_prob_11-594-126.pdf (accessed 27 October 2021).

Will of Sidney Venables of Donnington Lodge, Iffley Road, Oxford. Probate granted 26 July 1913.

Will of Thomas Wisdom of Chipping Norton. Made 6 January 1746. Available in Ancestry.co.uk

Directories, Encyclopaedias and Registers

England and Wales Return of Owners of Land 1873, Volume 2 (London: George Edward Eyre and William Spottiswode, 1875).

Hibbert, Christopher and Edward Hibbert (eds.), *The Encyclopaedia of Oxford* (London and Basingstoke: Macmillan, 1988).

Kelly's Directory of Berkshire, 1903 (London: Kelly's Directories Ltd., 1903).

Kelly's Directory of Oxford, 1930 (London: Kelly's Directories Ltd., 1930).

Kelly's Directory of Oxford, 1932 (London: Kelly's Directories Ltd., 1932).

Kelly's Directory of Oxford, 1933 (London: Kelly's Directories Ltd., 1933).

Kelly's Directory of Oxford, 1949 (London: Kelly's Directories Ltd., 1949).

Notes and Queries, Vol. 2, Eleventh Series, July–December 1910 (London: John C. Francis and J. Edward Francis, no year given).

Polk's World Bank Directory 1972 – International Section (Englewood, CO: R.L. Polk & Company, 1972).

Savage, Richard, *The Registers of Stratford on Avon in the County of Warwick. Marriages 1558–1812* (London: William Pollard & Co., 1898).

The India Office List and Burma List for 1945 (London: HMSO, 1945).

The India Office List for 1928 (London: Harrison and Sons Ltd, 1928).
The Law Advertiser, Vol. 2 1824 (London: J.W. Paget, no year given).

Theses

Graham, Malcolm, *The Suburbs of Victorian Oxford: Growth in a Pre-Industrial City*, University of Leicester, Ph.D. thesis, 1985.
Hingkanonta, Lalita, *The Police in Colonial Burma*, Department of History, SOAS, University of London, Ph.D. thesis, 2013.

Interviews

Telephone interview with Cynthia Byrt, 18 February 2021.
Telephone interview with Aubrey J. Capel, 13 May 2021.
Telephone interview with Roy Lecky-Thompson, 24 February 2021.
Telephone interview with Tom Lecky-Thompson, 4 March 2021.
Telephone interview with Elaine Pearce, 18 February 2022.
Transcript of family interview with Florence Lecky-Thompson (undated).

Books and Monographs

Allen, Brigid, *Morrells of Oxford: The Family and Their Brewery 1743–1993* (Stroud: Oxfordshire Books and Alan Sutton Publishing, 1994).
Badcock, John, *The Making of a Regency Village: Origin, History and Development of Summertown in 1832*, ed. Christopher Hicks, with introduction and essay by Ruth Fasnacht (Oxford: St Michael's Publications, 1983).
Ballard, Adolphus, *Chronicles of the Royal Borough of Woodstock. Compiled from the Borough Records and Other Original Documents* (Oxford: Alden & Company, 1896).
Ballard, J.G., *Kingdom Come* (London: Harper Perennial, 2008).
Berry, Victor, *Summertown: Towards an Integrated Community*

(Oxford: Oxford Civic Society, 1971).

Butler, A.J., *The College Estates and Advowsons held by the College: Brasenose College Quatecentenary Monographs, Vol. 1 – General* (Oxford: Clarendon Press, 1909).

Chaouche, Sabine, *Student Consumer Culture in Nineteenth-Century Oxford* (Cham, Switzerland: Springer Nature, 2020).

Childs, James Rivers, *Reliques of the Rives (Ryves)* (Lynchburg, Virginia: J.P. Bell Company, 1929).

Chrosthwaite, Charles Haukes Todd, *The Pacification of Burma* (London: Edward Arnold, 1912).

Collins, Irene, *Jane Austen: The Parson's Daughter* (London: The Hambledon Press, 1998).

Collison, Peter, *The Cutteslowe Walls: A Study in Social Class* (London: Faber and Faber, 1963).

Cook, Sir Edward Tyas, *The Life of John Ruskin, Vol.1 – 1819–1860* (London: George Allen & Company, 1911).

Cox, Mieneke, *The Story of Abingdon Part IV: Abingdon: An 18th Century Country Town* (Abingdon: Leach's the Printers, 1999).

Crook, John, *A History of the Pilgrims' School and Earlier Winchester Choir Schools* (Shopwyke Hall, Chichester: Phillimore and Co., 1991).

Davies, Mark, *Stories of Oxford Castle: From Dungeon to Dunghill* (Oxford: Oxford Towpath Press, 2005).

Dibdin, Michael, *Dirty Tricks* (London: Faber and Faber, 1991).

Dodson, Michael, *The Life of Sir Michael Foster, Knt* (London: J. Johnson and Co., 1811).

Donnison, David, *Last of the Guardians: A Story of Burma, Britain and a Family* (Newtown: Superscript, 2005).

Eddershaw, David, *The Story of the Oxfordshire Yeomanry Queen's Own Oxfordshire Hussars 1798–1998* (Banbury: Oxfordshire Yeomanry Trust, 1998).

Fairfax-Lucy, Alice, *Charlecote & the Lucys: The Chronicle of an English Family* (London: Victor Gollancz Ltd., 1990).

Fasnacht, Ruth, *A History of the City of Oxford* (Oxford: Basil Blackwell, 1954).

Fasnacht, Ruth, *How Summertown Started* (Oxford: The Vicar and Churchwardens of the Parish of Summertown, 1969).

Fasnacht, Ruth, *Summertown since 1820* (Summertown, Oxford: St Michael's Publications, 1977).

Fenby, Charles, The other Oxford: The Life and Times of Frank Gray and his Father (London: Lund Humphries, 1970).

Forster, Henry Rumsey and Richard Plantagenet Temple Nugent Brydges Chandos Grenville, Duke of Buckingham and Chandos, *The Stowe Catalogue: Priced and Annotated* (London: David Bogue, 1848).

Furdell, Elizabeth Lane, *The Royal Doctors 1485–1714: Medical Personnel at the Tudor and Stuart Courts* (Rochester, New York: University of Rochester Press, 2001).

Galbraith, Georgina (ed.), *The Journal of the Rev. William Bagshaw Stevens* (Oxford: Oxford University Press, 1965).

Geare, John Gullet, *Farnham, Essex Past and Present* (London: George Allen & Sons, c. 1909).

Gliddon, Gerald, *Somme 1916: A Battlefield Companion* (Stroud: The History Press, 2009 edition).

Graham, Malcolm, *Images of Victorian Oxford* (Stroud: Alan Sutton Publishing, 1992).

Graham, Malcolm, *Oxford Heritage Walks – Book 6: On Foot from the High to Trill Mill* (Oxford: Oxford Preservation Trust, 2020).

Graham, Malcolm, *Wholesome Dwellings: Housing Need in Oxford and the Municipal Response, 1800–1839* (Summertown, Oxford: Archaeopress Publications, 2020).

Gretton, R.H., *The Burford Records: A Study in Minor Town Government* (Oxford: The Clarendon Press, 1920).

Hamilton, James, *A Strange Business: Making Art and Money in Nineteenth Century Britain* (London: Atlantic Books, 2014).

Harrison, Colin, *Turner's Oxford* (Oxford: University of Oxford, Ashmolean Museum, 2000).

Hawthorne, Nathaniel, *Our Old Home and Septimius Felton* (Boston: Houghton, Mifflin and Company, 1880).

Hearne, Thomas, Charles Edward Doble and David Watson Ronnie (eds.), *Remarks and Collections of Thomas Hearne, Volume 7* (Oxford: Oxford Historical Society at the Clarendon Press, 1906).

Hinchcliffe, Tanis, 'Landownership in the City: St. John's College, 1800–1968', in R.C. Whiting (ed.), *Oxford: Studies in the History of a University Town since 1800* (Manchester and New York: Manchester University Press, 1993), pp.85–109.

Hinchcliffe, Tanis, *North Oxford* (New Haven and London: Yale University Press, 1992).

Horton-Smith, L.G.H., *The Baily Family of Thatcham and later of Speen and of Newbury, all in the County of Berkshire* (Leicester: W. Thornley & Son, 1951).

Howard, John, *The State of the Prisons in England and Wales* (London: W. Eyres, 1777).

Howe, Anthony, 'Intellect and Civic Responsibility: Dons and Citizens in Nineteenth-Century Oxford' in R.C. Whiting (ed.), *Oxford: Studies in the History of a University Town since 1800* (Manchester and New York: Manchester University Press, 1993), pp.12–52.

Hunt, William Holman, *Pre-Raphaelitism and the Pre-Raphaelite Brotherhood, Vol.1* (London and New York: Macmillan Company, 1905).

James, P.D., *Time to be Earnest: A Fragment of Autobiography* (London: Faber and Faber, 1999).

Jesse, John Heneage, *Memoirs of the Court of England: From the Revolution in 1688 to the Death of George the Second. Volume 3* (London: Richard Bentley, 1843).

Jewesbury, Eric C.O., *The Royal Northern Hospital 1856–1956: The Story of a Hundred Years' Work in North London* (London: H.K. Lewis and Co. Ltd., 1956).

Kennedy, Julie, *The Changing Faces of Summertown and Cutteslowe* (Witney: Robert Boyd Publications, 1995).

Kinchin, Perilla, *Seven Roads in Summertown: Voices from an Oxford Suburb* (Oxford: White Cockade Publishing, 2006).

Knapp, Oswald G., *A History of the Chief English Families Bearing the Name of Knapp* (London: O.G. Knapp, 1911).

Leigh, Michael, *The Collapse of British Rule in Burma: The Civilian Evacuation and Independence* (London: Bloomsbury Academic, 2018).

Lisle, Nicole, *Life in Miniature: A History of Dolls' Houses* (Barnsley: Pen & Sword Books, 2020).

Littell, Eliakim, and Robert S. Littell (eds.), *Littell's Living Age, Vol.181* (Boston: Little and Co., 1884).

Lively, Penelope, *The House in Norham Gardens (London: Penguin, 2016).*

Loudon, Jean Claudius, *The Suburban Gardener, and Villa Companion* (London and Edinburgh: Longman, Orme, Brown, Green and Longmans, and W. Black, 1838).

Macintyre, Ben, *Agent Sonya: Lover, Mother, Soldier, Spy* (London: Penguin, Random House, 2020).

Major, Susan and Sarah Murden, *A Right Royal Scandal: Two Marriages That Changed History* (Barnsley: Pen & Sword History, 2016).

Manning, James Alexander, *The Lives of the Speakers of the House of*

Commons from the Time of King Edward III to Queen Victoria (London: George Willis, 1851).

Marshall, Jenner, *Memorials of Westcott Barton in the County of Oxford* (London: John Russell Smith, 1870).

Mavor, William, *General View of the Agriculture of Berkshire* (London: Sherwood, Neely and Jones, 1813).

Maybury-Lewis, David, *Manifest Destinies and Indigenous Peoples* (Cambridge, MA: Harvard University Press, 2009).

McGuiness, Patrick, *Real Oxford* (Bridgend, Wales: Seren, 2021).

McKenna, Joseph, *The Gunmakers of Birmingham 1660–1960* (Jefferson, NC: McFarland & Company, 2021).

Mead, Helen, *Whence and Whither: 150 Years of Reformed Church Worship in Summertown* (Oxford: Harold Copeman, 1994).

Morgan, John Ainsworth, *Oxford Observations* (New York: F.H. Hitchcock, 1925).

Morris, Jan, *Oxford* (Oxford: Oxford University Press, 3rd edition, 2001).

Olcott, Charles S., *The Country of Sir Walter Scott* (Boston and New York: Houghton Mifflin Company, 1913).

Olusoga, David and Melanie Backe-Hansen, *A House Through Time* (London: Picador, 2020).

Palmer, F. P. and Alfred Crowquill, *The Wanderings of a Pen and Pencil* (London: Jeremiah House, 1846).

Parkes, Mary, *Art Monopoly. Deception in the Publication of Engravings. A Free… Exposure of the Printsellers' Association… Together with Suggestions by Way of Remedy* (London: John K. Chapman & Co., 2nd ed. 1850).

Prince, Alison, *Kenneth Grahame: an Innocent in the Wild Wood* (London: Faber Finds, 2011).

Rana, Bhawan Singh, *Rani of Jhansi* (New Delhi: Diamond Books, 2004).

Rawlinson, W.G., *The Engraved Work of J.M.W. Turner: Vol.1 – Line Engravings on Copper 1794–1839* (London: Macmillan and G. Ltd, 1908).

Roberts, W., *Sir William Beechey, R.A.* (London and New York: Duckworth and Co., and Charles Scribner's Sons, 1907).

Romilly, Samuel, *The Speeches of Sir Samuel Romilly in the House of Commons, Volume 2* (London: James Ridgway and Sons, 1820).

Rosen, Adrienne and Janice Cliffe, *The Making of Chipping Norton: A Guide to Its Buildings and History to 1750* (Stroud: The History Press, 2017).

Ruskin, John, *Fors Clavigera: Letters to the Workmen and Labourers of Great Britain – Volume 3 of The Complete Works of John Ruskin* (New York: Bryan, Taylor & Company, 1894).

Rylands, William Harry (ed.), *The Four Visitations of Berkshire Made and Taken by Thomas Benolte, Clarenceux, anno 1532… and by Elias Ashmole, Windsor Herald, for Sir Edward Bysshe, Clarenceux, anno 1665–1666, Volume 2* (London: Harleian Society, 1908).

Scargill, Ian D., 'Responses to Growth in Modern Oxford', in R.C. Whiting (ed.), *Oxford: Studies in the History of a University Town since 1800* (Manchester and New York: Manchester University Press, 1993), pp.110–30.

Scott, Ann, Mervyn Eadie, Andrew Lees, *William Richard Gowers 1845–1915: Exploring the Victorian Britain* (Oxford: Oxford University Press, 2012).

Shanes, Eric, *Turner's England: A Survey in Watercolours* (North Pomfret, Vt: Trafalgar Square Publishing, 1990).

Sherwood, J. and N. Pevsner, *The Buildings of England: Oxfordshire* (London: Penguin, 1974).

Sinclair, J.G., *Portrait of Oxford* (Sturry, Kent: Veracity Press, 1931).

Smith, Hannah, *Georgian Monarchy: Politics and Culture, 1714–1760* (Cambridge: Cambridge University Press, 2006).

Snow, Peter, *Oxford Observed: Town and Gown* (London: John Murray, 1991).

Stapleton, Mrs Bryan, *Three Oxfordshire Parishes: A History of Kidlington, Yarnton and Begbroke* (Oxford: Clarendon Press, 1893).

Steane, Elaine, *Soapsud Island: Oral Histories of Sunnymead, Oxford* (King's Lynn: Biddles Books, 2018).

Stevenson, W.E. and H.E. Salter, *The Early History of St. John's College, Oxford* (Oxford: At the Clarendon Press for the Oxford Historical Society, 1939).

Symonds, Ann Spokes, *The Changing Faces of North Oxford: Book One* (Witney: Robert Boyd Publications, 1997).

Symonds, Ann Spokes and Nigel Morgan, *The Origins of Oxford Street Names* (Witney: Robert Boyd Publications, 2010).

Thomas, Sir Miles, *Out on a Wing: An Autobiography* (London: Michael Joseph, 1964).

Thorne, James, *Rambles by Rivers: The Thames, Vol. 1* (London: C. Cox, 1847).

Thorne, R.G., *The House of Commons 1790–1820* (London: Secker & Warbourg, 1986).

Tuckwell, William, *Reminiscences of Oxford* (New York: E.P Burton and Company, 1908).

Tyson, Geoffrey, *Forgotten Frontier* (Calcutta: W.H. Targett & Co. Ltd, 1945).

West Hagbourne Village History Group, *Windsor Hakeborne: The Story of West Hagbourne* (West Hagbourne: West Hagbourne Village History Group, 2000).

Wharton, Thomas, *The History and Antiquities of Kiddington* (London: J. Nichols, Son and Bentley, 3rd ed., 1815).

White, Herbert Thirkell, *A Civil Servant in Burma* (London: Edward Arnold, 1913).

Whitehead, J.W.R. and C.M.H. Carr, *Twentieth-Century Suburbs: A Morphological Approach* (London and New York: Routledge, 2001).

Wigram, Spencer Robert, *The Cartulary of the Monastery of St. Frideswide at Oxford, Volume 1* (Oxford: At the Clarendon Press for the Oxford Historical Society, 1895).

Winrow, Gareth M., *Whispers Across Continents: In Search of the Robinsons* (Stroud: Amberley, 2019).

Young, Desmond, *Try Anything Twice* (London: Hamish Hamilton, 1963).

Zaleski, Philip, 'Stratford Caldecott: A Brief Biography' in Francesca Aran Murphy (ed.), *The Beauty of God's House: Essays in Honor of Stratford Caldecott* (Eugene, Or.: Cascade Books, 2014), pp.273–80.

Articles

Anderson, James, 'The Operation of the Early Nineteenth-Century Property Market', *Construction History*, 24 (2009), pp.63–81.

Chalus, Elaine, '"My Lord Sue": Lady Susan Keck and the Great Oxfordshire Election of 1754', *Parliamentary History*, 32, 3 (2013), pp.443–59.

Dallas, Eneas Sweetland, 'A Summer Day at Cumnor', *Once a Week*, 13 (9 September 1865), pp.321–8.

Dodsworth, I.C., 'The Chawley Brick and Tile Works, Cumnor', *Oxoniensia*, 41 (1976), pp.348–54.

Dyos, H.J., 'The Speculative Builders and Developers of Victorian London', *Victorian Studies*, 11 (Summer 1968) – 'Supplement: Symposium on the Victorian City (2)', pp.641–90.

Forsyth, Ann, 'Defining Suburbs', *Journal of Planning Literature*, 27, 3 (2012), pp.270–81.

Godfrey, Walter H., 'Burford Priory', *Oxoniensia*, 4 (1939), pp.71–88.

Gorsky, Martin and John Mohan, 'London's Voluntary Hospitals in the Inter-War Period: Growth, Transformation or Crisis?', *Nonprofit and Voluntary Sector Quarterly*, 30, 2 (June 2001), pp.247–75.

Graham, Malcolm, 'The Building of Oxford Covered Market', *Oxoniensia*, 44 (1979), pp.81–92.

Graham, Malcolm, 'Housing Development on the Urban Fringe of Oxford 1850–1914', *Oxoniensia*, 55 (1990), pp.147–66.

Hart, Harold W., 'The Horse Trams of Oxford, 1881–1914', *Oxoniensia*, 37 (1972), pp.221–5.

Kuchta, Todd, 'Semi-Detached Empire: Suburbia and Imperial Discourse in Victorian and Edwardian Britain', *Nineteenth-Century Prose*, 32, 2 (Fall 2005) – Special Issue on Cultural Studies of British Imperialism, pp.173–208.

Lamouria, Lanya, 'Financial Revolution: Representing British Financial Crisis after the French Revolution of 1848', *Victorian Literature and Culture*, 43, 3 (2015), pp.489–510.

Mayo, John, 'Britain and Chile 1851–1886: Anatomy of a Relationship', *Journal of Interamerican Studies and World Affairs*, 23, 1 (February 1981), pp.95–120.

Minn, H., 'A Manuscript History of Summertown', *Oxoniensia*, 11–12 (1946–7), pp.152–65.

Morris, R. J., 'The Friars and Paradise: An Essay in the Building History of Oxford, 1801–1861', *Oxoniensia*, 36 (1971), pp.72–103.

Osmond, Anson, 'Building on the Beaumonts: An Example of Early 19th-Century Housing Development', *Oxoniensia*, 49 (1984), pp.301–25.

Stevens, Walter, 'Oxford's Attitude to Dissenters, 1646–1946', *Baptist Quarterly*, 13, 1 (1949), pp.4–17.

Tedeschi, Martha, '"Where the Picture cannot go, the Engravings Penetrate". Prints and the Victorian Art Market', The Art Institute of Chicago, *Art Institute of Chicago Museum Studies*, 31, 1 (2005), pp.9–90.

Thompson, F.M.L., 'Life after Death: How Successful Nineteenth Century Businessmen Disposed of their Fortunes', *The Economic History Review*, 43 (1990), pp.40–61.

Thompson, F.M.L., 'The End of a Great Estate', *The Economic History Review*, 8, 1 (1955), pp.36–52.

Ward, Lucina, 'Quaestio Vexata: Collecting Arundel "Chromos" in America and Australasia', *Australasian Journal of Victorian Studies*, 24, 1 (2020), pp.28–50.

Zaleski, Carol, 'Stratford Caldecott (1953–2014)', *VII: Journal of the Marion E. Wade Center*, 31 (2014), pp.6–8.

Newspapers

Airdrie and Coatbridge Advertiser
Berkshire Chronicle
Bicester Herald
Boston Guardian
Bradford Observer
Buckingham Advertiser and Free Press
Civil and Military Gazette (Lahore)
Cork Advertising Gazette
Cork Constitution
Dundee Advertiser
Englishman's Overland Mail
European Magazine, and London Review
Hampshire Chronicle
Hereford Journal
Instructor and Select Weekly Advertiser

Lancashire Evening Post
Leeds Mercury
Leeds Times
London Courier and Evening Gazette
Morning Herald (London)
Morning Post
Oxford Chronicle and Reading Gazette
Oxford Journal
Oxford Mail
Oxford Times
Oxford University and City Herald
Oxfordshire Weekly News
Reading Mercury
Portsmouth Evening News
Shipley Times and Express
Tailor and Cutter
The National Magazine
West Kent Guardian

ACKNOWLEDGEMENTS

Firstly, many thanks to all the staff at The Book Guild who have helped in the production and marketing of the book. Their willingness to support the publication of the book is greatly appreciated.

Staff at the National Archives, the Bodleian Library and at the Oxfordshire History Centre all helped in finding materials and documentation. I am also grateful to the people working at the Woodstock Museum and, in particular, Carol Anderson.

My special thanks go to the relatives of the people mentioned in this book. The information that they provided has proved to be invaluable. In particular, I would like to express my gratitude to Tommy Bull, Janine McMinn, Libby Shade, John de Lucy, Jorge Brain, Linda Thurman, Sheila and Paul Wheatley, Aubrey J. Capel, Mandy Wood, Julie van Onselen, Yvonne Tye, Christine Knowles, Elaine Pearce, Barry and Laura Sheehan, Keith Hollingsworth, Charles Brookson, Helen Brookson, Roy Lecky-Thompson, Tom Lecky-Thompson, Julia Matthews-Parsons, John Catley, Gill

Walker, Stephanie Jenkins and Rosalind Gurney. My thanks also go to Elaine Chalus, Cynthia Byrt and to Catherine Matthews.

I am grateful to Ülker Sayın for reading over earlier drafts of certain chapters, Begüm Zorlu for her photography, and Tolga Yılmaz for the map. Thanks also to Malcolm Graham for his close reading of the whole text.

Last, but not least, my warmest thanks go to Nazan. Carefully checking each chapter she has been a constant pillar of support and a source of encouragement.

INDEX